CW01310960

Tarot Insights

By

Laurie Watts-Amato, Ph.D.

authorHOUSE

1663 Liberty Drive, Suite 200
Bloomington, Indiana 47403
(800) 839-8640
www.AuthorHouse.com

© 2004 Laurie Watts-Amato, Ph.D.
All Rights Reserved.

No part of this book may be reproduced, stored in a retrieval system, or transmitted by any means without the written permission of the author.

First published by AuthorHouse 11/10/04

ISBN: 1-4184-8329-X (sc)
ISBN: 1-4184-8330-3 (dj)

Library of Congress Control Number: 2004095224

Printed in the United States of America
Bloomington, Indiana

This book is printed on acid-free paper.

Cover illustration of the Fool from The Starlight Tarot
by Laurie Amato

Illustrations from the Rider-Waite Tarot Deck, also known as the Rider and the Waite Tarot, reproduced by permission of U.S. Games Systems, Inc., Stamford, CT 06902 USA. Copyright 1971 by U.S. Games Systems, Inc. Further reproduction prohibited. The Rider-Waite Tarot deck is a registered trademark of U.S. Games Systems, Inc.

TABLE OF CONTENTS

CHAPTER ONE INTRODUCTION TO THE TAROT 1
CHAPTER TWO THE MAJOR ARCANA 9
    THE FOOL: BECOMING........................9
    THE MAGICIAN: INTENTION................................12
    THE HIGH PRIESTESS: MEMORY........................16
    THE EMPRESS: NURTURING................................19
    THE EMPEROR: POWER........................22
    THE HIEROPHANT: BELIEF................................25
    THE LOVERS: CHOICE 28
    THE CHARIOT: CONTROL 31
    STRENGTH: COOPERATION................................34
    THE HERMIT: WISDOM 37
    THE WHEEL OF FORTUNE: FATE 40
    JUSTICE: CONSEQUENCES 44
    THE HANGED MAN: SACRIFICE........................47
    DEATH: REWARD 50
    TEMPERANCE: INTEGRATION 53
    THE DEVIL: DISTORTION 56
    THE TOWER: FEAR 60
    THE STAR: GUIDANCE................................63
    THE MOON: CHANGE........................66
    THE SUN: CONSCIOUSNESS 69
    JUDGMENT: REDEMPTION 72
    THE WORLD: FULFILLMENT................................75
CHAPTER THREE THE MINOR ARCANA........................78
    THE ACE OF PENTACLES: TRANSITION 78
    THE TWO OF PENTACLES: COPING 82
    THE THREE OF PENTACLES: COMMITMENT................85

THE FOUR OF PENTACLES: POSSESSION 88
THE FIVE OF PENTACLES: DEPRIVATION 91
THE SIX PENTACLES: COMPENSATION 95
THE SEVEN OF PENTACLES: EXPECTATION 99
THE EIGHT OF PENTACLES: WORKING 102
THE NINE OF PENTACLES: WAITING...........................105
THE TEN OF PENTACLES: REVELATION......................109
THE PAGE OF PENTACLES: FOCUSING 113
THE KNIGHT OF PENTACLES: POTENTIAL 117
THE QUEEN OF PENTACLES: ACCEPTANCE 120
THE KING OF PENTACLES: HARVEST 123
THE ACE OF CUPS: EMANATION 125
THE TWO OF CUPS: ATTRACTION.................................128
THE THREE OF CUPS: GRATITUDE 132
THE FOUR OF CUPS: REJECTION 135
THE FIVE OF CUPS: LOSS 138
THE SIX OF CUPS: GIVING 142
THE SEVEN OF CUPS: DESIRE...145
THE EIGHT OF CUPS: SEARCHING.................................149
THE NINE OF CUPS: GRATIFICATION 152
THE TEN OF CUPS: HOPE 155
THE PAGE OF CUPS: INSIGHT 158
THE KNIGHT OF CUPS: HESITATION 161
THE QUEEN OF CUPS: REPRESSION 164
THE KING OF CUPS: DRIFTING.......................................167
THE ACE OF SWORDS: THINKING..................................170
THE TWO OF SWORDS: AVOIDANCE 173
THE THREE OF SWORDS: PAIN 176
THE FOUR OF SWORDS: PERMANENCE 179
THE FIVE OF SWORDS: VICTORY...................................182

THE SIX OF SWORDS: CIRCUMSTANCE 185
THE SEVEN OF SWORDS: CONSCIENCE 188
THE EIGHT OF SWORDS: LIMITATION 191
THE NINE OF SWORDS: AWAKENING 195
THE TEN OF SWORDS: FORGIVENESS 198
THE PAGE OF SWORDS: INFLUENCE............................ 201
THE KNIGHT OF SWORDS: OVERREACTION 204
THE QUEEN OF SWORDS: TRANSFORMATION 207
THE KING OF SWORDS: RATIONALIZATION 210
THE ACE OF WANDS: OPPORTUNITY 213
THE TWO OF WANDS: OBJECTIVITY 216
THE THREE OF WANDS: VISION 219
THE FOUR OF WANDS: SECURITY 222
THE FIVE OF WANDS: CONFLICT 226
THE SIX OF WANDS: APPROVAL.................................... 230
THE SEVEN OF WANDS: RESISTANCE......................... 233
THE EIGHT OF WANDS: GOALS 237
THE NINE OF WANDS: VIGILANCE 241
THE TEN OF WANDS: PERSEVERANCE 244
THE PAGE OF WANDS: INTUITION 247
THE KNIGHT OF WANDS: RESTRAINT 250
THE QUEEN OF WANDS: SEPARATION 253
THE KING OF WANDS: ADAPTING 256
CHAPTER FOUR READING THE TAROT....................259
APPENDIX...267
BIBLIOGRAPHY 270

CHAPTER ONE
INTRODUCTION TO THE TAROT

All teems with symbols. Wise persons are they who
in any one thing can read another.

—Plotinus

We are all fortunetellers. We tell ourselves that we will die young or live forever; we will be prosperous or live in poverty; we will find the perfect partner or live alone. The unintentional predictions we make every day shape our destiny and determine the course of our lives. Because our predictions can become self-fulfilling prophecies, our expectations of the future can create reality.

In the Middle Ages, many deeply religious peasants believed that the world would end on the anniversary of Jesus Christ's death in 1000 C.E. Because their belief was absolute, they refused to plant their crops in the spring. So, when the world didn't end as planned, they all starved to death. Although this is a very literal example of a self-fulfilling prophecy, this story does warn us to be careful in how we approach the Tarot. A gypsy proverb states that "there are always two sides to a prediction," and we would be wise to consider several possible interpretations of the cards before acting on their sage advice.

We may wish to avoid a literal interpretation of the cards, for the Tarot's guidance is cloaked in metaphysical symbolism. To properly connect with the cards, it is necessary to understand this symbolic language of the Tarot. As a metaphysical system, the Tarot relies upon fairly ordinary scenes to communicate its hidden message. So each card contains familiar scenes of celebration, working, and travel, which we can easily understand. It is only when we look beneath the surface of these pedestrian images to find their symbolic and psychological meaning that we can fully comprehend the power contained within the cards.

The Tarot's power lies, not in its magical ability to reveal the future, but in its ability to reveal ourselves. The cards of the Tarot are cleverly disguised representations of our deepest desires and thoughts. By getting in touch with these deeper emotional issues, we can better understand ourselves and make better decisions based upon self-knowledge. When we use the cards therapeutically, the Tarot has the potential to heal us. Unlike conventional therapies, which may take many months of treatment to uncover unconscious fears or motivations, the Tarot immediately mirrors our deepest problems, so we can directly confront them. Although a Tarot reading cannot replace traditional counseling, it always gives us good counsel.

There are many reasons why we consult the wisdom of the Tarot. Most of us want to be prepared for future events, particularly if we have experienced sudden catastrophic events in the past. In this case, the Tarot is used as a window to the future, guaranteeing that we will never be caught unawares again. If we fear the future, we may need the Tarot's reassurance that everything will turn out well. Tarot readings can also provide us with a reality check if we become too optimistic about future events. Although many of us want to explore the future with the Tarot, most of us consult the cards to obtain sage advice.

In ages past, a person could easily consult the elders of his community for advice about personal matters. In this way, the younger members of the community could benefit from the elders' life experiences and wisdom. In today's fast-paced society, which encourages isolation, this type of multigenerational advice is simply not possible. Not only do we usually live many miles from older members of our family, we easily dismiss our elders' advice as being too old-fashioned. This leaves us with very few people we can turn to for the answers to our problems. However, we can always use the Tarot for guidance. Its sage advice is always available, offering us eternal wisdom in pictorial form.

While we may be eager to seek others' counsel, most of us fail to carry out the advice we are given simply because it does not originate within ourselves. When we are given explicit advice from others, we reject it because the advice is based upon the other person's life experience rather than our own. Like looking through someone else's eyeglasses, we quickly realize that what will correct another person's problems will not necessarily correct ours. The advice the

INTRODUCTION TO THE TAROT

Tarot offers us is fundamentally different from the advice we seek from others because the Tarot's guidance originates solely from within ourselves. If we are doing a reading for ourselves, we shuffle the cards and pick those cards that bring wisdom into our lives. We then choose particular interpretations for each card and then analyze the resultant meanings within the context of our life experience. This well-thought-out advice that we give ourselves in the form of a Tarot reading is usually accepted and acted upon enthusiastically because we have successfully figured out the answers for ourselves. Tarot gives us the opportunity to become our own wise woman or wise man who knows that all the answers we seek to life's questions are inside each one of us.

The Tarot uses the language of pictorial symbolism to impart its ancient wisdom. From pictorial alphabets such as hieroglyphics to great works of art, the most profound knowledge has always been communicated through images rather than words. Because we can read whatever we like into a picture, it is the perfect portal to self-knowledge. The Tarot is a magic mirror in which we can see ourselves, although not too clearly. This is because symbols like the Tarot simultaneously conceal and reveal their hidden meanings. The symbol, standing for something else, conceals what it denotes while it reveals a deeper meaning. When we use the Tarot, we begin to think symbolically instead of literally. This is a very valuable skill that can greatly enrich our lives because great wisdom can be obtained through deciphering the symbolic elements in life. Symbolism gives us a context in which to understand our experience, and the Tarot provides a perfect symbolic system in which to see ourselves.

Before we can learn the Tarot's symbolic language, we need to understand the structure of the Tarot deck. The seventy-eight cards of the Tarot consist of twenty-two Major Arcana cards and fifty-six Minor Arcana cards. The Major Arcana is numbered from zero to twenty-one while the Minor Arcana is divided into four suits: pentacles, cups, swords, and wands. Each of these suits consists of fourteen cards numbered one through ten, with the addition of four court cards: the page, the knight, the queen, and the king.

The twenty-two cards of the Major Arcana symbolize the metaphysical world over which we have little control, but which often controls us. This is the realm of archetypes, gods and goddesses, or divine intervention. The Major cards also represent all the influential people who have shaped our personalities. Depicted on these cards are our mother, father, siblings, and spouses. Influential events are represented as well: birth, death, anniversaries, and catastrophes. The minor cards reflect the world we are familiar with, full of people, places, and things. We can also see our all too human nature in the Minor Arcana, as they show us our capacity to love, hate, desire, give, take, create, and destroy. In total, the Tarot represents the nature of reality: the cups are lessons about the nature of love; the swords reflect the nature of conflict; the wands are the nature of time and energy; the pentacles symbolize the nature of the environment; and the Major Arcana show the nature of universal laws. The seventy-eight cards of the Tarot are an all-encompassing system describing our fateful journey through life as a journey through the cards.

In order to fully understand the symbolic meaning of the Tarot, it is necessary to orient ourselves within the scenes presented on the cards. Although it is tempting to focus exclusively on the interesting actions of each character on the card, the entire scene must be carefully viewed to completely understand the whole story the card is trying to tell us. Like ourselves, the people on the cards can only be understood within the context of their environment.

Each section of the card represents a part of our experience. The right side of each card represents the future, while the left side is the past. So a woman on the card who looks toward the left is actually contemplating her past. Anything in the upper portion of the card is symbolic of our conscious motivations, while the bottom can show us underlying motivations. The position of the people in the scene also produces a noticeable background and foreground. Anything in front of the figure on the card is something that must be faced, even if we do not wish to acknowledge it. The background, which should never be disregarded, is often symbolic of something we have left behind such as a memory, a fear, or past guilt. Many of the scenes also take place at night, and these nocturnal landscapes symbolize the unconscious. Although most of the cards depict outdoor scenes, a few feature indoor areas such as a church or a bedroom. These interior spaces are reflective of the thoughts and feelings we have inside ourselves, whereas the exterior scenes are the communication of these thoughts and feelings to others. It is always best to consider the entire scene because, when we read the Tarot, our intuition may instinctively draw us to certain parts of a card to find the particular meaning that is needed.

Everyone naturally likes to categorize their experiences, and Tarot reading is no exception. The first thing we usually do after we have picked a particular card is to immediately categorize it as either a good card or a bad card. On the surface, the card shows either a fortunate or an unfortunate occurrence, so we believe the picture to be either a good or a bad omen. However, the Tarot is not a group of ordinary pictures, and all is not what it seems. If we delve deeply into the symbolic meaning of the cards, we can see that even the worst catastrophe pictured can be a disguised representation of a positive experience. Even if we take the cards at face value, we quickly realize that the Tarot is a magical world in which the normal law of cause and effect does not apply. Giant hands suddenly materialize out of clouds, fish appear inside cups, and angels magically appear. Many of the cards also contain contradictory messages and confusing paradoxes. Because we have entered a topsy-turvy world that bears little resemblance to our own view of reality, we have no factual basis upon which to judge whether a particular card is good or bad. In the strange world of the Tarot, good fortune may result in tragedy, while bad fortune may be a strike of good luck.

To fully understand the symbolism of the Tarot, we need to mentally project ourselves into each card. When we use our imagination, we can become the entire scene we are contemplating. We are everything on the card: the people, the water, the sky, the cups, the mountains, the trees, and the animals. This may not be as unbelievable as it seems because Tarot cards illustrate the ancient belief in animism, which attributes life to inanimate objects. So, the Tarot's Sun and Moon cards have human faces, a queen converses with her cup, and pentacles naturally grow on trees. When we consider the objects on the cards to be living, breathing entities, it becomes much easier to identify with them. With a little imagination, we can envision all the object's characteristics as our own: the trees our slow but steady growth; the rocks our steadfastness; the soaring birds our objectivity; and the flowing water our ability to change. The landscape of the Tarot becomes our inner landscape as we perfectly reflect all the qualities contained in each scene.

Of course, we most easily identify with the people portrayed on the cards. During a reading, their attitudes and actions become our own. However, we also have many people in our lives that could be represented by the people on the cards, and sometimes it is difficult to distinguish between ourselves and others in a reading. Is the Page of Cups an immature aspect of ourselves, or does he represent our son? Actually, both interpretations are correct. The people whom we invite into our lives are usually hidden reflections of ourselves. Their positive qualities and problems are often ours as well, although it is far easier to see their foibles than our own. For this reason, the characters on the cards simultaneously represent ourselves and others.

Just as the people close to us are projections of our best and worst qualities, the Tarot is a projective instrument designed to reflect our image back to us. Psychologically, we project our thoughts and feelings onto the cards so we can objectively examine them. The Tarot also cleverly circumvents the common defense mechanism of denial. For example, it is impossible to deny our angry feelings when we are confronted by cards in a reading depicting angry, defensive people. The cards continually give us an outside perspective on ourselves and our situation. They show us a problem that must be faced, or a relationship that must change. Most importantly, the Tarot gives us the opportunity to use these insights in order to change our lives for the better.

The earliest Tarot decks were created in the fifteenth century, but the most popular deck today is the Rider-Waite Tarot. This is also called the Waite-Smith deck in honor of the artist who illustrated this series of cards, Pamela Coleman Smith. The original designs for the cards were drawn in 1909 by Ms. Smith under the direction of Arthur Edward Waite, a member of the Hermetic Order of the Golden Dawn. Tarot cards had been produced for hundreds of years, but this was the first deck to feature pictorial scenes on both the Major and Minor Arcana. Previously, the Minor cards were decorated with the

INTRODUCTION TO THE TAROT

appropriate number of pips, similar to modern playing cards. The addition of scenes to the Minor cards made the Tarot much easier to use because the reader could easily relate to pictures instead of abstract suit signs. Although the deck was published in 1909, the traditional appearance of the Tarot was preserved by setting all the scenes in the medieval period. The costumes featured on the cards date this as the late Gothic period (1450–1550), which is when the first Tarot cards appeared in fifteenth-century Italy. After its initial appearance in 1909, the Rider-Waite deck went out of print, but was reprinted decades later. The Rider-Waite Tarot illustrates this book, and is available in most major bookstores.

As well as being a Tarot designer, Pamela Coleman Smith was also a set designer for stage plays at the turn of the century. Her influence as a set designer can be seen on many of the cards, for several cards have a double line close to the bottom of the card, which could be the bottom of a backdrop. This painted curtain appears on the Four and Two of Pentacles, as well as the Ten and Two of Cups. It is possible that Ms. Smith may have envisioned the Tarot as an elaborate stage play involving seventy-eight different scene and costume changes.

If we consider the Tarot to be a pictorial representation of a play, then we can envision ourselves as eager participants in this age-old drama. As actors, we need to wear the appropriate costumes for our roles and perform the correct actions onstage. The roles we play may be the clown (the Fool), the moral authority (the Hierophant), or the mother (the Empress). As we assume each character, we find ourselves subtly changed by the ever-changing demands of each role. Sometimes we are the hero of the melodrama, and sometimes we are the villain. In a similar fashion, we are changed by our interaction with the Tarot. Playing with the cards gives us the opportunity to see the many possibilities in life because each time we shuffle the cards, the storyline changes.

The remainder of this book is devoted to a detailed explanation of the many meanings of all seventy-eight cards of the Tarot. Each card represents a special quality we need to develop, an action we need to take, or an experience we need to undergo in order to grow. For example, we may need to develop the quality of gratitude (the Three of Cups), act with perseverance (the Ten of Wands), or experience loss (the Five of Cups). The divinatory meanings given for each card are more complex than the standard meanings such as, "You will soon take a journey by water." These types of divinatory meanings are the simplest interpretations for the cards because they are limited to concrete predictions that can be confirmed or denied by future events. The Tarot is far more than a predictive device. It is an important tool for self-development. The cards can help us develop our full potential by helping us understand ourselves. It is this self-knowledge that is the real predictor of future events, not the cards.

CHAPTER TWO
THE MAJOR ARCANA

THE FOOL: BECOMING

When you come to the edge of all you know, you must believe one of two things: there will be earth to stand on, or you will be given wings to fly.

—Anonymous

The Fool stands on the edge of a precipice and blithely gazes up at the heavens. Like the Fool, some of us constantly live on the edge, where one wrong step can send us plummeting to earth. So, we begin our journey into the Tarot with our first lesson: life is a very risky business. In order to avoid a tragic fall, we need to watch where we are going, both emotionally as well as physically. By far, the greatest risk we take in life is to love, for we know in our hearts that someday we may lose the one we love. To follow one's heart is to step off into an unknown future where we can either soar to great heights or fall heartbroken into an abyss of despair. Nevertheless, like the Fool standing precariously on the edge of a cliff, we dare to risk everything. We may not know how our journey of the heart will end, but we do know that the love we feel on this wonderful journey is our only destination.

In many ways, the Fool represents the idealism of youth, capturing a time in which we envisioned unlimited opportunities. The Fool personifies beginnings and the limitless possibilities found at the start of our journey. Eternally optimistic, the Fool has an adventurous spirit that cannot be contained within the physical world. The certainty of his dreams guides him along a path of endless possibilities, until he reaches the edge of the cliff. It is at this point that his positive imagination gives him wings to soar into the sky. His potential is as unlimited as the infinite universe. His life is the fulfillment of his dreams.

The Fool's only companion on his journey is his faithful little dog, and, as anyone who has owned man's best friend can attest, dogs are perfect examples of unconditional love. If we had to choose only one virtuous quality to take along with us on our journey through life, hopefully it would be unconditional love. To love someone even though they are fundamentally different from us is a wonderful gift. Our unconditional love can also extend to those people who have hurt us in the past. By loving and forgiving our enemies, we free ourselves from the heavy burden of anger, which can weigh us down on our journey. The Fool carries his satchel gently balanced on his shoulder, indicating that the baggage of guilt or anger that we bring with us from the past shall be lightly borne.

The freedom of the vagabond lifestyle is also expressed in the Fool card. As the happy wanderer, he is perfectly free to come and go as he pleases. Traveling without any predetermined plan or direction, he follows the pathless path guided only by chance occurrence or twists of fate. Although we carefully plan our days, believing that we control our destiny, the Fool tells us otherwise. Despite all our carefully laid plans, life has a way of taking us where it wants us to go. These strange destinations may not be our thoughtfully planned itinerary, but we need to visit them for the advancement of our souls. When we find ourselves bound for one of these unknown destinations, it is wise to adopt the Fool's outlook on life. Remaining open to new experiences, he feels total trust in a universe he is confident will always provide for his true needs.

The Fool is a free spirit, and our most precious freedom is the right to simply be ourselves. As the first card in the Tarot, the Fool represents the spiritual essence of who we are. It is our most important task to remain true to that essence during the course of our lives. However, like most freedoms, our essence is usually only attainable through struggle and conflict. This is because our essence is not what our parents want us to be or what society expects of us, but rather a subtle prompting from deep inside ourselves to follow our true path in life. This can naturally lead to serious conflicts with others who want us to be just like them. The Fool follows the path of self-determination, going only where his dreams will take him. This gives him the freedom to be true to his own nature and live according to his own view of reality. When we identify with the Fool, we have the courage to make our dreams come true, regardless of the social consequences.

This is not to say that we have absolute freedom to do whatever we wish. On this journey that we call life, we carry with us certain psychological limitations. Like the Fool carrying his satchel, we are always carrying the burden of the past with us. We carry our personal histories with us wherever we go, and it is these problems of the past that create sensitivities to certain issues in the present. For example, if we had overbearing parents, we may persistently avoid the commitment of marriage for fear of being controlled by our spouse. Unfortunately, in trying to scrupulously avoid reproducing the unpleasantness of the past, we may fail to watch where are going in life and fall off the cliff of our own negative expectations. On the other hand, if these limiting patterns are identified, we can regain our freedom to choose what direction is best for us.

The Fool represents youthful adolescence and, therefore, the opportunity to grow. As we go through life, we accumulate various experiences that help us grow beyond our present state of awareness. As we learn from these experiences, we continually evolve into better and, hopefully, wiser people. The Fool is only a starting point for our journey, for we are continually developing wisdom. Life is a journey of becoming more of who we are meant to be and of fulfilling our life's true purpose. The journey the Fool takes through the remaining cards of the Tarot represents this journey of self-discovery.

When the Fool appears in a Tarot reading, it indicates that we may be trying to hold onto unrealistic expectations from our youth. We may need to let go of these youthful expectations if we want to proceed. The Fool also represents our identity and, because he is nearing the edge of a cliff, he may also symbolize an identity crisis in the near future. Instead of falling victim to changes that threaten our identity, we can use them to discover a new self and a new life brimming with possibilities. The Fool represents the adventure of life, in which each day can be a new beginning.

THE MAGICIAN: INTENTION

Magic has power to experience and fathom things which are inaccessible to human reason. For magic is a great wisdom, just as reason is a great public folly.

—Paracelsus

    The Magician silently stands before a wooden table upon which sit representative elements of the four suits of the Minor Arcana. The wand, sword, cup, and pentacle placed upon this table are a three-dimensional representation of a Tarot reading, for readers customarily lay out their cards on a table in order to read them. The Magician is the reader who must cleverly discern the meaning contained in the cards' placement. Furthermore, the Magician's stance tells us that he is not an ordinary fortuneteller, but rather is a person skilled in the art of divination. While his right arm points upward, his left arm is pointing down, symbolizing the channeling of divine energy from above to below. Divination is the revelation of divine guidance to those of us below on this earthly plane of existence. It is through a Tarot reading that we may know our divine purpose and align ourselves with it.

    Actually, there are two types of magicians. The first is the stage magician with whom we are all familiar. He entertains his astounded audience with his trickery, making objects magically disappear and reappear. He lives in a magical world of illusion, in which things are not what they appear to be. Some Eastern religious traditions also see life as an illusion; however, if this is true, it is an illusion which is real in its consequences. The actions we take in the real world (the way we rearrange the objects on the table) determine the experiences we will have in this life. It is up to us to use the power of our free will to make correct choices that will result in positive consequences. Like the Magician, we have the power to rearrange our lives according to what we desire. The only illusion is our belief in powerlessness.

The stage magician expertly uses misdirection to create his magic tricks. The master of illusion cleverly focuses his audience's attention on a particular object while he carries out his magical operation out of sight. Our attention can also be misdirected by strong emotions. When we are emotionally overwhelmed, our attention is focused upon our feelings rather than rational thoughts. Anger or fear quickly captures our complete attention, causing us to ignore the important consequences of our actions. Even pleasant emotions can become powerful distractions. The joy we feel when we unexpectedly receive a dozen roses from our boyfriend may temporarily distract us from his philandering ways, or the excitement generated by a financial advisor's get-rich-quick plan may divert our attention from the great financial risks involved. Fear is expertly used by politicians, who frequently lead our attention away from a poor economy by focusing attention on international threats. In the Magician card, the table represents our field of attention, where we must intently focus our energy upon the issue at hand without becoming distracted. We need to be very careful that the objects within that field of attention are not manipulated by others into a shell game in which we are constantly fooled into looking in the wrong place for the wrong object. We must use selective attention to focus on the indisputable facts of the matter or on important clues to someone's character, instead of the artificial distractions of shallow promises.

Our bodies can be another source of distraction. Physical pain can divert our attention away from certain emotions that we want to repress. Many pain syndromes such as migraine headaches or back pain may be an attempt to focus our attention on the body's ills instead of on socially unacceptable feelings. Pain immediately gets our full attention, so it is the perfect distraction from the seething anger or overwhelming panic that we keep carefully buried beneath conscious awareness. If we are to outwit the conjuring magician inside us, we will need to focus our attention on what is really bothering us.

The second type of magician is the ceremonial magician who practices magick. Magicians of this type believe they can alter events through the use of rituals and spells. Instead of asking a higher power to intercede on their behalf, they believe in their own magical ability to change their circumstances. This is the fundamental difference between magick and religion: magicians use their own abilities to control events, while the religious person asks God to control events for them. Another important difference is that ceremonial magick is basically egocentric, while religion is egoless. Magick is based upon personal will, whereas religion is firmly established upon the belief in God's will. If the spell does not work, the magician has only himself to blame, whereas unanswered prayers can only be blamed upon omnipotent wisdom.

Although it differs from religion, magick has many positive benefits. Because it gives us a sense of control, the practice of magick can get us in touch with our sense of personal power. It is particularly effective in counteracting feelings of helplessness and powerlessness that arise when we are faced with uncontrollable situations. Magick also creates optimism. The first law of magick is to firmly believe in what we wish to manifest. One must clearly envision the intended goal of the magical operation if it is to succeed. This automatically creates a belief in a brighter future and encourages an optimistic outlook. The Magician in the Tarot teaches us that an optimistic viewpoint coupled with a belief in ourselves can create powerful magic in our lives.

The first step in any magickal operation is always to develop our intention. Before we can perform magick, we must carefully consider exactly what we want and then form a precise plan of action to obtain positive results. This is a crucial step because the success or failure we experience in life is not at the end of our endeavors, it is at the beginning. The intention we have at the start of any project will automatically lead us to the result. The type of partner we initially choose or the type of business we start can lead us to either triumph or disaster. Beginnings are vitally important, and the Magician's assignment as the number-one card in the Tarot reflects the importance of carefully focusing our energies at the start of any project.

When the Magician appears in a Tarot reading, we need to be wary of someone whose charisma hides a deceiving nature. Carl Jung theorized that magicians represent the negative father complex, a constellation of ideas revolving around a "bad" father figure. Negative father figures typically try to emasculate their sons and denigrate their daughters by imposing their own stringent beliefs. So, it may be necessary to examine the ways in which an overbearing father may influence our present behavior. If we identify with the Magician's power, we have the ability to defeat negative influences from our past. Just like the beautiful, cultivated garden in which the Magician stands, we have the power to transform negative relationships, situations, and behaviors into positive growth experiences.

THE HIGH PRIESTESS: MEMORY

Study the past if you would divine the future.

—Confucius

An impassive high priestess holding a scroll serenely sits between two massive pillars. This is a card of hidden meanings and secrets because the High Priestess wears a veil symbolizing the many veiled layers in life. As each veil is lifted, there is veil upon veil behind. The Torah scroll that the High Priestess holds is partially hidden by her veil, while the tapestry behind her conceals a Tree of Life diagram within its design. Behind these mysterious concealments are the waters of the unconscious, where all the secrets we hide from ourselves are contained. All mysticism and science are attempts to see through the veil of existence that obscures the true meaning behind the material world. There is a powerful desire within us to know all the hidden things in life, but we uncover them at great peril. The High Priestess is the guardian of doors that should remain unopened. As the spiritual gatekeeper of the many realms beyond our normal experience, she may deliberately prevent full understanding of many situations. The truth, if revealed, may be detrimental to ourselves or to those we love. Family secrets, unsolved mysteries, or past lives should remain hidden until we are ready to deal with the serious ramifications of their disclosure.

The High Priestess is the only card in the Tarot that contains a written document, the Torah scroll. Writing is man's greatest achievement because recorded experience can be disseminated to others so they are able to learn from the written word rather than through trial and error. Our personal history is recorded in our minds as memory. Like an open book, memory provides us with the opportunity to learn from past experience so we don't repeat previous mistakes in the future. However, sometimes our memory can be very selective, only recalling the best or the worst part of past experiences. The best way to maintain objectivity about the past is to keep a daily journal. We can record experiences as they happen and write down our feelings about important events. When we reread the journal entries months or years later, we can be assured that we are reviewing an accurate recollection of events for the time in question. Reviewing past journal entries can also be very insightful, as they can magically transport us to the places where we triumphed or failed. More importantly, the journal reflects our personal growth over the years. Looking over past journals, we can clearly see that disturbing issues in the past are no longer important issues in the present, or that we seem to be confronting the same problems today as yesterday. Journals, by chronicling the everyday events in our lives, help us to better understand ourselves through our relationship with the past so we can create a better future.

Like a furled or unfurled scroll, memories can be either lost or found. We may choose to lock away disturbing memories in the unconscious, where we believe they can no longer hurt us. Retrieving these lost memories can take years of concerted effort. When we finally do remember the past, there is always a danger that our memory may be distorted. Historical truth is often falsified by our preconceived ideas and our own vested interest. For example, our deceased father was either a perfect parent or a monster, while the boss we previously worked for was either a tyrant or a saint. These distortions are not the reality we lived through, but they do serve a vital purpose. By reconstructing the past, we can envision ourselves in a better light so we can heal old wounds.

Memories can also come unbidden into our awareness. While driving our car, for example, we suddenly remember an old college friend we haven't thought about in years. While these vivid memories are usually dismissed as flights of fancy, it is wise to respect their sudden emergence into consciousness. This intrusion of the past may provide important answers to present problems. The old college friend we suddenly remembered may have exhibited a positive quality such as tenacity that we realize we need to develop right now. Reminiscing about the friend, we suddenly remember that she was also a thief, and this could be a subtle reminder to lock our doors and windows. If we take the time to carefully look at our memories, we find that the past is a dim reflection of the present. By looking at the hidden messages contained in our memories, we may be able to better understand our present circumstances and correctly divine the future.

The High Priestess is also symbolic of another quality we need to develop: emotional self-sufficiency. Her flowing robes cascade into a pool of water on the ground. This indicates that she is the source of the water flowing through all the other cards in the Tarot. Because water represents the emotions, the High Priestess is also the source of her own emotional fulfillment. Like the High Priestess, we need to be responsible for our own happiness rather than shift this responsibility to our partners or children. By being the wellspring of our emotional well-being, we can always choose to be happy whether or not someone else plays a vital role in our lives. Like the temple pillars, we can find the inner strength to emotionally support ourselves independently of others.

When doing a Tarot reading, we must remember that the intuition we use to divine the future is only the memory of the past. We recognize the Tarot's truth because, in the recesses of our mind, we already know the fateful outcome. Another aspect to this card is the negative mother complex. Like the Magician, she may represent a far-less-than-perfect parent who was either neglectful or abusive.

THE EMPRESS: NURTURING

It is the marriage of the soul with nature that makes the intellect fruitful and gives birth to imagination.

—Henry David Thoreau

In this card, a beautiful woman in a flowery dress sits in a tranquil garden. The Empress is a very powerful figure because she represents Mother Nature in all her benevolence and cruelty. Mother Nature's wrath can destroy us with tornados, hurricanes, droughts, or floods. As Demeter, goddess of grain, she also can sustain us with a bountiful harvest and beautiful weather. One of Mother Nature's greatest gifts is the miracle of birth. The Empress is pregnant and personifies the nurturing found in motherhood. A mother is caring and protective, and it is these qualities that are present in the Empress card. The heart-shaped shield resting at her feet symbolizes her instinct to protect anyone who is young or unable to protect themselves. Anything that needs caring attention will automatically come under her protection. This may include nascent ideas or embryonic feelings that need protection from others' criticism until they are fully developed.

The Empress leans against a large pillow decorated with a design resembling a supportive spinal column. Mothers are the true support systems of the family, for they soothe the fretful, encourage the discouraged, and praise the disheartened. We need to develop these nurturing qualities within ourselves so we can become our own support systems. Just as the womb is a sheltered space for the growing fetus, we must find our own private place in which to nurture our ideas, feelings, and spirituality. Then we can develop the backbone necessary to firmly stand up against anything that threatens our personal growth. In this way, we become good mothers to ourselves.

Motherhood includes nurturing personal development, as well as creating new life. While the road we follow as parents is predetermined (diapers, tricycles, PTA meetings), the road to self-development is not as easily laid out for us. There are many paths to choose from including the arts, sports, education, or spirituality, each of which offers limitless opportunities for growth. Once we have chosen the path that best suits our temperament and innate abilities, we can go through the difficult process of giving birth to ourselves. Each skill mastered and every small step taken on the road to self-improvement brings us closer to becoming a brand-new person. Eventually, the growing potential we carry like an embryo within us will develop into great accomplishment.

However, there are two important prerequisites to self-birth. The first of these is adequate gestation time. We must give ourselves the necessary time to grow by setting aside time each day to devote to self-improvement. Whether it is learning meditation, learning to play an instrument, or learning to read the Tarot, we need to schedule time that will be used exclusively for our new undertaking. We will also need to develop patience because, like pregnancy, growth takes a considerable period of time. The process cannot be rushed, but rather should be completed in its own time frame.

The second prerequisite to birth is, of course, labor. We will get out of a situation only what we put into it, so we need to complete the fundamental work necessary to achieve our goals. Labor is required to manifest our dreams, even though it may be a painful process. There is an inborn tendency in all of us to search out pleasure, while avoiding pain. Our dreams can be sabotaged when we direct our energies toward satisfying immediate pleasures rather than concentrating on laborious, long-term goals. This pleasure principle is symbolized by the Empress card, where we find the immediate gratification of needs such as sex (pregnancy), hunger (wheat), and thirst (water). This card provides us with a subtle warning not to get distracted by momentary pleasures that can detour us from the important process of growth.

Self-development, like pregnancy, always necessitates change. The birth of a child changes the mother's life forever. Likewise, self-development is not just the addition of some new skill to our repertoire, but is the cause of fundamental change in our lives. When we transform something in our environment, we are transformed.

Women are by nature transformers who have the innate ability to change one thing into another: blood into milk; feelings into art; or ideas into reality. These things that we create also create us by changing how we perceive ourselves and our world. As our project grows, we can grow along with it. The achievement we experience in the outside world reflects our inner transformation.

In divination, the Empress encompasses issues revolving around our mothers. The Empress is the perfect image of what Jung termed the positive mother complex: nurturing, loving, and sympathetic. This idealized image of our mothers can sustain us in our darkest hours, for we know that we are truly loved. If our mother is not available, substitute mother figures can readily be found in the workplace or in friendships with other women. If this fails, then we can always be good mothers to ourselves by nurturing our interests, supporting our goals, and loving ourselves.

The final interpretation for this card in that of compromise. In the Greek myth of the coming of spring, the goddess Demeter had to compromise with the lord of the underworld, Pluto, to be allowed to see her daughter Persephone for part of the year. The number three on the Empress card also reflects a third alternative midway between two opposing desires. This tells us that we may have to find a suitable compromise in our conflicts with others if we are to succeed.

THE EMPEROR: POWER

Self-reverence, self-knowledge, self-control.
These three alone lead to sovereign power.

—Alfred, Lord Tennyson

A stern-faced Emperor sits regally upon his throne, surveying his vast empire. Emperors acquire their power by conquering distant lands and then forcing their ruthless will upon the conquered. In our lives, there are countless situations in which other people routinely force their will or beliefs upon us. The first persons to assert their authority over us were our parents, who exerted a tremendous influence in our lives. Our fathers did not necessarily have to possess an authoritarian personality to influence our behavior. The archetypal father, whom the Emperor symbolizes, asserts his authority by virtue of just being our parent. Because displeasing our father could jeopardize our loving relationship, we quickly learn to acquiesce to his demands. Even after we have grown up and our parents have died, we can still be tyrannized by our parents' ideals, which continue to rule our lives. Eventually, we can become totally dependent upon any outside authority, trusting their power rather than our own. However, by becoming aware of our parents' effect upon us, we are able to develop an inner authority independent of external influence.

The typical father in Western society is a good provider who works hard, but who remains disinterested in what is happening in the home. Fathers may, like the Emperor, be encased in their emotional armor, preferring to be emotionally remote. Hopefully, as childrearing becomes a shared activity between fathers and mothers, this situation will change. Nevertheless, many of us carry around the heavy armor of a patriarchal culture that subtly rewards us for performance and independence while failing to acknowledge vulnerability, intimacy, or sensitive feelings. While this armor may keep the outside world from intruding upon us, it also prevents us from touching others. Western culture, which the Emperor represents, has become increasingly insensitive to others' differences, vulnerabilities, and needs. As for ourselves, we need to recognize our ingrained insensitivity to others and then consciously strive to become more tolerant and understanding. Developing active listening techniques and a compassionate disposition can help us defend ourselves from our own damaging defenses. Other defensive attitudes that we need to be aware of are cynicism and negativity. We can wear our cynicism like a suit of armor, protecting ourselves from disappointment. Negativity is another form of protection, for by always expecting the worst possible outcome in every situation, we will never be disillusioned. Nevertheless, learning to trust in a positive outcome is an important step toward abolishing the tyranny of our inner Emperor.

The Emperor, unlike many of the other cards, represents the real world with all its inherent demands and immense responsibilities. The glacial mountains in the card's background reflect the cold, harsh reality which we must sometimes face. Our hostile environment often forces us to adapt to its demands, however, reluctantly. Economic recessions, disastrous weather, or the sudden loss of a loved one can, like an authoritarian emperor, force us to leave our homes or relationships. Exigent circumstances beyond our control may require us to deal with a difficult reality we would rather not confront. The Emperor within us is forced to immediately attend to problems and make authoritative decisions. We must take care of problems as they arise instead of holding onto the delusion that the problematic situation will miraculously improve on its own. By finally recognizing the demands of the external world, we can effectively rule our domain.

As an authoritarian ruler, the Emperor symbolizes the incessant demands made upon us by ourselves and others. Demands in the workplace and at home can be overwhelming at times. While constantly fulfilling others' demands can spare us the anxiety of free choice, it leaves us little leeway for self-direction. Submitting to others' demands may make our lives predictable but essentially not our own. There must be a balance between the needs of others and our own needs. We may also play the role of Emperor by constantly demanding that everyone do everything our way. Unfortunately, since most of our demands are usually ignored, we are left feeling very frustrated and angry because of others' flagrant disobedience. Rather than playing the role of benevolent dictator, we might strive to elicit others' cooperation instead. Politely asking for what we want usually results in greater compliance, not to mention a friendlier environment. Paradoxically, we can still hold onto our imperial authority, even if our first decree is to rescind all demands.

When the Emperor appears in a reading, it naturally reminds us of our fathers. Whether we view him as a benevolent protector or a harsh disciplinarian, our father is a very influential person in our lives. The Emperor symbolizes the positive father complex in which our father's beliefs and attitudes have become our own. We may follow him into the same profession or uncritically accept his every word as law. In a larger context, we may be dominated by someone or something that reminds us of our beloved father. Large corporations or universities can become institutionalized parents who we hope will protect and care for us as our father once did. Although it gives us a sense of power to align ourselves with large institutions, the power we really need to access is within. True self-empowerment is not conferred by our fathers or by corporations, titles, or salaries, but rather is bestowed by ourselves.

THE HIEROPHANT: BELIEF

Man makes holy what he believes as he makes beautiful what he loves.

—Ernest Renan

In this card, the Hierophant gives his ritual blessing to a pair of kneeling monks. As a religious figure, the Hierophant personifies religious belief and faith in things unseen. Personal beliefs, whether in God or in ourselves, form the intangible bedrock upon which our entire reality is built. What we believe about ourselves and the world around us affects every aspect of our lives, including our self-esteem, relationships, and careers. When we strongly believe that doors will be closed to us because of our race, age, or sex, they will be. When we fatalistically believe that we do not deserve to have a fulfilling relationship, we will fail to have one. As a famous French anthropologist once remarked, "Beliefs are real in their consequences." So, to understand the circumstances of our lives, we need to fully understand the origin and consequences of our most cherished beliefs.

Religious and cultural beliefs are so firmly ingrained in our consciousness that we are totally unaware of their powerful influence. Our national heritage may value traditional roles for men and women, so we believe we must have children at an early age, or we must be the sole breadwinner for our family. Beliefs, like physical characteristics, can also be inherited from our parents. This is particularly true of parental beliefs revolving around the nature of the world and our place in it. Some parents view the world as a dangerous place full of imminent disaster, while others see life as an adventure. When we internalize these parental beliefs without question, our parents' outlook on life becomes our own. When we are young, our parents seem to be as infallible as the Pope because, as sons and daughters, we believe their every word is the gospel truth. As we get older, our experiences in life tend to validate our parents' belief system. In fact, we can go to great lengths to find situations that reinforce our pre-existing beliefs. For example, if a divorced mother believes that all men eventually abandon their wives, then her daughter will promptly find a man who will abandon her at the first opportunity. Whether the belief we hold is valid or not is unimportant, so long as we can find justification for it in the real world. In this way, beliefs are real in their effect upon our lives. We become what we believe.

Like the massive pillars behind the Hierophant, beliefs support our entire world. However, beliefs can also be very limiting, just as the walls of a great cathedral enclose sacred space. Although we would all like to break out of the enclosure of our restrictive beliefs, there are two reasons why we often fail to change core beliefs. First, the nature of belief dictates that we cannot believe in one thing and its opposite at the same time. If we believe everyone will try to swindle us, we cannot concurrently believe in trust. The stronger our convictions, the less inclined we will be to accept alternate beliefs. This naturally narrows our awareness, and our beliefs become very restricted. Second, many of our most cherished beliefs are largely unconscious and, therefore, are not accessible to awareness. It is only through our dreams and oracles like the Tarot that we can access our hidden beliefs about ourselves.

The most important beliefs we hold are religious principles. Whether we call it a morality complex or a superego, religious belief establishes certain standards of behavior that we ideally would like to live by. In this context, the Hierophant is seen as a religious leader giving his blessing to his ideological offspring who must conform to the prescribed moral code. However, if we receive our moral guidance from popular culture rather than organized religion, we can quickly become lost in a sea of contradictory beliefs. Modern society has embraced a form of moral relativism in which there appear to be no clear-cut distinctions between right and wrong. Like the background of the card, moral conduct seems to be a grey area in which there always seem to be mitigating circumstances to explain our transgressions. In our lives, we must be certain that we are not making flimsy excuses for hurting others. The Hierophant, as a reflection of our conscience, represents our inner sense of morality regardless of what society dictates. Our self-imposed standards of behavior will guide us through the labyrinth of moral choices to the right destination.

The Hierophant is also the supreme religious instructor, representing the many teachers we encounter in life. On our spiritual journey, life experience is often our only teacher. However, experience is a very harsh instructor because it usually gives the crucial test first and then follows it with the lesson to be learned. Life experience, although valuable, can cost us time, money, or even our lives. Nevertheless, we continue to attract certain experiences in order to learn important lessons from them. What we learn largely depends upon our ability to objectively understand our role in what happens to us. If we can take personal responsibility for our actions, then the lesson will be well-learned.

Everyone we meet in life is a potential teacher, but the people who school us in life's most important lessons may not be paragons of virtue. Sometimes the best teachers are those who teach by negative example. When our parents or friends make major mistakes with their health, their finances, or their relationships, we can find the place where they went wrong and vow never to go there.

Because we tend to teach what we most need to learn, teaching others can also provide us with important lessons. So, when we read the Tarot for others, we also read for ourselves. If we listen carefully to what we say when we are reading for others, we will undoubtedly hear the advice we most need to hear echoed in our words. As the Hierophant card clearly shows, we are both the student and the teacher.

THE LOVERS: CHOICE

I am always content with what happens, for I know that what God chooses is better than what I choose.

—Epictetus

This card shows Adam and Eve in the Garden of Eden just before their tragic fall from grace. Although this biblical story is central to Judeo-Christian belief, this mythical account of the first human beings reflects a wide range of problems inherent in life including the nature of relationships, the lure of temptation, and the power of choice. While the previous card, the Hierophant, emphasized obedience to religious authority, the Lovers shows the tragic consequences of disobedience. When Adam and Eve ate the forbidden fruit, they were immediately thrown out of the garden and transformed into earthly creatures who would have to endure the many hardships of material existence.

Psychologically, to be cast out of the Garden of Eden is to be rudely ejected from a place of safety and security where a loving nurturer provided everything we needed in life. In other words, we must leave the innocent, carefree world of childhood to enter the demanding and restrictive adult world. Childhood is a paradise to which we can never return, although it continues to exist in many forms of fantasy. When we fervently wish that things were the way they used to be, we have entered the world of the Lovers, where we nostalgically long for a former time in our lives before our fall from grace. Before the disease, the divorce, or the disappointment, there was an idealized past that was perfect. In reality, the past was probably just as difficult as the present. The Lovers card reflects this tendency to adopt a romantic view of the past while ignoring the present. In this case, our fall from grace takes place when we realize that our past paradise is an illusion and we are involuntarily cast into the harsh reality of the present.

The Garden of Eden story is also a classic tale about the power of choice. Adam chooses to disobey God by eating the forbidden apple and then suffers the dire consequences of his decision. In the story of our lives, we have chosen to disobey the authority of our parents so we could assert our independence. Growing up entails making our own decisions based upon personal rather than parental values. As adults, we may have attained freedom of choice, but we cannot choose the consequences of our decisions. Every choice we make results in loss because we must leave behind all the other alternate selections. Since choosing one thing naturally precludes another choice, we have to cope with the resultant lost opportunities. While we may regret missed opportunities, it is unwise to dwell upon all the roads not taken. Instead, it is better to realize that, given how the alternatives were perceived at the time, we made exactly the right choice.

Just as there are two people on the Lovers card, we can make decisions in either one of two ways: consciously or unconsciously. Conscious decisions are based upon self-awareness, whereas unconscious decisions are based upon hidden agendas we are largely unaware of in our lives. Conscious awareness creates freedom of choice, while unconsciousness produces compulsive behavior. For instance, a woman with an alcoholic father chooses to marry an alcoholic. This is not a well-considered decision, but rather a compulsive need to unconsciously re-create her childhood. Because we are always prone to unconscious motivations, any decision-making process must include self-knowledge. When, like the Lovers, there is a union of the unconscious with conscious awareness, we will be able to make positive choices.

While we certainly have many more choices in life than in ages past, we sometimes fail to notice the many moral choices we make each day. In the Middle Ages, such ethical choices were codified by the Church as the seven deadly sins and the seven moral virtues. The Lovers card, because it depicts the first time humans had to choose between good and evil, represents the crucial choices we must make between virtue and vice in everyday life. So, when the Lovers card appears in a reading, we are advised to either develop one of the seven virtues or renounce one of the seven deadly sins. Exactly which of these saving virtues or deadly sins we need to work on can be shown to us by the other cards in the reading. Fourteen of the Tarot's Major Arcana cards correspond to each of the seven vices and virtues, so their appearance in a reading can alert us to the particular moral choices we must make.

The first of the seven virtues is temperance, represented by Temperance in the Tarot. To be temperate is to do all things in moderation, and this is demonstrated by the angel of Temperance carefully blending the contents of his two cups. The second virtue is justice, symbolized by the scales held by the woman in Justice. Fortitude is another important virtue, symbolized by the woman resolutely holding the lion's jaws in the Strength card. The virtue of prudence is illustrated by the Moon, as it represents the careful way we must traverse a moonlit path. Faith is represented by the personification of religious belief, the Hierophant. Hope is embodied by the Empress, because the unborn child she carries gives her renewed hope for a better future. The final virtue is charity, symbolized by the woman in the Star who generously pours out her water for all eternity.

The seven deadly sins are illustrated, not surprisingly, by some of the most negative cards in the Tarot. The Tower symbolizes the vice of anger as it shows the destructive power of wrath. The vice of gluttony is represented by a very rotund Devil, while the Hanged Man exemplifies sloth due to his inability to move. The World, containing man's many desires, represents the vice of greed. The Sun, with its central position in the solar system, symbolizes the vice of pride. The Wheel of Fortune is envy because those unfortunates at the bottom of the wheel usually envy those at the top. Finally, the naked figures of the Lovers symbolize the vice of lust. By carefully examining a Tarot reading in the light of these vices and virtues, we can become more aware of the ethical basis of our problems.

THE CHARIOT: CONTROL

One who rules his spirit is better than one who takes a city.

—The Bible

In the seventh card of the Major Arcana, a triumphant warrior proudly stands in his swift chariot. Since the chariot is a means of conveyance, it symbolizes a necessary transition in our life from one place to another. This could be the transition of middle age, the passage from being a student to becoming a teacher, or simply moving to a different location. With its constant movement, the Chariot reminds us that it is the journey, not the destination, which is important. This process of change will challenge our abilities, and we may need the courage of a warrior to complete our transition. The charioteer is the laurelled hero who valiantly confronts his fears and continues on his journey despite his apprehensions.

To successfully maneuver a chariot, the driver must carefully control the animals that are pulling it along. Likewise, the Chariot card reflects all the control issues we have in our lives. The first and most important type of control is self-control. While we usually complain about others' control over us, outside influence is very small compared to the control we have over ourselves. In an era in which there is rampant drug and alcohol abuse, there are obviously many among us who are having serious problems in the area of self-control. This lack of control is like a runaway chariot heading toward the edge of a cliff while the charioteer holds on for dear life. When we relinquish control, we let substances or others take complete control of our lives while we are passively carried along toward disaster. We can also be carried away by our emotions. Anger or sorrow can carry us to a barren land devoid of joy. Even if we do feel emotionally out of control at times, we always have some control over our actions. Trying something new, even though we are afraid, or persevering when we feel discouraged takes an enormous amount of self-control. It is this heroic self-control that leads to the triumphant procession pictured on the Chariot.

Like the driver who skillfully uses his reins to guide the animals pulling his chariot, we must learn to use our sense of self-control wisely. Too much control can be just as damaging as too little. The Chariot card illustrates man forcefully harnessing his animals in order to control them, and this may mirror our own domineering way of controlling our animal instincts and passions. Typically, men repress more of their feelings than women in the belief that giving their emotions free rein would show weakness. However, too much control over feelings can lead to psychological difficulties. Because feelings are also a vital part of communication, consciously controlling the expression of our feelings can result in damaged relationships. Some of us also feel the need to maintain strict control over our social behavior and appearance, mistakenly believing that these are the only things we can control in an unpredictable world. Eventually, we will discover that, like a horse reined in too tightly, retaining too much control over our appearance or our passions only hinders our progress.

The invisible connection between the charioteer and his harnessed animals mirrors the underlying control issues found in every relationship. Some of us fear being controlled by those around us, while others wish to exert their control over men and women at every opportunity. Those who dread the thought of someone else pulling the strings usually assert their independence by avoiding intimate relationships or by starting their own businesses. People who wish to control others seek positions of authority or become petty tyrants at home. There are also those who subtly control us through the invisible reins of guilt and fear in order to elicit our cooperation. The Chariot card advises us to become more aware of the controlling forces that surround us so we can take control of our lives.

Like the charioteer, we find that moving forward in life requires motivation. While we are harnessed to time's chariot, we must find something that moves us to take action. Aristotle theorized that all human actions derive from one or more of seven causes: chance, nature, compulsion, habit, reason, passion, or desire. As the seventh card in the Major Arcana, the Chariot represents these seven motivations for our behavior. Just as the chariot leaves the walled city, all of these motivations either take us away from a negative situation or propel us toward a positive outcome. We need to be in touch with our underlying motivations because it is our inner drives that determine our destination.

In a reading, the Chariot often represents a career persona, for it is in the world of work that we venture forth in order to triumph. Work in the world can become a vehicle for growth. Although we tend to base our self-worth upon the success of our relationships, the self-assurance gained through professional accomplishment can take us a long way in life.

STRENGTH: COOPERATION

Mastering others requires force; mastering the self needs strength.

—Lao-Tzu

In this card, a courageous woman gently closes the mouth of a ferocious lion. Her strength lies in her extraordinary ability to subdue wild animals. This gift of magically overpowering the king of beasts derives from her vital connection with her own nature and the nature that surrounds her. When we are in touch with universal forces, we have nothing to fear from man or beast.

In the previous card, the Chariot, the charioteer forcefully subdued his animals by harnessing them to his vehicle. The woman of Strength, by contrast, does not forcefully coerce the lion, but rather seems to gently elicit his cooperation. Through nonverbal communication, she has expressed her wishes, and the lion has magically complied. In fact, the lion seems as docile as a domestic cat, for he seems to be licking the woman's hand. She has gently tamed the beast instead of forcefully overpowering it. There is a vital lesson in this: if we wish to impose our will on the world around us, we must first be in complete harmony with our environment. When we align our will with the greater forces surrounding us, we find not only strength, but victory as well. This is the essence of cooperation, whether we are cooperating with nature, or our fellow travelers. This card advocates a natural, synergistic approach to issues such as health, or relationships in which we actively work with the forces of nature. If we follow the woman's example, we can work with others' personalities instead of trying to change them, or we can consider natural alternatives for health problems.

The woman of Strength has effectively domesticated the wild, man-eating lion. This is reminiscent of the socialization process we all go through as children. Through our parents' love and concern, we are gradually taught to behave well, have good manners, and eventually become good citizens. A large part of this process is devoted to controlling our animal instincts so that we do not act in socially unacceptable ways. We are taught to control our immediate desires for toys, revenge, and food. However, as adults, we may still have some difficulty in controlling these impulses. The Strength card shows us that we can foster a good relationship with our strongest impulses by domesticating our wildest desires. Just as the gentleness and affection of the woman gradually transforms the wild beast into a docile pet, we can learn to tame our desires by gently coaxing them to obey our commands. Like the wild lion, our desires seem to have a separate will of their own, but we can gradually bend their will to align with ours.

The title of this card alludes to the newly found courage, confidence, and capability of women today. While in times past many women were just as afraid of their strength as men were afraid of their weakness, twenty-first century women have befriended their inner strength. Like the woman pictured, they refuse to feel threatened by their own power. Instead of projecting their power onto male authority figures or institutions, they have learned to develop their own personal authority. Rather than focusing on their weaknesses and ineffectiveness, they have decided to concentrate on developing their strengths instead.

Paradoxically, the real strength of women lies in their ability to yield. The woman's bent-over posture clearly shows that "she stoops to conquer." In other words, sometimes to be strong, it is necessary to adopt a weak posture. Women have known for centuries that submission can be used as a subtle form of power if it is used correctly. Sometimes it is better to acquiesce rather than to waste precious energy fighting losing battles. Yielding in arguments can also quickly disarm an opponent, for he soon discovers that there is nothing of substance to fight against. Although this yielding strategy may go against our combative nature, it often produces very positive results.

The woman of Strength is interacting with a male lion, and this shows that she is making friends with the masculine side of her personality. In some women, this relationship with their inner male can be all-consuming, leading to a Diana complex. These women exhibit masculine characteristics while they firmly reject the traditional roles of wife and mother. Because they identify with the masculine, they may also choose professions usually reserved for men. The Strength card shows us that getting in touch with our masculine side is a very positive experience which can confer many benefits.

In a reading, Strength reflects our need to assert our masculine natures. It is time to realize that the problems we face may need a forceful solution. The ability to act decisively and remain confident in our decision is definitely a masculine strength. Also, because the woman's attention is directed toward closing the lion's mouth, we need to examine our ability to keep our own mouths shut. What we say can hurt others, and restricting our criticism or anger could definitely improve our relationships.

THE HERMIT: WISDOM

Knowledge dwells in heads replete with thoughts of other men; wisdom in minds attentive to their own.

—William Cowper

The Hermit is the wise old man of the Tarot. He stands alone on a mountaintop, holding aloft his lantern shining brightly in the darkness of night. Traditionally, the Hermit has been seen as a wisdom figure that, having attained spiritual enlightenment, now shines his light upon the path below so that others may follow. In this card, we are both the guide and the guided as we attempt to map out our journey through life. Sometimes our guide is the wise man pictured, while at other times, we may be led by the Fool; however, it is important that we keep to our course and continue climbing. Even if the course we have chosen is steep and long, we can be assured of success if we have a light to guide us.

Because we are all travelers in the dark, we must have a light to illuminate our path into the unknown. We need not fear the dark so long as we are guided by the light of a higher purpose. This light can be love, parenthood, spirituality, or any lofty ideal. The illumination of a higher purpose helps us to see where we are going and gives us courage when we are surrounded by our darkest fears and doubts. The light guides us in our passionate search for something better in life and in ourselves. Even a small act of selflessness, such as comforting a crying child, can help us connect with the best in ourselves. It is truly better to light one small candle than to curse the darkness. A life filled with purpose transports us to the mountaintop, where we can transcend our limitations.

The Hermit is also symbolic of the unconscious. Often, in order to find the best in ourselves, we must traverse the darkness of the unconscious. Exploring the dark aspects of our minds takes great courage, but the inner journey can lead us to a lofty destination. In order to enter into the unknown depths of ourselves, we will need to contact our inner wise man. Inner wisdom is always available, although it may appear in many forms. Our dreams are often far wiser than we are because they access a wisdom far greater than our own. The Tarot is another wise counselor, always eager to show us the right path or discourage us from going down the wrong road. The wisdom of the unconscious may also reveal itself in the lyrics of a song we can't get out of our heads, or a sudden flashback to a childhood memory. To access this hidden wisdom, all we have to do is focus our attention on the fleeting thought, the momentary memory, or the dream that is too soon forgotten. The wisdom we seek is within. We have only to listen.

The Hermit looks down from his lofty mountain peak at the dramatic scene far below. From high above, he is viewing his own life in perspective. It is only when we can elevate ourselves high above the circumstances of our lives that we can clearly see where all the different experiences fit together to form the story of our lives. The Hermit personifies the observing self who accurately perceives all that happens inside and outside ourselves. This wise observer carefully notices all of our accomplishments and failures without passing judgment. The observing self is that part of ourselves which remains detached from everyday experience in order to view life objectively. Remaining compassionate, we quietly gaze down from a tremendous height to lovingly observe everything we do in our lives. Gaining this lofty perspective has a calming effect upon the mind because we can be emotionally detached from the troubling situations in which we find ourselves.

We automatically gain this heightened perspective when we look upon our lives in retrospect. The Hermit gains his perspective by facing left, signifying that he is looking toward the past. An event in the past that we thought at the time was earthshaking, turns out to be a small bump in the road when we look back upon it. We should assume that whatever problem we may be experiencing in the present will be seen as either inconsequential or a blessing in disguise when we review it in the future. By treating the present as the past of some distant future, we can accurately judge our circumstances. We should, like the wise hermit, try to see everything in retrospect. Because life can only be understood backwards, it is wise to mentally project ourselves into a future where we can gain some perspective.

The Hermit voluntarily seeks isolation, living by himself in a secluded area. His ability to live without human contact is very reflective of modern man's essential alienation from his fellow man. Loneliness and isolation are widespread problems in the modern era, due in large part to our insular lifestyles. First, we grow up and quickly move away from our family. Then, we isolate ourselves within our homes, within our cubicles at work, and within our cars. Physical isolation soon evolves into psychological alienation, and we essentially become hermits.

Although alienation is usually seen as a basic problem of modern life, it can also be seen as a positive step in human development. Isolation encourages individualism, allowing us to follow our unique path. Without pressures from others, we are free to be ourselves and live life on our own terms. When we feel the sadness of isolation, it is wise to consider that a sense of belonging is often paid for by the high cost of conformity.

In a reading, the Hermit's silence can reflect unspoken problems. To live in silence with our troubles is to invite emotional hardship. Instead, we can make an effort to contact others with similar problems so we can benefit from their experience.

Although the Hermit is a solitary figure, he does offer wise counsel about relationships. The appearance of the Hermit in a reading does not necessarily predict that we will find ourselves alone. Rather, this card means we will be wiser in choosing future partners or in sustaining a relationship. This wisdom may come from unfortunate experiences, but we must treasure the wisdom we gain.

THE WHEEL OF FORTUNE: FATE

Submit to fate of your own free will.

—Marcus Aurelius

The Wheel of Fortune rotates human affairs, determining the fortunate or unfortunate circumstances of our lives. Of medieval origin, the Wheel of Fortune traditionally shows the changing fortunes of four men who are attached to a giant revolving wheel turned by the goddess Fortuna. On the top of the Wheel is a crowned king symbolizing worldly success, while on the bottom, another man lies prostrate in the mud. As the Wheel makes its circular revolution, the men switch places, as their fortunes change for better or worse. This card beautifully illustrates that our fate, whether it is great wealth or disastrous accident, is bestowed by the goddess. However, it is very difficult for most of us to believe in supernatural forces beyond our personal control determining the major events in our lives. Believing in self-determination, most of us think that our positions in life are earned, rather than bestowed by impersonal celestial forces. Nonetheless, fateful encounters can change the course of our lives forever, and whether we consider them blessings or curses, we cannot easily escape our destiny.

Take, for example, the story of the woman who, shortly after her wedding, suddenly discovered that her new husband was secretly a drug addict. She immediately divorces him and moves to another country where, a few years later, she meets another man and remarries. Soon after the wedding, she discovers he is also a drug addict. The moral of this sad but true story is that we are destined to have certain unalterable life experiences in order to grow. In fact, if we look back on our problems, we find that they are all very similar. There is always an older woman at work who we can't seem to get along with, or there is always a financial setback just as we are getting back on our fiscal feet. However, the Wheel of Fortune does not repeat the exact same experiences again and again. The Wheel is not a circle; it is a spiral on which we repeatedly travel to similar experiences. Each time, we circle around the spiral to a similar experience but at a higher level. With each successive revolution of the Wheel, we are brought back to a similar event, but each time we are a more mature person who is able to cope with the situation differently. In this way, we can gradually make progress in dealing with what the Fates have decreed.

While we travel along the circumference of the Wheel of Fortune on our circular journey, the Wheel becomes a vehicle for developing virtue. Those who have experienced the many ups and downs of life soon develop the virtue of humility, for it is impossible to have excessive pride when suffering disaster. Even the pride we may feel when we finally reach the pinnacle of success is quickly tempered by the realization that, as the Wheel slowly revolves, we may soon be back where we started. Feelings of exaltation or degradation quickly become relative when we discover the cyclical basis of experience. While in prosperous times we should be humble, in difficult times we need to develop the virtue of patience. Misfortune does not last forever, and we must patiently wait until the stars change their fateful positions in the heavens, until our body heals, or until the goddess Fortuna turns her eternally revolving Wheel of Fortune. Although patience is a virtue born of adversity, these words to the wise remain: "This too shall pass."

Virtuous behavior, however, does not guarantee material success. The Wheel of Fortune in the Waite-Smith Tarot is composed of both an inner and an outer wheel. The larger wheel represents the outer world of materialism, while the smaller wheel is the inner world of ethical values. Most of the time, these two wheels spin in opposite directions. They are at cross-purposes with one another. For example, corporate profits must be sacrificed for a cleaner environment, and whistle-blowers routinely get fired. The rise of virtue often brings about our downfall in the material world, while a financial windfall can usher in the temptation of newly affordable vices. As William Shakespeare said, "Some men rise by sin, some by virtue fall." This sage observation on the operation of the real world may force us to reconsider our ambitions. Before we blindly pursue our fortune, we need to carefully define what constitutes success in the spiritual and material worlds.

Our attitude toward good or bad fortune is far more important than the fortunate or unfortunate circumstances in which we find ourselves. Because our fate is beyond our control, one of our first reactions to a change of fortune is usually to blame or praise an omnipotent God. We may believe that misfortune is a fitting punishment for our sins or that good fortune is God's reward for our good behavior. Actually, these beliefs may have more to do with human psychology than religious dogma. By believing that our actions directly cause God's wrath or reward, we still remain in control. If, on the other hand, we view fate as an impersonal and erratic force in the universe, over which we have absolutely no control, we can feel totally helpless in the face of destiny. Helplessness, and her sister hopelessness, do not encourage us to become better people. This is because, when confronted with a predetermined destiny, most of us just want to give up. Since we feel nothing we do can change our fate, we do nothing. Although our lives may indeed be largely controlled by fate, it is unwise to be fatalistic. To believe that every event in our lives is predetermined destroys self-determination and the human spirit. Instead, we must cling to the slender hope that what we do makes a meaningful difference in our lives and in the lives of others.

The rotating Wheel of Fortune also illustrates an optimistic or pessimistic outlook, for we usually see ourselves as either on the way up or on the way down. Optimists naturally look for the best in themselves and in the world around them, while pessimists always expect the worst. Needless to say, our prevailing attitude can have serious consequences when we are confronted with misfortune. Pessimists view misfortune as a permanent situation ("This will never change"), and unjustly blame themselves for any reversal of fortune ("It's my entire fault that the company went out of business"). Optimists see their situation quite differently. They view misfortune as temporary ("I'll be able to get another job") and impersonal ("I know it's the poor economy not my job performance that resulted in my dismissal"). We can learn to be optimistic by believing in the transitoriness of experience and by telling ourselves that things always turn out for the best. An optimistic state of mind will assure us that, as the Wheel of Fortune turns, we will naturally ascend after the fall.

In a reading, the Wheel of Fortune represents the cyclical nature of events. Each yearly cycle brings us back to events that happened at the same time in previous years. Sometimes we have strong emotional reactions on the anniversary of a traumatic event. The anniversary of any tragic event such as a death, divorce, or accident can force us to relive the terrible feelings caused by past misfortune. This anniversary reaction may even be unconscious as we find ourselves inexplicably depressed at the same time each year. The appearance of the Wheel of Fortune in a reading can help us acknowledge these elusive feelings and, hopefully, come to terms with them.

JUSTICE: CONSEQUENCES

The hope of all who suffer.
The dread of all who wrong.

—John Greenleaf Whittier

The imposing figure of Justice sits holding her traditional sword and scales. The Tarot's Justice is not the familiar representation of legal justice that adorns courthouses, but rather is the symbol of divine justice. Societal justice meted out by the judicial system is hindered by human beings' limited awareness, while divine justice can clearly see the entire truth of all earthly matters. Unlike legal justice, the figure of Justice in the Tarot is not blindfolded, for she is all-seeing. Because injustice is the prevailing condition in our world, we must place our faith in a justice that transcends the boundaries of space and time. Divine justice operates in incomprehensible ways to invisibly balance the affairs of the world.

In our limited view, we feel justice is correctly operating in our lives if we get exactly what we desire. Contrarily, we feel a great sense of injustice when we fail to receive the things we want, or if we have been victimized in any way. In our way of thinking, we should automatically receive the positive rewards we deserve, while avoiding any penalties. In reality, life does not work this way. Whether we attribute our plight to karma or poor judgment, we all must face deprivation and suffer inexplicable losses during the course of our lives. Our reaction to these problems is usually to immediately complain that life is unfair. There seems to be no justice in the world, at least not for us. However, what we term justice is thinly disguised self-interest. We rarely consider our previous behavior or the feelings of others when we complain of being treated unfairly. In other words, we tend to miss the bigger picture.

Far beyond our limited concept of justice is divine justice, an ultimate authority far above our understanding. It portions out to us exactly what we truly deserve while punishing us for past transgressions. Divine judgment takes into consideration all personal and financial relationships between people in order to correctly apportion what is needed to balance the scales of justice. As harsh as this belief may be, there is a hidden benefit in believing in the laws of karma. If we truly believe in divine justice, we will never feel victimized. The problems and joys we experience in life are seen as merely a supernal accounting, using pain or pleasure as the currency. By placing our faith in this eternal system of checks and balances, we can set aside our bitterness in favor of complete acceptance of our lot in life. Everything is exactly as it should be because there is always a just outcome.

Justice is one of the four cardinal virtues, providing ethical direction in our relationships with others. When we believe in the concept of justice, we acknowledge that every action in our lives has important consequences. Every interaction disturbs the stable equilibrium of Justice's scales because every action transforms us into either debtors or creditors. To balance the scales, we will have to pay in some way for our mistreatment of others. Likewise, any kindness we extend to others will be returned to us in the future. This simple yet obscure formula for ethical conduct should greatly influence our relationships with others, but it seldom enters our thinking. Although we always consider the legal ramifications of our actions, the moral consequences of our behavior are usually lost in the pursuit of self-interest. Because the actions of today create our destiny tomorrow, we should always attempt to carefully examine our present conduct with divine justice in mind.

The Tarot's Justice is also concerned with the decision-making process. Courts of law routinely make decisions based upon legal precedent. We may also base our decisions upon previous experience, but it is better to use the Justice card as a guide to making sound decisions. Justice holds balanced scales in her hand, encouraging us to carefully weigh all the issues before making up our minds. It is particularly important to consider both sides of a matter in order to make an impartial decision. Both the advantages and disadvantages of an important decision need to be carefully considered. This can be easily accomplished by making two lists, one in favor of following a particular path and the other listing opposing reasons why we should not continue on the path. This listing must include the interests of all involved parties, not just ourselves. In this way, we are able to balance our needs with the needs of others. When our two lists are finally compared, we will be able to make our decision based upon what is best for us and for those around us.

To balance the scales of justice, it is necessary to either remove a heavier element from one side or add more weight to the other side. In our lives, we can maintain our balance by either eliminating certain activities or adding new ones. Because balance is the point between excess and deficiency, we may need to cut back on anything considered obsessive or addictive in nature while devoting more of our energy to neglected parts of our lives. For example, if we obsessively pursue our work, we neglect both our health and our family. Making time for exercise and family activities is a workable solution. The Justice card advises us to re-evaluate our priorities to assure a more balanced lifestyle.

In a reading, the Justice card indicates a satisfactory solution to our problems. Like a judicial verdict, it signifies the end of a series of troubling events, so we may finally get on with our lives. However, when the problem is internal rather than external, the verdict becomes self-imposed. Just as a court of law determines the guilt or innocence of the accused, we often become our own judge and jury. Our crime begins with the breaking of a self-imposed rule that, in our minds, should never be broken. Our conscience is the policeman who arrests us, while our defense attorney is our mind's attempt to rationalize our behavior by presenting reasonable excuses. The judge is our inner critic, who constantly condemns our criminal behavior. Finally, our sentence is a combination of guilt and misery administered to ourselves over a long period of time. Because judging ourselves too harshly can result in depression or self-destructive behavior, we may wish to administer a more lenient sentence. This leniency is based upon the premise that we have limited awareness that does not give us the supernal wisdom needed to accurately judge ourselves.

THE HANGED MAN: SACRIFICE

The important thing is this: to be able at any moment to sacrifice what we are for what we could become.

—Charles Du Bois

The Hanged Man finds himself suspended upside down from a tree branch. He appears to be completely immobilized, eternally stuck in a situation from which he is unable to extricate himself. We have all been, at one time or another, in his position. When we are stuck in a dead-end job, or find ourselves in the never-ending line at the motor vehicle office, we are having a Hanged Man experience. Being unable to move usually results in feelings of powerlessness and frustration. However, the Hanged Man of the Tarot remains oddly serene. By completely accepting his powerlessness, he has found inner peace. There comes a time in all our lives when we must accept our own limitations and the pain these limitations produce. When we continue to try our best in unchangeable circumstances, we have completed a heroic task. If we can persevere in our efforts without being paralyzed by fear or immobilized by helplessness, we have succeeded admirably. In order to cultivate the serenity necessary to endure, we must have complete trust in a higher power. This is echoed in the words of St. Paul, who said, "When humans are the most powerless, God is the most present." The Hanged Man is prevented from falling by a slender rope attached to his ankle. Our trust in God is that slim thread which suspends us high above our troubles and keeps us from fatally falling into despair.

Another theme contained in the symbolism of the Hanged Man is that of sacrifice. While the Hanged Man is essentially a pagan symbol, it is closely related to the crucifixion and sacrifice of Jesus Christ. Hanging, whether upright or upside down, represents the essence of sacrifice in which a person is killed in order to fulfill a higher purpose. Perhaps we cannot escape the pain of life, but there must be a reason for our suffering. A higher purpose gives our sacrifice meaning and makes our pain bearable.

Love always requires sacrifice. In our lives, we make sacrifices daily for our loved ones. Whether we are sacrificing for our children or supporting our partner's ambitions, we always give our love along with our best effort. Like the Hanged Man, who sees the world upside down, sacrifice demands that we shift our perspective from what we selfishly want for ourselves to what we can selflessly give others. Actually, this card could probably be re-titled "The Hanged Woman," because women seem to naturally embrace the concept of self-sacrifice by always putting others' needs above their own.

Sometimes, we have to sacrifice an important part of ourselves in order to make progress. Spiritual progress requires that we sacrifice our egos, so we may transcend the limitations of our thinking. Also, some of our most cherished beliefs must be abandoned if we are to finally grow up. The Hanged Man is firmly attached to the tree, and it is our attachment to our family tree that often immobilizes us. Family expectations can tie our hands, leaving us suspended, with few options. Letting go of our perfect son or dutiful daughter persona can liberate our unique talents so we may develop our full potential. We may also need to sacrifice our belief in human perfectibility as well by choosing to accept the flaws of those closest to us.

One of our greatest sacrifices is detailed in the Old Testament. In biblical times, animal sacrifice was used to petition God for mercy. When man was in need of God's help, an animal sacrifice was made to secure God's favor. Although barbaric by modern standards, animal sacrifice fulfilled an important symbolic purpose. The animal that was killed represented the sacrifice of man's instinctual, animal nature. Today, we must also sacrifice our animal natures in order to maintain our health or sustain a stable family life. Like the Hanged Man, we may have to endure a great deal of physical discomfort when we decide to relinquish our animal passions. However, we must remember that the rewards more than make up for our pain. The necessary losses we voluntarily endure help us become the persons we were meant to be.

It is also possible to sacrifice for the wrong reasons, and when this happens, we can become as stuck as the Hanged Man. The twelfth card of the Major Arcana is associated with the element of water. Because water naturally reflects everything upside down, the Hanged Man is actually a reverse image formed by his reflection in the water. Similarly, sacrifice can quickly turn into a distorted reflection of our own egos. When we need constant acknowledgment or rewards for the sacrifices we have made, we are bolstering our egos in the performance of good deeds. This can easily lead to the development of a martyr complex as we constantly complain that we are never appreciated for all we have done for others. Martyrdom produces depression and bitterness because the martyr genuinely believes that other people do not value his self-sacrifice. When we become too attached to sacrifice, it is time to explore the reasons why we are causing ourselves so much unhappiness.

It is also possible to sacrifice the wrong things in life. Sometimes, we sacrifice our true selves in the pursuit of money, a new lover, or social acceptance. When we sacrifice our integrity to satisfy our aspirations, we eventually discover that ambition is not the best compass by which to guide our lives. Finally arriving at our longed-for destination, we may find that we have left irreplaceable parts of ourselves behind.

In a reading, the Hanged Man represents an irresolvable problem. Since a workable solution cannot be found, the advice given in this card is to totally accept the problem. When we fully realize that diets don't work, things will never be the way they were, or he's not going to come back, we must accept our fate. Nevertheless, there can be a great sense of release in accepting the mystery of failure. If we can finally cease struggling at the end of our rope, we can attain freedom.

DEATH: REWARD

Things do not change; we change.

—Henry David Thoreau

    The Grim Reaper, dressed in a suit of black armor, stands ready to mow down four unfortunate souls. This is the card we all dread, but are destined to get sooner or later. We all live with the specter of death. For some, the approaching hoofbeats are a distant rumble, while others hear the loud clattering, crashing in their ears. The Death card naturally instills fear when it appears in a reading, and is the primary reason why some people adamantly refuse to have their cards read. This has resulted in some very clever ways to avoid the omen of death present in a Tarot reading. In some cultures, when the Death card is drawn, the querent immediately kills an insect to safely fulfill the Tarot's grim prophecy! The Death card forces us to confront our fear of the end of our existence on earth, and our dread of the afterlife as we envision it. Non-existence is terrifying enough, but when the Christian hell of fire and brimstone is even remotely considered as our eternal resting place, we understandably have great difficulty in accepting death. Hopefully, the Tarot's rendition of death can guide us through the fear of our demise.

    To resolutely face death takes the faith of a clergyman, the courage of a king, the optimism of youth, and the wonder of a child. The four figures who confront the Grim Reaper in the Death card reflect these different ways in which we can cope with death in our lives. Faith, represented by the bishop, can dispel our fears if we strongly believe in a benevolent creator. Courage, symbolized by the fallen king, sometimes temporarily fails us when we are faced with our own mortality. Even those of us who are not immediately threatened by death must be courageous, for it takes real courage to maintain a meaningful connection with the world when we are confronted daily with the transitoriness of life. Optimism, represented by the adolescent girl, is the positive attitude that must be our constant companion in the face of death. Wonder, symbolized by the little girl, is our remarkable ability to view death as an amazing adventure rather than as a punishment.

As long as we view death as a divine punishment, we will fear it. As a punishment, death appears to be the ultimate contradiction. In the Tarot, as in life, Death approaches the saint and the sinner, the powerful and the weak, the rich and poor alike. If death was a fitting punishment, the guilty would perish while the innocent would be spared. Another contradiction is that we have been brought up to believe in the rewards of virtue, but no matter how good we behave, we will all die someday. We also believe that some people must die for committing terrible atrocities, for this is their well-deserved punishment. However, if we look at death from the perspective of the Hanged Man, we could see that, in all likelihood, life is the punishment, while death is our reward. This is not an entirely new concept, as Christians have often spoken of the deceased as having "gone to his reward." This is life's greatest mystery, aptly summarized by the Greek philosopher Lucan, who said, "The gods conceal from men the happiness of death, that they may endure life." Envisioning an idyllic afterlife can help to eradicate our ingrained fear of death, so we can celebrate eternal life.

Our fear of death is also directly connected to our self-esteem. Most of us are afraid we will die before we have had the opportunity to prove our self-worth. After we have had a close brush with death, our first reaction is usually to review the life we had led up to that fateful point in time. This life review is often discouraging because we realize we have failed to accomplish many of the goals we set for ourselves. Finding our lives lacking, we desperately try to prove our worth as soon as possible by pursuing our lifelong dreams. However, as long as our self-worth is based upon accomplishment rather than our intrinsic worth as human beings, we will never be able to successfully surmount our fear of death.

The fear of dying also can conceal the wish to murder. Take, for example, the man who becomes so infuriated that he wants to strangle his wife. This abhorrent idea is buried very deeply in his unconscious; however, he soon develops asthma. In his asthmatic choking, he experiences both his intention to choke his wife and self-punishment for his forbidden death wish. Although some of us harbor ill feelings for our loved ones, these dire desires must be interpreted symbolically rather than literally. What we actually wish for is to be permanently rid of the problem this person poses to us. We wish the problem would die, not the person. By focusing on the problem instead of our anger, we can find a workable solution.

In a reading, the Death card signals an important transformation. Because every transformation begins with an ending, we should become aware of the small deaths that herald new beginnings. Being fired or sending our children away to college may seem like the end of the world, but they are actually transformational opportunities. We must reinvent ourselves, because the people we were no longer exist. As we are carried along on our journey from birth to death, we die many times. We can, like the pleading bishop on the card, resist the many endings that naturally occur. Our old self may want desperately to survive, even if it is miserable. While we may fear the changes transformation brings, we must realize that transformation is the reason for our existence.

TEMPERANCE: INTEGRATION

The golden rule in life is moderation in all things.

—Terence

The luminous angel of Temperance carefully pours the contents of one golden cup into another. As he blends the two liquids together, a wonderful transformation takes place. The angel reflects man's superhuman ability to transform everything he touches. Although we often fail to notice it, our everyday actions have a great impact on the world around us. What we say and what we do changes the world for better or worse, so we must be very conscious of our actions. When we try to carefully pour the contents of one cup into another, we must concentrate in order to prevent spilling the liquid. Likewise, we need to concentrate our attention on what we are eating, watching, reading, thinking, and doing so that we do not waste our time. Focusing on the present moment can have far-reaching consequences because deliberate actions create a more purposeful life.

The interchange of liquid between the two cups in Temperance is reminiscent of the sharing that forms the basis of any relationship. When two people connect, their lives intermingle like the blending of two liquids. However, not all of us like to be blended in this way. This card symbolizes the delicate balance we must maintain between merging with someone else and keeping our own identity intact. If we pour all of the contents of our cup into our lover's cup, we will have nothing left but an empty cup. On the other hand, if we don't share enough of ourselves, we can hardly hope to have an intimate, loving relationship. We must be willing to share our life, but not surrender it. There should always be a part of our lives which remains exclusively ours. This may be a favorite hobby, our artwork, or our spirituality. There must always be something wonderful we do by ourselves, for ourselves. By developing separate interests, we often become more interesting because we have more of us to share with others. Each person should encourage their partner to develop outside interests so they can develop their full potential. In this way, we learn to respect each other as unique individuals who can bring their special qualities into the relationship. We cannot lose ourselves in a relationship in the unrealistic hope that our partner will love us more. Although we have a responsibility to love and care for one another, our primary responsibility must be to ourselves.

The Temperance card also illustrates the differences in giving and receiving between the two sexes. In general, men are reluctant to share because they fear intimacy. They feel their autonomy will be severely compromised by a committed relationship. Women, on the other hand, are more than willing to share because they fear aloneness. So, like the two cups pictured, women usually abundantly give while men reluctantly receive. This unequal situation is based upon the misconception that we cannot experience true intimacy and independence at the same time. The cups that the angel of Temperance holds are not changed by the water shared between them. They remain essentially the same. Likewise, we can keep our individuality while sharing parts of ourselves in a relationship.

The angel of Temperance pours out his blessings just as we pour out our love for another person. We give our beloved our hearts, our energy, and our time, while asking for little in return. When we fall in love, we experience a great outpouring of emotion that, like a swift current, can quickly transport us far away. Before we get carried away, we must carefully determine if our potential partner is a worthy vessel for our love. Just as a particular cup may not be the right receptacle for the type of liquid poured into it, some people are not worthy of the love we wish to bestow. Our love must be tempered with wisdom, lest we waste it like spilled water.

Just as the contents of the two cups merge to become one, we are constantly trying to integrate the opposing parts of our personalities into a cohesive whole. There is a blending of male and female energies that occurs naturally as we grow older. We also gradually learn to integrate our positive and negative attributes, becoming less defensive of our weaknesses and less identified with our strengths. If we are pursuing a spiritual path, we begin to apply spiritual knowledge to problems in the real world in order to create a synthesis of both worlds. Integration is a vital step in our growth, for the whole is always much greater than the sum of its parts.

The final integration is the hallmark of Temperance. It is to integrate our desire to gratify our instinctual impulses with prohibitions against fulfillment of those desires. To be temperate is to practice restraint in satisfying our desires. Temperance is not the nullification of desire, nor is it complete abstinence. On the contrary, desires must be acknowledged. The natural desire for sensual enjoyments such as food, wine, or sexual pleasure has preserved the human race for hundreds of generations. It is only when these natural desires degenerate into selfishness that they become destructive. When the satisfaction of desire becomes a self-centered pleasure, we automatically become intemperate. Temperance seeks to balance our selfishness with selflessness, resulting in moderation. When we control our temper, eat moderately, and practice restraint, we effectively blend our wants and needs into a unified whole.

When Temperance is present in a reading, we are advised to use restraint in all of our activities. Like the two cups pictured, we must practice moderation in both giving and receiving. Giving too much to others makes them overly dependent upon our generosity, so they never learn self-sufficiency. Receiving too much food, alcohol, or possessions can be just as destructive. We can avoid excessive giving and receiving by focusing on the Temperance card. Like a guardian angel, the virtue of temperance can protect us from ourselves.

THE DEVIL: DISTORTION

> The world is the best of all possible worlds, and everything in it is a necessary evil.
>
> —Francis Herbert Bradley

The Devil card in the Tarot is an intentional distortion of the Lovers card. Adam and Eve have been transformed into demons enslaved in the dark, while the angel of the Lovers has been replaced by a grotesque devil. This bizarre transformation of good into evil develops when love is absent. Evil in our world is caused by disappointed, despised, or frustrated love. The absence of love also causes an absence of light, plunging us into the pitch-black hell pictured on the card.

The Devil in the Tarot is a distortion of evolution, having the wings of a bat, the torso of a man, and the horns of a goat. This grotesque conglomeration of animal parts mirrors the distorted image we have of ourselves that threatens to enslave us. Some of us are preoccupied with small defects in our appearance (usually the size or shape of a body part), or with a temporary incapability we may have (usually our intelligence or competence). Like the huge figure of the Devil, we have allowed these erroneous beliefs to grow all out of proportion. Seeing ourselves as disreputable or disfigured, when this is far from the case, is a clear distortion of reality. This preoccupation with what we wrongly believe is wrong with us shatters our self-esteem and leaves us prisoners of our own self-denigration. However, this delusion will persist only so long as we allow it. By focusing attention on our many positive qualities, we can regain our perspective. When we thoroughly enjoy who we are, the devil will not loom as large.

The partners on the Devil card, as the shadow couple of the Lovers, also reveal the dark side of the relationship between the sexes. While the Lovers card is a celebration of the bond between men and women, the Devil experiences their relationship as equal parts cruelty and exploitation. The Lover's choice to fully enter into a loving commitment has been perverted into a form of slavery in which one partner owns the other. As the chains of domesticity tighten around the couple's necks, they can only fantasize about their escape. Many relationships degenerate into this hellish entrapment as love turns to hate.

The evolution of a relationship, from the paradise of the Garden of Eden found in the Lovers card to the underworld of the Devil, is an all too familiar story. Infidelity, boredom, and stress all contribute to the breakup of a couple. However, one of the most overlooked reasons for marital decline is the shadow. Just as the Devil's torch casts shadows upon the wall, we all cast our shadows upon each other. Because of childhood conditioning, we have all formed a negative, shadowy image of the opposite sex. This causes us to see our mate, not as he or she really is, but rather as a demon with horns and a tail. As a result, we never really see our partner clearly.

The shadow can also contain the undeveloped or unacceptable parts of ourselves that we keep hidden in the unconscious. Married couples have an unconscious agreement to live out each other's shadow side. One partner will be assertive and aggressive because his partner cannot consciously recognize these qualities in herself. The trouble arises when one of the partners ridicules the other for expressing these same qualities, thinking them to be separate from themselves. What they don't realize is that the quality they soon learn to dislike in their partner is actually a hidden aspect of their own personality. By consciously developing our undeveloped shadow qualities, we will be less likely to blame our partner for our own inadequacies.

Blame is another theme found in the Devil card. Since the devil has many features of a goat, scapegoating is a very apt meaning for this card. Here again we find the darker side of the Adam and Eve story, for when God asked Adam why he had eaten the apple, he blamed Eve. When Eve was asked the same question, she immediately blamed the snake! This story of blame in the Garden of Eden shows us that scapegoating has been with us from the beginning of time, and is very likely to remain with us.

The purpose of blame is to protect the fragile ego from being damaged by self-condemnation. If we believe someone else is responsible for our wrongdoing, we can cleverly escape self-reproach, while making ourselves look innocent in the process. Instead of taking responsibility for our actions, we develop an accusatory attitude that shifts the focus away from ourselves and onto someone else. This is reflected in the Devil by the man and woman who look at each other while ignoring the devil in the background. This situation in which evil lurks in the back of our psyches was perfectly expressed by the Greek philosopher Seneca when he said, "Other men's sins are before our eyes while ours are behind our backs." To avoid the tendency we all have to blame others for our misdeeds, it is helpful to make a list of all the ways in which we are personally accountable for our present difficulties. We will need to face our dark side if we are to make any progress toward the light.

Most of our personal demons arise from the past, which is another reason why the Devil is standing in back of the couple. The darker side of our nature may originate in the distant past and indirectly involve many generations of our family. Child abuse, alcoholism, or violence can be transmitted from generation to generation, like an evil disease afflicting past and present family members. Parents who have been abused in their early years unconsciously enslave their children with the same shackles that crippled them. Seen in this light, the chains secured around the couple's necks in this card represent the unbroken chains formed by generations of addicted or abusive family members, who are each a link in the tragic chain of behavioral inheritance. When we finally decide to stop our hurtful behavior, we break this human chain of behavioral inheritance so that our children will not have to suffer as did previous generations.

In divination, the Devil symbolizes any relationship in which we feel enslaved or persecuted. These feelings may develop into a persecution complex in which we harbor delusions of being constantly cheated or harassed. Jealousy is another situation where we feel enslaved by our partner's possessiveness. Situations we are forced to stay in because of financial dependency are also reflected in the Devil card. Only self-respect and assertiveness can effectively break the chains that hold us prisoner.

THE TOWER: FEAR

I will never be sure of anything again.

—Second Officer, R.M.S. Titanic

A lofty tower is suddenly hit by a bolt of lightning, causing its occupants to plummet to earth. This card represents situations in life we would most like to avoid: accidents, catastrophe, and chaos. Sudden catastrophe has a lingering psychological impact much greater than the initial trauma. The most common repercussion stemming from catastrophe is devastating disillusionment. Catastrophe not only has the potential to destroy the body, it also can destroy the fundamental beliefs we have about personal safety. Suddenly, the world is a frightening and unpredictable place full of malevolent people. Even if we are involved in an accident that is no one's fault, we are still faced with the realization that we live in an indifferent universe that does not seem to care about our well-being. Like the lightning-struck tower, catastrophe ushers chaos into our ordered world and changes us forever.

The Tower's scene of imminent death strikes terror in our hearts, as we are all too familiar with the destructive capabilities of man and nature. This card mirrors many of our greatest fears including being totally out of control, being hurt in an accident, having our home destroyed, or losing a loved one. Any of these real possibilities will produce tremendous anxiety; however, most of our worst fears are totally unfounded. The imminent catastrophes we picture in our minds (the boat will sink, or we will get a dreadful disease), never really happen. This constant catastrophic thinking is based upon "what if" scenarios. "What if my mother falls and breaks her hip?" "What if I lose my job?" Our minds are filled with catastrophic scenes in which we maximize the risk of danger while minimizing our ability to cope with the aftermath. Like the two figures falling from the tower, we envision a terrible disaster and soon find ourselves falling into feelings of total helplessness. Replacing catastrophic questions such as, "What if the plane crashes?" with life affirming statements such as, "I will arrive safely and have a wonderful vacation," often helps to alleviate unnecessary anxiety. We can also build our self-confidence by remembering times in the past when we successfully coped with an emergency. We need to remind ourselves that the probability of being involved in a catastrophic event is extremely low, while the odds of frightening ourselves daily can be very high.

Tragically, the panic-stricken man and woman on this card have decided to jump out the windows of the tower, rather than face incineration. In our lives, we make many important decisions based upon fear. We decide to avoid certain activities which make us overly anxious or which may remotely put us in harm's way. Not all decisions based upon fear are the wrong ones, but we must distinguish between realistic and unrealistic fears. Unrealistic fears usually originate in childhood. Overprotective parents, particularly around issues of danger or illness, may have instilled unwarranted fears in their children. Also, the real dangers of childhood abuse or neglect can easily produce fears these earlier traumas will be repeated in adulthood. The Tower could also reflect the death of one or both of our parents, which understandably produces fears of abandonment at any age.

Whether our fears are realistic or unrealistic, we can use the Tower card to evaluate our fears. The Tower has three windows representing three different viewpoints. The first window is our perception of our fear including any worst case scenarios that may come to mind. The second window is our view of the real world showing us the cold, hard facts surrounding our anxiety. This would include the actual odds of our fear becoming a reality. The third window is our new viewpoint based upon a realistic assessment of possible future events after looking through the previous windows. Although neither one of these three viewpoints can totally eliminate our fears, they do give us alternate ways to view our reality. Hopefully, by using this method, we can make decisions based upon our best interests rather than our fears.

The figures falling from the tower have absolutely nothing to hold onto and, therefore, illustrate overwhelming feelings of insecurity.

The secure tower that supported the couple has been completely destroyed. In our lives, emotional security is not built of mortar and stone; it is fashioned from loving relationships. Like the falling victims, our insecurity originates in the fear that we cannot survive without the support of those we love. The catastrophe pictured is the possibility of losing a loved one, for our emotional survival depends upon them being there for us. We fear the failure of our support system, feeling that when we fall the next time, there will be no safety net to catch us. Nevertheless, we may gradually recognize our ability to be self-supporting and to survive independently without assistance.

In a reading, the Tower warns of the dangers of climbing too high or getting too angry. Like Icarus, who fell because he flew too close to the sun, we can reach too high and expect too much. When our unrealistic expectations are not met, we fall and become emotionally incapacitated. However, if we keep both of our feet planted firmly on the ground of reality, we can't fall very far. We may also want to look carefully at the lightning that destroys the tower, as it is symbolic of the destructive potential within us all. Angry outbursts can be like a bolt of lightning, destroying in seconds what took many years to build. Although we are usually advised to get in touch with our anger, it would be wiser to explore the hidden emotions that cause our fury. The two falling figures on this card experience fear and helplessness, and it is these two strong emotions that actually trigger our rage. Perhaps instead of getting in touch with our anger toward someone else, it would be healthier to examine our own feelings of vulnerability.

The Tower provides a final warning about disastrous relationships. We may be involved in a destructive relationship that threatens to tear down our self-esteem. Like the ill-fated couple, we should be very wary of individuals who are destroying themselves and who are determined to take us with them.

THE STAR: GUIDANCE

Ideals are like the stars. You can choose them as your guide, and following them, you reach your destiny.

—Carl Schurz

On a starry night, a beautiful woman pours water out of two golden pitchers. Sailors have used the stars to successfully navigate the seas, bringing them safely to remote destinations. As a faraway destination, the stars have always represented man's eternal destiny. Our fate is said to be written in the stars, but it seems that only Tarot readers or astrologers know where we are headed. The Star represents the act of divination that is actually receiving divine guidance from a very remote source. By reading the stars or the Tarot, we can connect to the right path leading us to our destiny.

While the movement of all the stars influences our fate, this Tarot card refers to a particular star in the heavens. In ancient Egypt, the greatly anticipated star of Isis would appear on the horizon to herald the coming of the yearly flooding of the Nile. The annual flood watered the parched land so that crops could be grown and famine could be averted. This yearly renewal of life-giving water is very similar to the renewal of love, faith, or idealism we periodically experience. We can fall in love with our partners again and again through the years, or rekindle romance with a lost love. Perhaps we can reaffirm our faith by attending religious services or by developing spiritual practices such as meditation. Enthusiasm is renewed when we remember the ideals we strived for in the past. These periodic renewals get us in touch with the essence of who we are and the potential of who we can be.

The ancient Egyptians understood the yearly appearance of the star on the horizon to be a symbol of their hope that the terrible drought threatening their survival would be broken by the rising waters of the Nile. We also experience dry spells, but it is precisely when we feel most disheartened that we must hope for the best. The darker the night, the more brilliant the stars shine. In the dark night of the soul, the star of hope sustains our ability to cope and helps us maintain a positive outlook. Hope is the comforting belief that our situation will get better, the dawn will break, or the stars will change their fateful positions in the sky. When we look heavenward, we will see small points of light reflecting our hope in a better future.

The woman in the Star uses two golden pitchers to pour out her nourishing water onto the ground. A pitcher is specifically designed to pour out whatever is poured into it. For this reason, pitchers naturally symbolize selfless giving, and the Star card becomes the virtue of charity. The woman pictured charitably shares her water without thought to her own needs. Her charity knows no bounds, as her cascading waters appear to be a never-ending stream of ceaseless giving. We can certainly try to emulate the Star by becoming more charitable to others. Our belief in scarcity, however, may cause us to hesitate when it is time to give. Most of us think that if we give to others, we may run out of the necessary things we want for ourselves. The Star contradicts this viewpoint by showing an endless supply of water emanating from the generous pitchers. Contained in this card is an underlying message that the universe, symbolized by the starry heavens, will always provide for all our needs.

Although charity is its own reward, there are certain universal laws of cause and effect that cause us to directly benefit from charitable giving. Like the ripples in the pond, charity can have many far-reaching effects including an increase in our own good fortune. When we are caught in unfortunate circumstances, it is often a good idea to help others, because what we give will be returned to us. Just as the water the woman pours onto the parched ground slowly flows back into the pond, our charitable deeds will come back to us when we need assistance. The universal law symbolized by the Star is that we give in order to receive.

In a reading, the Star symbolizes many essential qualities we need to develop. These qualities are represented by the eight stars on the card and include self-nurturing, self-reflection, self-acceptance, self-confidence, self-revelation, self-healing, self-expression, and self-actualization. The exposed breasts of the woman on the card reflect her ability to nurture by breast-feeding, and the two flowing pitchers probably symbolize this outpouring of milk for the hungry infant. She is the good mother who unselfishly offers herself as a source of nourishment for her growing child. In our lives, we can become self-nurturing by being good mothers to ourselves and by giving ourselves what is essential to our well-being. When we nourish our interests and goals, we feed our souls. Another way we can nurture ourselves is through remembering our dreams, the visions of the night. Dreams are the vital nourishment we receive nightly from our unconscious. However, if we fail to write them down upon waking, they return to the depths of the unconscious just as the Star's water is poured back into the deep pond. Recalling our dreams and integrating their cryptic message into our conscious awareness provides us with the nourishment of wisdom.

When the woman gazes at her reflection in the pool of water below, she is practicing self-reflection. Like the woman staring at her own nudity, we may need to look at the naked truth of our lives. Instead of covering over our problems with lies, it is better to courageously face our true selves. This new honesty will automatically produce self-acceptance. Just as the woman seems perfectly comfortable with her nudity, we can learn to be comfortable with ourselves. Nudity also takes a tremendous amount of self-confidence, which is another quality we may need to develop. If we are confident enough, we can decide to fully reveal ourselves to others. Self-revelation, whether in analysis, intimacy, or art can be an important breakthrough. Being able to fully express our emotions through writing, dance, or poetry is also essential. All of these activities can contribute to self-healing because an outpouring of emotion can rejuvenate our bodies and spirits. Finally, we may reach a level of self-actualization where we can realize our full potential.

THE MOON: CHANGE

Life is a shadowy, strange, and winding road.

—R. G. Ingersoll

The eighteenth card of the Tarot is a moonlit landscape filled with shadowy figures and unseen perils. This is a landscape of fear where our minds conjure up terrifying thoughts. In this atmosphere of foreboding and dread, we must somehow find our way through the darkness down a moonlit path. The moon has been called the lantern of the night, but its dull illumination only intensifies the shadows, making us more aware of the dangers lurking in the dark. Unable to see clearly, we are thrust into a place of heightened anxiety where we fear the worst will surely happen.

The moon is our constant companion on our dark journey through the unfamiliar terrain of the unconscious. Although we traverse this foreign territory each night in our dreams, the world of dreams seems to be as unfamiliar as a lunar landscape. We awake feeling we have been to a mysterious land in which nothing made any sense. Nonetheless, our dreams are the royal road to the unconscious and should be carefully examined. Our nocturnal journeys can open up new vistas in our waking life if we have the courage to follow the wisdom of our dreams.

Just as the sun's brilliant rays are reflected on the moon's surface, the qualities of the moon reflect our characteristics. First, the moon exerts a powerful influence on the earth, most notably controlling the rising and falling tides. We may find ourselves unduly influenced by family or friends to the extent that we have very little control over important decisions. More importantly, others may be influencing how we feel about ourselves. Our parents or spouse can create a lunar pull toward negative feelings that we must firmly resist with all our strength. We could also be under the influence of powerful drugs that can control our behavior. Each time we allow people or substances to affect us, we relinquish a small part of our power. If this continues, we will end up like the dark, lifeless moon, receiving our only light from a distant source.

Another way in which we resemble the moon is in our ability to change. The moon's appearance changes from night to night in an eternal cycle of light and dark. Our emotions also naturally wax and wane, which is something we need to keep in mind when we are in the depths of despair or experiencing panic. Emotions never continue at their peak intensity for very long, and we can be assured that even the most distressing feelings will not last forever. Just as the moon gradually brightens in the sky, we can look forward to a brighter emotional outlook. The moon may also represent changeable friends who may prove to be inconstant companions. Just as the moon's appearance varies, our friends may suddenly become undependable people who readily leave us to cope on our own.

Central to this card's meaning is the winding path that fatefully leads toward the distant mountains. This well-worn path indicates that we have traveled this road many times before. However, this particular path is definitely the wrong road. It is the road of negative thinking which, while very alluring, will essentially lead us nowhere. This is the perilous path of regret, guilt, and self-pity. Like the path on the card receding into the faraway mountains, this path also connects us to the distant past. We constantly relive past tragedies or mistakes until these destructive thoughts form a well-worn path in the mind. When we continually replay our worst experiences, we automatically re-experience accompanying emotions such as the anger of betrayal or the terror of an accident, until we are emotionally exhausted. A better alternative is to stop this trip down bad memory lane as soon as possible. When we first become aware of our negative thoughts from the past, we should say firmly to ourselves, "Don't go down that road." This is a torturous path we no longer have to travel.

The path winds its way between two imposing towers that form a fateful gateway. The towers act as a restrictive passage showing us that there may be only one way out of our present situation. The two towers seem ominous, and the farther we veer away from one tower, the closer we get to the other. This is a classic double bind in which no course of action can have a satisfactory result. Being literally between a rock and a hard place, we can avoid one menacing tower only by risking proximity to the other. The Moon is a card of contradictory messages and inescapable dilemmas that sometimes only serve to confuse us. Seeing no reasonable way out, we can only proceed with caution.

Guarding the moonlit path is an odd assortment of animals: a wolf, a dog, and a lobster. Mythologically, these animals are threshold guardians that rise up to test our determination and intelligence. Usually, the guardian will ask the traveler to either solve a difficult riddle or perform a courageous feat before the traveler is allowed to pass by safely. On a psychological level, these animals represent our regressive and depressive tendencies that we need to subdue before we can continue on our journey of self-awareness. Just as the lobster emerging from the pool resists the pull of the tide, we need to resist the regressive pull that wants to bring us back to our old, self-destructive ways. On a more positive note, the lobster can also symbolize our struggle to come out of a deep depression, emerging a wiser, stronger person. After we have victoriously emerged from the oppressive waters, there are still those remaining problems represented by the wolf and the dog. Both animals are closely related, but wolves have a wild nature whereas dogs are tamed creatures. Our uncontrollable animal instincts are understandably fraught with danger, but there is also a danger in being too domesticated. If we become too civilized by worshiping the norms of society, we can evolve into creatures resembling well-trained dogs. Nevertheless, if we closely follow the path that is equidistant from the dog and the wolf, we can find a careful balance between the wild side of our natures and the domesticated side.

THE SUN: CONSCIOUSNESS

Child of nature, learn to unlearn.

—Benjamin Disraeli

While the last four cards have been shrouded in darkness, the Sun shines brightly. Here, a beautiful child rides a wild horse through a sunlit garden. The sun is the supreme source of energy, providing essential warmth and light to the earth. Every living thing is dependent upon the sun for its survival and growth. We also have fundamental sources of energy that we depend upon to revitalize our lives. Family and friends can sustain us with their encouragement, while a spouse's support can help us to fulfill our full potential. Appreciating a good book, a beautiful painting, or a lyrical piece of music can also energize us. Energy can also come in the form of activities we love such as favorite hobbies or participation in sports. Like the sunflowers that naturally turn toward the light of the sun, we are naturally attracted to these sources of abundant energy. Recreational activities renew our vitality and enthusiasm by reconnecting us to the profound joy of life. Like a small child, we can thoroughly enjoy playing with our toys, whether they are sports cars or Tarot cards. Connecting with the vital energy of our favorite things brings sunshine into our lives.

The Sun is also the light of conscious awareness. To be conscious is to be fully aware of what one is doing or thinking. In order to shed light on our behavior, it is necessary to become self-aware of our activities. This, in turn, requires us to slow down our actions. For example, when we gobble down a hamburger at a fast-food restaurant, we are probably not thinking about what we are eating. Perhaps we're thinking about how late we are for an appointment, or we are ruminating about a recent argument with our spouse. On the other hand, we could choose to slowly enjoy a home-cooked meal, while thinking about all the necessary steps involved in getting the meal on the table: the farmer harvesting his crops, the truck driver delivering food to the supermarket, and our partner finally cooking the meal for us. Bringing conscious awareness into even a seemingly insignificant event such as eating a meal can heighten our appreciation of the small things in life. It also makes us aware of all the people we have never met who have helped us in unseen ways, for to be fully conscious is to recognize the fundamental interdependence of all people and all things.

In contrast with the unconscious processes symbolized by the Moon, the Sun represents our ability to bring unconscious material into conscious awareness. Through various techniques, we can become conscious of underlying problems or unconscious actions. One of the simplest techniques is to keep a daily journal. Writing down our feelings and actions allows us to review them weeks or months later when we have a more objective point of view. Keeping a food diary can help us become more aware of exactly what we are eating so we can modify our eating habits. If we have a problem with negative thinking, jotting down each negative thought as it arises and then rewriting each one as a positive affirmation can often help us overcome a pessimistic attitude. Recording our experiences exteriorizes them so we can look at them objectively and, hopefully, change the way we view them.

The interior changes we seek are portrayed by the small child basking beneath the glorious sun. Mythologically, this is the divine child whose birth heralds a new era of important change. This birth is usually associated with the birth day's sunrise that ushers in a new day for mankind. This child of God is a potent symbol of positive change in our lives. Childhood is a time of newness and unlimited possibility as the curious child discovers the world for the first time. Like a child, we can make a fresh start by changing our residence or simply changing our way of thinking. Our self-esteem can also be renewed. We can tell ourselves that our birth matters because we were put on this earth for a purpose no less important than that of a divine child.

Positive change also occurs when we free ourselves from being our mother's daughter or father's son to becoming an independent child of God. To attain this boundless freedom portrayed by the

Sun's exuberant child, we may have to unlearn the lessons we have been taught by our parents. Our well-meaning parents tried to protect us by teaching us distrust, intolerance, and fear. Babies are born without such beliefs and only acquire them by emulating their parents. To achieve the child's natural unknowing state, we need to consciously learn to unlearn the restrictive lessons our parents carefully taught us in favor of a more open attitude. The child sitting on his unbridled horse with his arms open wide reflects this new open-minded outlook. His innocence also illustrates what Zen Buddhists call "beginner's mind," a consciousness devoted to living life without preconceived ideas. Like a brick wall separating us from the light, formal education and acquired beliefs can screen us from the perception of powerful truths. The child of the Sun, having no such limitations, reflects the divinity within us all.

However, the Sun card also depicts a serious obstacle that prevents us from getting in touch with our divine selves. The brick wall pictured forms an impenetrable barrier between ourselves (the child) and our Higher Self (the sun). This opaque wall is formed from the brick and mortar of our ingrained beliefs about space and time. We learn early in life that the world is made of objects separate and distinct from ourselves. Our perception of time, based upon the earth's revolution around the sun, creates a past, present, and future. Although these learned concepts of space and time are useful, they form a barrier to our understanding of a mystical reality that transcends the material world. Because this impenetrable wall of belief is erected so early in our lives, we find it difficult to access any alternate realities such as contact with our Higher Selves. The wall can only be torn down by our refusal to limit our perceptions to the five senses and our refusal to believe in the restriction of time. If we realize that this barrier is only an illusion, it will disappear, leaving us in the brilliant light of the sun.

In divination, the Sun's brilliance can expose issues we would rather keep hidden. This is a secret garden surrounded by a wall of lies we have built to protect ourselves. Secrets are hidden from others precisely because their exposure to the light of day would also expose our wrongdoing. Secret addictions, love affairs, or notorious pasts may soon be exposed to the bright light of truth.

JUDGMENT: REDEMPTION

Only what we have wrought into our character during life can we take away with us.

—Baron Alexander von Humboldt

The Last Judgment is announced by the archangel Gabriel blowing his heavenly horn. This is the day of final judgment for mankind when the world ends. Although the Last Judgment is understood biblically to be sometime in the distant future, its influence is felt every day of our lives. Somewhere in the dark recesses of our minds, we realize that our actions on earth will eventually be judged by a supernal tribunal. Hopefully, this knowledge will act as a spiritual wake-up call, propelling us to do good deeds and to restrict destructive actions.

Focusing on eternal judgment immediately puts our lives in perspective, for we realize that the purpose of human existence is to attain a higher state of consciousness. Like the naked people on the card, we are born into this life with nothing and can only bring our consciousness with us into the afterlife. So, it is imperative that we raise our spiritual consciousness during our brief lifetime. When we return to our source at the end of our days, the spiritual progress we take with us will determine our fate in the afterlife. When we reach our final destination, the trappings of the ego are stripped away like discarded clothing. Gone are the accomplishments, status, and wealth that defined our life on earth. Ultimately, we will be judged by our divine essence: who we have become rather than what we have attained. If we can focus daily on our spiritual progress and act in a kinder, more compassionate way, we will never fear eternal judgment, for we know we have fulfilled our spiritual responsibility.

On a psychological level, Judgment is symbolic of unconscious material rising up into conscious awareness. Like the resurrection of the dead, it is necessary to understand our unearthed memories in the light of day. The unconscious is the mind's depository for past experience, but the buried past occasionally becomes unearthed. The archangel Gabriel is a messenger from the unconscious whose resounding trumpet triggers the resurrection of repressed memories. A familiar smell or a furtive glance can immediately bring us back to a place left long ago. Because a family is pictured on the Judgment card, this memory probably took place in our parental home. The memory may not necessarily be traumatic, but may be the key to the solution of our current difficulties. By retrieving lost childhood memories, we may also be able to understand the origin of our present behavior as well. Like the family liberated from their claustrophobic coffins, we can finally awake to a new freedom by making peace with the past.

Judgment also clearly shows us that the past is not as dead and buried as we had previously believed. Past loves and old resentments can certainly be resurrected if we are given the right stimulus. This is particularly true of what we hear. Just as the sound of Gabriel's trumpet wakens the dead, our dead feelings for a past lover can be reawakened when we hear an old love song playing on the radio. Likewise, overheard conversations can trigger long-buried feelings of resentment or envy. When the past is suddenly remembered in this fashion, our first reaction may be to disregard its unsettling message. However, nothing happens by chance, and the reactivation of a distant memory may cause us to consider the lessons of past experience. The painful reasons why we left our previous lover or the resentment that caused us to quit our job may be lessons we do not want to repeat in the future. Triggered memories can be a prophetic warning that the past will become the future if we fail to change.

Death of a loved one can also reawaken painful memories. The loss of a loved one causes memories of previous deaths to resurface. Death causes us to emotionally revisit the somber places where others have died and thrusts us into re-experiencing our grief. This can naturally also resurrect any unresolved past issues we had with the deceased. However, the Judgment card shows us that it is never too late to communicate with those who have departed, for they are always with us in spirit. Although this may appear to be a one-way conversation, we can still send the departed our forgiveness and heartfelt prayers. Even though this may not completely resolve our problems with the deceased, it will certainly help resolve our grief.

On this card, the grey people rising up from their graves also mirror the human capacity for self-renewal. Like many of the other cards in the Major Arcana, Judgment is concerned with personal transformation. While many of the other cards portray change as something that is thrust upon us, the change pictured in Judgment is predicated upon death. There can be no glorious resurrection until a part of us has died. This card is the cemetery of the self, for the self must die so that we may become the person we are destined to be. When we voluntarily kill off our old, destructive ways, we must have faith that we will be born again. Just like an unknowable afterlife, we may not be able to clearly see exactly what this new life will be like. Nevertheless, our belief in the process of positive transformation will guide us safely through to the other side.

In divination, the Judgment card represents the resurrection of an essential part of ourselves we thought had been dead and buried long ago. There is a reawakening of dreams, values, beliefs, or skills we have left behind. This is an opportunity to begin again or fulfill youthful aspirations.

Finally, the eternal salvation pictured on the Judgment card may resemble a messiah complex in which we wish to take on the role of someone else's personal savior. Some of us feel the need to constantly try to save others from themselves by offering them more help than they really need. We may have to free ourselves from our salvation fantasies before our help inadvertently creates helplessness in others. Although it may be difficult to acknowledge, the pain that we valiantly try to save others from may be an integral part of their spiritual progress in life.

THE WORLD: FULFILLMENT

Nothing brings you peace but yourself.

—Ralph Waldo Emerson

In the last card of the Major Arcana, a beautiful woman dances inside a laurel wreath. When we think about the world, we naturally imagine the world outside ourselves full of people, places, and things. Mystics have seen a far different world in which there is no essential division between the exterior world and ourselves. They see everything in the universe merging into a harmonious whole, like an oval wreath having no beginning and no end. Everything is connected because all is one. Although we seem to be physically separated from those around us and from the world that surrounds us, this is a clever illusion. Every tear that has ever been shed is ours and every heartbeat is our own. Even the Tarot cards that we hold in our hands are part of ourselves. There is nothing in the universe that is not vitally connected to us. We may have fleeting glimpses of our oneness with the universe, perhaps while watching a magnificent sunset or while holding our child for the first time. It is very important to keep this ephemeral vision as part of our daily life, constantly reminding ourselves of our essential union with the cosmos. As Marcus Aurelius said many centuries ago, "The universe is a single life comprising one substance and one soul."

Because our eyes deceive us into thinking we are separate from everything else, we sometimes feel very isolated and alone. Yet a part of us desperately wants to restore the vital connection we have with the universe. We want to merge with the all-encompassing One in order to cure the unbearable loneliness of separate existence. In pursuing this lost connection with the cosmos, we may try to connect with nature, art, or meditation to purposely open up the boundaries that divide us from the oneness we seek. Any experience that causes a temporary transcendence can be used to escape the separateness that imprisons us. This can include fasting, sensory deprivation, or even becoming totally engrossed in a good book.

The interconnected physical world is also invisibly connected to the metaphysical realm. Matter and spirit are mirror images of one another, and this is reflected in the two identical wands that the woman in the World carefully holds. Her hidden message to us is that there are actually two worlds: the ordinary world of the senses and the ethereal world of the spirit. Everything in the world with which we are familiar is a dim reflection of the spiritual realm; therefore, everything we come into contact with in the universe can directly connect us with the metaphysical dimension. This is the basis of the magical belief in correspondence that underlies the effectiveness of the Tarot. When we read the Tarot, the symbols on the cards connect our earthly experience with the spiritual plane. Because all things, including Tarot cards, are spiritual teachers, the physical world in which we exist cannot be summarily dismissed as what the Eastern traditions call Maya, or illusion. The world is not an illusion; it is an allusion. Everything in the physical world alludes to a greater truth in the spiritual realm. Therefore, to connect to the spiritual realm, we must go through the ways of the world, not around them.

If we fail to meaningfully connect to the wholeness of either the mundane or spiritual worlds, we can feel fragmented. Disconnection from God or our fellow man makes us feel somehow incomplete. This is a particular problem for women, for most women need meaningful relationships in their lives to feel connected to the world and to feel complete. Feelings of incompleteness are like a gaping hole in our lives, similar to the hole created by the wreath surrounding the women of the World. This gaping space cannot be filled with money, food, or entertainment. Although we often attempt to fill it with anything and everything, no relationship or accomplishment can fill the emptiness within us. The only thing that will fill this hole within each of us is ourselves. Just as the dancing woman fills the empty space created by the wreath that surrounds her, we can fill our emptiness with ourselves. By learning to love and appreciate ourselves just the way we are, we will not need to eternally search for someone or something to make us feel complete. Although we have been led to believe that we can be complete human beings only when we finally attain success or receive the love we have always wanted, nothing outside ourselves can make us feel whole.

As the culmination of the Major Arcana, the woman of the World looks back upon the curious journey she has taken through the other cards. She started her journey as the Fool, an androgynous being blithely walking toward the edge of a cliff. In the course of her adventures she has gone on to endure bad parenting, become pregnant, internalized the laws of society and religion, made critical choices, learned important lessons about control, gotten in touch with her inner strength, and climbed a mountain. Further along in her journey she has had to accept the inevitability of change, learned the consequences of her actions, had her world turned upside down, confronted her own mortality, learned moderation, confronted evil, survived catastrophe, regained hope, became aware of her conscious and unconscious motivations, and been reborn. This is the journey of life. Perhaps we will not have all these exciting experiences in one lifetime, but experiencing even one of the events symbolized by the Tarot's Major Arcana can be a turning point in our lives. These profound occurrences transform us so that we never see ourselves or the world in the same way again.

CHAPTER THREE
THE MINOR ARCANA

THE ACE OF PENTACLES: TRANSITION

It is a narrow gate and a hard road that lead to life and only a few find it.

—The Bible

The Ace of Pentacles acts as a fateful doorway into the hidden mysteries of the Minor Arcana. In this card, the oval wreath encircling the woman in the World (the last card of the Major Arcana) is transformed into the hedge's oval opening in the Ace of Pentacles, leading to a new awareness. Leaving the archetypal world of the Major Arcana, we enter an enchanting region containing the four suits of the Minor Arcana. Through this narrow gate, we move from the transpersonal realm into the world of our daily life: work and relationships. However, it is also an entrance into parts of ourselves that are usually inaccessible including hidden fears, underlying motivations, and secret desires.

Each of the four suits of the Major Arcana have their roots in Carl Jung's four psychological functions. Cups are equated with the feeling function and are concerned with the emotions. Swords represent the thinking function found in the world of intellectual matters and ideas. Wands are equated with the function of intuition and, hence, with the world of imagination. Finally, the suit of pentacles is linked with the sensation function, which emphasizes our relationship with the physical world around us. It is here that we begin our journey.

Pentacles are an exceptionally worldly suit, and many of the cards reflect this by showing agricultural pursuits such as gardening and farming. In this suit, there is a definite concern for our place in the world and our relationship with our surroundings. Because the work we do directly connects us to the world at large, many of the cards depict workmen. Here, man is seen as the toolmaker, utilizing hoes, hammers, and chisels to make his mark in the world.

On a deeper level, pentacles show us our underlying feelings toward our work. It is usually quite easy to recognize the positive feelings we have about our jobs. A sense of accomplishment when we've learned a new skill, new abilities, and pride in continuing to do a good job certainly build ego strength. On the other hand, reoccurring difficulties in the workplace can usher in feelings of anger, powerlessness, or inferiority. The money we earn (and which pentacles symbolize) can also make us feel worthy. Pentacles are ultimately about our sense of self-worth, and in Western cultures it is often our job that determines our self-respect. Because our culture tends to overemphasize economics, it may be helpful to put work into perspective. After all, pentacles are not the only cards in the deck!

However, the suit of pentacles goes far beyond the traditional work ethic. In medieval Italy, the suit of pentacles was called denari. This was also the word for mirror because both coins and mirrors were circular in shape. In money matters we can often clearly see ourselves, because the world of commerce is a reflection of our heart's desire. Money can be symbolic of our need for nurturance, and often a desire to be loved masquerades as a desire for wealth. Also, inheritance comes with many emotional strings attached to it, as each heir calculates just how much he was loved by the deceased. Although pervasive, money is an emotionally charged element in our lives that underscores many relationships.

Sometimes when we are doing a reading, it is very perplexing to see a spread containing a preponderance of pentacles when the querent has just asked a question about her love life. Many cups in such a reading would be quite understandable, but pentacles seem to emphasize work relationships rather than personal attachments. However, by equating love with money, so to speak, the pentacles can answer any question. We merely have to visualize the pentacles on each card as symbolic containers of emotion. In this way, the people on the cards can either hold onto their feelings too tightly, cultivate them, or even give them away. In readings, we can easily see that pentacles are the emotional currency in our lives.

Historically, pentacles have been seen as coins, a very valuable commodity. The suit emphasizes what we value in life, particularly the things we've put our energy into. We value what we've made a commitment to, worked hard for, or even lost along the way. We may also need to examine what we are willing to pay for what we value in life. Ideally, no sacrifice may be too great, but the real world puts great constraints upon those who have high values. Because of this, many of the cards in this suit reflect the eternal conflict between idealism and reality.

In the Ace of Pentacles, this clash between idealism and reality is shown in the contrast between the angelic hand emanating from the cloud above (symbolizing what we desire), and the garden scene below (symbolizing the struggles inherent in the physical world). Gardens are places where the forces of nature are molded into a man-made design and so represent the hard work of transforming the world. The flowery hedge confines the landscape just as the circumstances of our lives sometimes restrict our hopes and dreams for the future. However, there is a way out of our present circumstances, because this card shows an opening through the impenetrable hedge. This entrance marks a period of transition between our old way of living and a new phase of life.

Life transitions often have a mysterious quality to them, as if they were somehow preordained. This is like a mysterious hand that suddenly emerges from a cloud offering us a new opportunity. However, upon closer inspection, we find that this wondrous opportunity presented itself because of our own inner growth. Eastern philosophies state, "When the student is ready the teacher will come." When we have an inner need to move beyond the setting in which we have become all we can be, then we can travel through the opening to head toward the distant mountains of our aspirations. To go through this opening is to be transformed.

In divination, the well-worn pathway on this card indicates that many others have trodden the same path before us. We may be able to benefit from their experience. Seek out someone who has successfully solved the present problem and ask their advice. We may also be following in someone else's footsteps. Perhaps we have taken the same career path as our parents. If so, the entrance in the hedge may lead us to go beyond our present career into a new field.

THE TWO OF PENTACLES: COPING

The storm is master; wind and waves play ball with men.

—J. C. F. Schiller

In this card, there is a young man on the shoreline trying to juggle two pentacles, while behind him two ships ride on the ocean's waves. Both man and ships are experiencing the ups and downs of life. Like the rising and falling ships on a stormy sea, we often seem to be at the mercy of our constantly changing emotions. This is particularly true when our fluctuating emotions are generated by someone else's actions. Compliments or praise cause us to soar upward, while an unkind remark sends us spiraling downward into depression or anger. We seem to vacillate hourly between pessimism and optimism, or confidence and self-doubt. Our juggler within tries to cope with these changing emotional situations and makes adjustments to keep all his balls in the air. Although, like the skillful juggler, we are usually quite successful in handling daily emotional vicissitudes, the way in which we cope can prove maladaptive in the long run.

As children, we all developed certain coping strategies to help us adapt to the unpredictability of our home environment. Perhaps we became ill or threw temper tantrums to receive attention from parents who usually ignored our needs. We may have tried to avoid our father's rage by learning to withdraw into ourselves. Once successful, these strategies became a pattern of behavior (similar to the pattern traced in the air by the pentacles on the card) that followed us into adult life. Unfortunately, these childhood survival skills can become maladaptive and destructive in adulthood. For example, a child who tries unsuccessfully to constantly please critical parents may later see their spouse or employer as a substitute parent. Still trying to please, this person often develops a submissive attitude and a lifetime of accommodation.

Another ineffective coping skill is manipulation. By the look of uncertainty on his face, the juggler appears to lack the confidence necessary to keep all his balls in the air. When we feel incapable of handling the seemingly uncontrollable circumstances of our lives, self-doubt quickly overwhelms us. Like the confused juggler, we may feel uncertain of where we stand either in a company or in a relationship. As our self-confidence ebbs, we try harder to control the externals in our lives, namely, the people around us. In an attempt to gain some measure of control, we often try to dictate the behavior of friends and family. This can easily lead to emotional manipulation similar to the juggler's manipulation of his pentacles. Like a juggler, who must constantly repeat the same dexterous actions, we repeatedly find ourselves manipulating others in order to elicit the desired response from them. However, there may be alternative ways of coping that we had not previously considered.

Just as there are two pentacles on this card, there are two very effective strategies for coping with many of life's problems. When a particular difficulty can be corrected, we first use problem-solving skills to find an answer. We immediately identify the problem and then concentrate our energies on finding a workable solution. For example, if we've lost our job, we will need to prepare a résumé and contact prospective employers. If we experience anticipatory anxiety about an upcoming job interview, we can cope by careful study and painstaking preparation. Problem-solving requires that we take constructive action, confronting our difficulties instead of avoiding them.

There are, however, some problems that do not have a solution. Debilitating illness or tragic loss cannot be so easily fixed, and we are often left alone to cope with our immutable destiny. In this case, we can use emotional reframing to help manage our distressing feelings. Reframing is based upon the belief that if we can't change a serious problem, at least we can alter our reaction to it. By changing the way in which we think about our problems, we can transform negative feelings of dread and anguish into a more positive outlook. Perhaps the loss we've suffered contains a hidden opportunity. Likewise, by reassessing our circumstances, we may find that the outcome is not as dire as we originally thought. Reappraisal of our problems in a positive light can help us find the small ray of hope locked within our hearts and the courage to face the inevitable.

In divination, this card reminds us of the woman who tries to juggle a family and career, or a businessman trying to juggle his finances. Whenever we feel we must maintain strict control over a situation, our lives quickly become out of balance. Juggling time, relationships, or resources can become so exhausting that we no longer enjoy life. Whatever area of our lives we need to keep in balance, we will need to be more flexible. Like a juggler who changes his position to accommodate the changing trajectory of his descending balls, we can learn to adapt to the requirements of each new situation. We can make adjustments to our workload by rescheduling difficult tasks and delegating authority to others. Ultimately, we may need to lower our personal expectations to get more out of life.

THE THREE OF PENTACLES: COMMITMENT

All are Architects of Fate Working in these Walls of Time.

—Henry Wadsworth Longfellow

In this card, we find three men collaborating on the construction of a medieval cathedral: a monk, an architect, and a mason. Sheltered beneath a graceful archway, each of these individuals has an important role in cathedral construction. Each represents an important aspect of ourselves that is essential for the successful completion of any creative project.

Every great undertaking starts with an idea, whether that undertaking is a medieval cathedral or a modern-day business. The monk on this card represents the ability to visualize a needed goal in life. He is inspiration, a word that not only means the stimulus of creative thought, but also denotes the Holy Spirit descending into man, and, thus, divine influence. Monks, as well as other religious persons, have always recognized the true source of inspiration and have understood the creative vision as sacred. This tonsured friar also personifies faith in our ability to maintain belief in ourselves and our personal vision. It is only by believing in things as yet unseen that we can maintain the fortitude necessary to achieve our desires.

Even though inspiration is a great impetus, enthusiasm alone will not generate results. Other parts of our personalities, depicted by the remaining two figures on the card, must come to the forefront to carry the project to its conclusion. The next step in construction is carried out by the architect holding the cathedral's blueprints. His job is to form the monk's idea into a concrete plan that can be used by the mason in actual construction of the building. This blueprint is vital, for it forms an integral bridge between the spiritual (inspiration) and the secular (construction), the dream and its materialization. Like the figures on the card, we should approach the future with a plan firmly in hand to guide us. A plan instills confidence that we can achieve our goals, and is an affirmation of intent. Our inner architect reminds us that, while many things in life come about unexpectedly while we curse the Fates, much of life can actually be created by our own design.

After the initial inspiration and careful planning, the final step is always action. This is personified by the stone mason who uses his powerful hammer of creativity to shape the church's decorative stone. Putting our plans into action is a crucial step in any undertaking; therefore, the Tarot's mason is shown in an elevated position above the other men. This is because while the monk and architect are both concerned with future results, it is the mason who must grapple with the hard work at the present moment. So, it is always important to put our energy and concentration into any task that is immediately before us. If we continue to dream, plan, and act, we can create a great work, whether it is the grandeur of a Gothic cathedral or the grandeur of our lives.

There is another important parallel between building construction and the formation of our lives. In the Middle Ages, it took several decades to complete a great cathedral. Obviously, this was a long-range goal which required great commitment from all those working on such a monumental project. Life also requires commitment. Many of the things we cherish most in life are those that require us to commit our time and energy. They also require sacrifice. In selecting a particular objective, we may have to give up other tempting opportunities that might interfere with an important goal. Those who are afraid of commitments (also known as those who are "keeping their options open") eventually find certain areas of their lives unfulfilling. Although they may have had many diverse experiences and relationships, they have failed to build a lasting structure in their lives.

While working within the framework of commitment narrows our options, it also creates a great opportunity to expand ourselves. Commitment builds character because it helps us develop self-discipline and fortitude. A true commitment also fosters maturity, for we must not only carefully choose between alternatives, we must also choose to deal with the outcome no matter what results. In this way, we are not so much building our lives as we are being built by our own endeavors.

The unfinished cathedral on this card indicates that some aspect of our lives is still under construction. The card not only advises us to start some type of self-improvement project in order to complete ourselves, but also subtly guides us toward what we could be working on. The men on the card are working on the left pillar, which is symbolic of the feminine. So, a man may need to work on developing his nurturing, feminine side and, similarly, a woman may need to develop her assertive, masculine side. Developing the contrasexual part of ourselves is one of the most important tasks in life because it creates balance. We cannot support ourselves with the singular pillar of either masculinity or femininity. It takes the strength found in both sides of our personalities to bear the full weight of life's challenges.

In the Middle Ages, the Gothic cathedral was known as "the Bible of the poor" because its statues of the saints and stained glass windows taught Bible stories to the illiterate masses. Each Tarot card is also a story in pictorial form. In a Tarot reading, our task is to translate pictures into words that hopefully can be understood within the context of the querent's life. Like the holy space created inside a cathedral, the story that we tell with the cards is the story of someone's life and should be considered sacred.

In the Three of Pentacles, there are three Gothic arches supporting the weight of the cathedral's walls. The pointed Gothic arch was a fundamental innovation that reduced pressure from above and made it possible to create much taller buildings. We may also need to reduce the pressure and stress of our lives in innovative ways. One of the most successful strategies for relieving stress is by utilizing the division of labor. Like the three different professions pictured, we may need to delegate work in a business or household in order for it to run smoothly. A heavy load shared between either people or pillars is much lighter and less stressful.

THE FOUR OF PENTACLES: POSSESSION

What gives life its value you can find—and lose but never possess.

—Dag Hammarskjold

In this card, we see an enthroned king tightly grasping one pentacle, while firmly placing his feet on two others and balancing a fourth on his crown. He appears to be a man of immense wealth and power, yet he looks unhappy. He is afraid of losing what he possesses, just as every monarch secretly fears losing his hard-won kingdom. The more we fear losing something, the tighter we hold onto it. We hold onto our jobs, relationships, resentments, bad habits, or fears. Even unproductive attitudes and harmful situations are clung to with great tenacity simply because they are familiar and comforting.

When something external is perceived to be essential to our well-being or self-concept, we naturally become anxious at the possibility of losing it. "What would I be without my job?" we ask. Giving up a lifelong career or meaningful relationship is seen as relinquishing an essential part of ourselves. So, we often hold onto these things much longer than is necessary, or even healthy. We stay in destructive relationships or dead-end jobs for fear of losing more than love or money.

This determined inability to let go of the things we deem important can have unforeseen consequences. The first of these is that we inadvertently create the situation we most hope to avoid—loss. By holding on too tightly, we lose what we want to possess, just as sand grasped too tightly runs through our fingers. A jealous spouse often creates a distrustful atmosphere of suspicion that can lead to divorce. Miserliness, whether in relationships or in the material world, can invite loss. Furthermore, by concentrating exclusively on what we have in the present, we may miss the opportunity to receive something better in the future. The paradox of this card is that we must let go of what we treasure in order to hold onto it.

The medieval city in the card's background is our own kingdom of fulfilled material aspirations. Interestingly, the way in which we handle the failures or triumphs of materialism can often reveal a hidden emotional outlook. Those who feel worthless may try to compensate by accumulating wealth in order to have undeniable evidence of their self-worth. For others, fears of financial insecurity are often a rationalized substitute for the emotional insecurity they often feel. Trying to obtain security from the outside world, we dearly hold onto what we can physically possess rather than the love and attention we really need. In this way, we are able to hide our true needs behind socially accepted accumulation, just as the unhappy king hides his heart behind one of the pentacles.

Material possessions are not the only things people want to hold onto. The miserly king may also represent someone close to us who has decided to withhold their affection or praise. Perhaps this person is trying to punish or manipulate us by ignoring our emotional needs. Kings are authority figures embodying power, and there is no greater power than love. To withhold love, for whatever reason, is to attempt to control someone in the worst possible way.

There may be other people in our lives who are simply unable to give us what we need. Whether we desire security, affection, or some other important need, we must admit that certain people may not have the maturity necessary to satisfy our most basic requirements. Some men cannot commit to a relationship, while some parents are deficient in their capacity to love their children equally. We must recognize that others' inability to give us affection is entirely their problem, rather than falsely assuming that we are unworthy or unlovable. It may be time to re-evaluate our bonds with irresponsible or selfish people before it adversely affects our self-esteem.

Whatever questions are asked of the Tarot, most of the answers can be found in this card because most problems stem from either the desire to possess something or the fear of loss. By carefully examining what we are afraid of losing, we may gain a greater awareness of the true source of our problem. When this card appears in a reading, it is time to consider what it is we are so desperately trying to hold onto such as our youth, money, status, or children. This list could include holding onto the current problem addressed by the reading. Sometimes a serious problem has a hidden value that makes us want to continue it. The current conflict may generate sympathy from others, provide drama in our lives, or keep us from examining an even greater problem we wish to avoid.

THE FIVE OF PENTACLES: DEPRIVATION

Life, misfortunes, isolation, abandonment, poverty, are battlefields which have their heroes; obscure heroes, sometimes greater than the illustrious heroes.

—Victor Hugo

In this scene, we find two homeless persons trudging through a snowstorm, the stained glass window above a silent witness to their suffering. These two lost souls are severely in need, being deprived of the necessities of warm clothing, food, and shelter. Here is a situation in which something essential to our well-being is painfully missing. This deprivation may be one of physical comfort, but it is more often an emotional or spiritual deprivation. Beyond the physical misery pictured, it is all too common to see a poverty of spirit, a poverty of hope, or a poverty of caring.

Underneath the busyness of daily living, there is often a deeply hidden neediness that is seldom acknowledged. Just as the homeless are so often ignored on the street, many of our most pressing emotional needs go unnoticed by us. Equating neediness with weakness, we ignore our unfulfilled needs until they suddenly surface as an addiction or physical ailment. This card asks us to identify the true needs, which are often hidden underneath our expectations of what we may want from a job or relationship.

Once we've acknowledged our innermost needs, we need to be more open in communicating our needs to others. The boy pictured wears a bell around his neck, indicating that he may be deaf and mute. His inability to speak mirrors our own inability to have our needs understood by others. We may have to learn to communicate our needs, or ask for reassurance that we are loved.

The neediness we often find so difficult to express in words usually originates in a childhood of neglect. Hobbling along on crutches in his torn clothes, the boy pictured epitomizes the neglected child. Children are naturally dependent upon their parents for their well-being, but not all parents are able to properly care for them. Just as the son trails after his mother, children have little choice but to follow the path of their caretakers even if they are not well-cared for. Lack of parental care forces the neglected child to carry unsatisfied needs over into adulthood where they have a negative impact on health, careers, and relationships.

Neglect, particularly the emotional deprivation caused by narcissistic, self-centered parents, can adversely affect adult relationships. Childhood deprivation affects the partners we choose when we grow up because it is very likely that we will be attracted to partners who are emotionally unavailable just like our parents. Like the wintry weather on this card, we will consistently choose partners who are cold and distant, therefore replicating our childhood deprivation. These ill-fated relationships based upon familiar childhood feelings of neglect usually fail because neither partner's emotional needs are being satisfied. Those persons with deprivation in their pasts need to be particularly careful to choose potential partners who are genuinely loving and caring. We need to learn to open our hearts to emotionally generous persons who can satisfy our emotional needs rather than ignore them.

Tragically, those who have experienced physical or emotional neglect often see themselves as unworthy of their parents' love. They have an underlying belief that there is something wrong with them, rather than realizing that their parents were simply unable to properly care for them. Instead of blaming his parents, the disabled boy pictured thinks of himself as defective and, therefore, unlovable. Furthermore, his self-blame leads to lack of self-esteem, shown by his ragged clothes. The real poverty for the mother and son in this card is a poverty of self-esteem, for their destitution mirrors their feelings of worthlessness.

The weakened ego resulting from neglect may also cause the impaired person to create failure and rejection in order to reinforce their belief in their own defectiveness. Those who always seem to attract bad luck may be unconsciously trying to convince themselves that they don't deserve good fortune. Positive affirmations such as, "I deserve happiness and wealth," are often needed to counteract these feelings of worthlessness. Like the stained glass window pictured,

THE MINOR ARCANA

affirmations can brighten our outlook and illuminate our path with a light that comes from within.

Because low self-esteem makes us feel unworthy of relationships or belonging to a group, it can quickly lead to alienation. Feelings of inferiority make us believe that we are always outsiders looking into lighted windows. Although we may want to belong, we are prevented from going inside by feelings of alienation that stop us from seeking the companionship we need. Feeling unforgiven and outside of God's grace, we may have also given up on the solace that spirituality gives us in times of need. We must find the inner strength to put our feelings of alienation aside in order to enter a spiritual sanctuary where we can find faith in the face of adversity.

Finally, deprivation can also solely be a state of mind. We feel terribly deprived each time we don't get what we feel we most deserve in life. This can make us feel just as miserable as the homeless figures on this card. No matter how prosperous we may be in most areas of our lives, having one major, unfulfilled desire can make us feel very poor. The child we never gave birth to or the fame we never attained can be the source of great dissatisfaction and the cause of depression. To counteract these insistent feelings of deprivation, it is helpful to make a daily list of the things for which we are grateful. By focusing, even momentarily, on what we have rather than what we lack, we may be able to gain a better perspective on our situation.

Deprivation also pervades our thinking when we constantly compare what we have with what others have acquired. We can feel a sense of relative deprivation when our neighbor buys a new car or when we imagine that our single friends must have more exciting love lives than we do. Others are certainly happier, richer, more attractive, or more loved than we are. Their pasts were untroubled, their futures brighter than ours. Like the boy on crutches, we can become crippled by envy, feeling we have nothing in comparison. However, by concentrating on what others have, we pass by our own inner light of specialness. As exceptional individuals, we have feelings that are quite different from others and dreams that are uniquely ours. Our chosen path may be difficult and impoverished, but it is our own. When we see things in this light, we come to realize that our struggle and deprivation have been present in our lives for a reason.

Paradoxically, deprivation can lead to a richer experience of life. Financial deprivation often results in a stronger person, determined to find a more prosperous future. Being deprived of loved ones can also help us develop compassion for others who have trodden the same lonely path. This ability to see misfortune as a necessity for personal growth is the true illumination offered by this card. In this new light, a problematic path can be understood as a hero's journey in which our greatest triumphs stem from adversity.

In divination, this card not only reflects financial insecurity, but poor relationships as well. The two people out in the cold depict a frigid estrangement from either family or friends. However, just as the woman's clothes appear to have been mended, the severed relationship can be patched up with diligent effort and a humble attitude.

Also, because there is a mother and her son on this card, it indicates abandonment by a father figure sometime in the past. This may have resulted from either death or divorce, but even a father who was physically present may have been emotionally absent because of his preoccupation with work or addictions. Fatherlessness is a profound loss that colors all of a person's experiences in later life. Loss of a father creates the wounded inner child pictured, who cannot proceed without some sort of external crutch instead of the strong, inner support usually generated by an internalized father figure.

If this card is any indication of the future, then there will be a very rough road ahead. Difficult times test our belief system, particularly our belief in ourselves and the world around us. Believing in a cold, cruel world leads to an impoverished view of reality in which the struggle for survival is the only focus in life. This survival mentality may also include social survival, in which we play our expected roles and industriously work at our jobs, while forgetting our dreams. Just as the people pictured continually move forward, we must progress past this limited viewpoint toward a wider belief in a universe of abundance.

THE SIX PENTACLES: COMPENSATION

> For everything you have missed, you have gained something else; and for everything you gain, you lose something else.
>
> —Ralph Waldo Emerson

In this card, a nobleman charitably dispenses coins to two beggars. This appears to be a card about the different social classes, particularly the stark contrast between the wealthy aristocracy and the wretched poor. On a more symbolic level, the Six of Pentacles reflects any unequal relationship where one of the parties has more power and authority than the other. Many of our interactions such as between boss and employee, husband and wife, or parent and child all have unspoken agreements covering who has the power in the relationship. We may need to be more conscious of the implicit consent we've given to those in power and decide whether we want the dynamics of such an unequal relationship to change.

Central to this card's meaning is the concept of noblesse oblige (nobility obliges). Historically, this is the social obligation of those of high rank to be kind and generous to those who are less fortunate. Although there are few persons who hold noble titles today, we all still have an obligation to behave in a noble fashion by generously donating money to the poor. With its balanced scales, the Six of Pentacles also is the Justice card of the Minor Arcana and as such reflects our need to correct social injustice wherever we find it. It also shows the price we are willing to pay for justice of any kind. Balancing the scales of economic or social inequality can be very costly, but it is an obligation we should assume with alacrity.

Charity also carries spiritual, as well as social meaning. The needy among us must often beg for the necessities of life. The word beggar derives from the Beghards, a thirteenth-century European brotherhood whose friars lived by begging. Today, many religious persons around the world beg for their daily bread as an expression of their faith in divine sustenance. Being totally reliant upon the charity of others then becomes symbolic of complete reliance upon a higher power for all that is received in this life. Therefore, there can be no shame in accepting the charity of others if we see the giver as simply an intermediary between a divine gift and ourselves.

Although charity is a spiritual virtue, most of us have serious reservations about giving to those who do not work for a living. Most of us believe, underneath our noble gestures, that charity encourages dependence. This is because, in most patriarchal cultures, any form of dependence is denigrated, while self-reliance is seen as a masculine virtue. Add to this a Protestant work ethic in which hard work is seen as a road to salvation and you have a built-in prejudice against the less fortunate. There is also a commonly held belief that these people could certainly do better if they would just work harder, as we do. These beliefs directly contradict the psychological reality we find so difficult to accept: people do the best they can given their present level of awareness. If they could manage their lives better, they would certainly do so. We must keep in mind that others may lack the skills and advantages we have acquired, or simply lack the resiliency to cope with life's many tragic losses. By withholding our scornful judgment, we can become more charitable in our thoughts toward others. Giving others the benefit of a doubt or trying to understand their unfortunate circumstances is a true act of kindness. Sending others our kind thoughts instead of harsh words is often the greatest gift of charity.

On an inner level, this card reflects our unspoken neediness and the ways in which others fulfill those needs. Some of us may unconsciously long for someone to take care of us, believing that everything in our lives would be perfect if someone would give us the love we've always wanted. However, if our happiness depends solely on others, we make our happiness someone else's responsibility. Not only can this be an unfair burden on our partner, but it also makes us less likely to seek out our own happiness within ourselves. A keen interest in a new hobby or finding pleasure in nature can generate inner contentment independent of others. We can then come into relationships able to give of ourselves instead of expecting to constantly receive from others.

We may also incorrectly assume that others automatically know exactly what we need. Whether we need a compliment, a hug, or a raise, it is important for us to express our needs. Just as the beggars ask for charity, we need to make our needs clear. This is because many times important people in our lives will give us only what they perceive we need rather than what we really desire. People usually give others what they themselves view to be important. For example, money may be given to us instead of the emotional support that is needed. Although what is given may not be what we need, we must understand that the gift is precious to the giver and, therefore, should be appreciated.

Spiritual assistance is also available when we ask for it, although otherworldly help is usually indirect and veiled. A book we happen to find serendipitously, a chance encounter with a stranger, or overhearing an enlightening conversation can all provide the answers for which we've been searching. These mysterious gifts of the universe give us what we truly need at just the right time.

Although we usually see ourselves as being either the giver or the receiver, sometimes beggar and benefactor are one and the same. Just as the nobleman's loss of his coins is the beggar's gain, we each must lose something important in order to gain something else. The universal law of sacrifice dictates that growth necessitates loss of one kind or another. So we find loss is a constant companion to gain. For instance, the joy of having children also entails the loss of much of our freedom. Other losses are less tangible; for example, in our struggle to grow, we may find ourselves giving up cherished beliefs. This card reflects life as a system of compensations in which we must sacrifice something we value in order to obtain something more desirable. While we may make these sacrifices gladly, it is important to realize the price we have paid for what we have gained and to evaluate if it has been worth the cost.

When this card appears in a reading, we need to examine the careful balance needed in giving to others. Because women in particular are very prone to helping others while ignoring their own needs, their lives can quickly become imbalanced. Many women have an underlying belief that they cannot be loved for themselves, but rather have to earn love by sacrificing themselves for others.

Their self-esteem becomes based entirely on their need to be needed, and they become emotionally dependent upon those who are dependent upon them. While it is important to be mindful of the needs of others, we also have a duty to respond to our own needs.

We can start to help ourselves by giving ourselves the gift of encouragement. The small deeds we accomplish daily should be acknowledged and applauded. Cleaning out the closet may seem like an insignificant task; however, we can certainly take pride in having done it. By giving ourselves a psychological pat on the back every day, we can give ourselves the encouragement we really need.

THE SEVEN OF PENTACLES: EXPECTATION

> Whether you tend a garden or not, you are the gardener of your own being, the seed of your destiny.
>
> —The Findhorn Community

The Seven of Pentacles shows a medieval serf patiently tending his crops. Interestingly, the fertile field has yielded an abundance of pentacles instead of the usual fruits and vegetables. This harvest of pentacles provides a far more important type of sustenance than ordinary food. The fruit of this tree is our own potential.

Farming has been used through the centuries as an apt metaphor for self-improvement, as it involves the development of something new. Just as the farmer sows his seeds in the spring, we need to cultivate new interests or talents in order to grow. Like tending to the needs of growing crops, we nurture these new interests until they come to fruition. This card affirms the necessity of growth and the fundamental value of self-improvement.

Self-improvement is paradoxical, for in trying to change ourselves we must be both the initiator and the object of change. In initiating self-change, we must have the necessary objectivity to see ourselves as something important to be worked upon, just like a beautiful garden. In this way, the serf pictured is both the gardener and the garden. As he contemplates his growing vines, he knows that the hard work of self-improvement will generate needed change. Eventually, he may even come to realize that he has changed so much that the person who initiated the change will have ceased to exist. Through his own strenuous efforts, he has become a different person.

Tending to our inner development requires both delayed gratification and patience. Just as serfs in the Middle Ages were required to give a percentage of their crops to the landowner, we may be required to give up some of the pleasures of today to achieve a lasting goal tomorrow. By postponing gratification, we will eventually reap a greater harvest down the road. Most importantly, as gardeners of our own lives, we need to cultivate the virtue of patience in order to delay gratification. As we invest time and energy in self-improvement with no guarantee of reward, patience is necessary so that we don't abandon our work prematurely. Just as the farmer must wait for his crops to mature, we must recognize the slow nature of human development and wait accordingly. The wise know that the fruit of accomplishment grows on the tree of patience.

Impatience is not the only saboteur of self-improvement. Failure to grow can also stem from either fear of failure or fear of success. When we attempt to grow we also sow seeds of self-doubt. We wonder whether success will be within our grasp, or if our efforts will ultimately be a waste of time and energy. If we fail, we fear ridicule from our friends and family. This fear of shame can be so extreme that we won't even attempt to make important changes in our lives for fear of being seen as foolish. On the other hand, if we succeed we often fear rejection from others who may be jealous of our success. We may also believe that the new person we have become as a result of our efforts may not be as well liked as the old reliable person we were. We may unconsciously believe that taking on a new role or new responsibilities will threaten important relationships. Although there is no magic formula for predicting the repercussions of self-improvement, we can believe in our ability to cope with future problems, should they arise. Positive affirmations such as, "I can grow as a person without threatening those things in life which are important to me," can be used daily to help alleviate any fear of success or failure that may arise.

Another useful tool to counter anxiety is preparation. Just as the serf prepares the fertile soil with his hoe before planting his seeds, we can lay the groundwork ahead of time in preparation for future problems. One of the most effective preparatory strategies is information gathering. This fact-finding mission can be in the form of library research or simply asking friends and relatives how they coped with a similar problem in the past. Self-help groups are also very useful, because talking to people who have gone through the same difficult experience reassures us that we can too.

THE MINOR ARCANA

Just as the serf must diligently rid his garden of unwanted plants with his hoe, we also need to weed out the fears we project into the future. For example, constant fears of future bankruptcy may motivate us to work longer hours, but the cost to our health and peace of mind can be exorbitant. Using fear as our primary motivation may produce some degree of success; however, it can make us miserable. To stay motivated, it is much better to focus our attention on past accomplishments rather than on an uncertain future. The serf pictured on this card gazes at the fruits of his labors located to the left (the past). It is in the past that we sow the seeds of future aspiration.

This card reflects our worries of earthy survival because, in ages past, the growth of a crop could mean either life or death. So, financial anxiety or job insecurity may be uppermost in our minds. Peace of mind can be attained through the realization that life has its financial cycles similar to the changing seasons. Farmers, as the guardians of natural cycles, know that timing is critically important in cultivating their crops. Likewise, we must plant and harvest our energies according to the seasons. New projects should, if at all possible, be initiated in the spring, the season of beginnings. Fall is the right time for leaving a situation or letting go of destructive habits. The coming of winter heralds a time for conserving energy, while summer is the season for nurturing creative projects or oneself. Part of the solution to the present problem can be found in aligning ourselves with the natural cycles in nature that govern our lives.

The old adage "you reap what you sow" also tells us that the present problem is a direct result of the past. An action taken long ago may have repercussions in the present, either good or bad. As the serf stares at what may be his family tree, we may also need to understand that the current problem may have deep roots in our ancestral past. Many of us are burdened by a family history of alcoholism or health problems that can have a negative impact upon our work or relationships. Tracing our problems back to their source in either our own past actions or the actions of our family can often lead to a satisfactory solution.

THE EIGHT OF PENTACLES: WORKING

If you're not working on yourself, you're not working.

—Anonymous

In this card, a skilled craftsman is hard at work manufacturing pentacles. Because he is literally making money, he symbolizes the world of commerce and work. Traditionally, this craftsman is seen as someone new to his workplace, an apprentice developing his skills. Through learning our craft, we develop a sense of achievement and confidence in our abilities. Once we've mastered our skills in the workplace, we start to identify with our jobs, hammering and forging an identity based upon our chosen profession. Our self-esteem rises as we see the fruits of our labors, but deriving all of our self-esteem from work can result in problems. Unfortunately, we may become entirely too dependent upon work as a source of our self-worth and erroneously believe that we are of value to others only as long as we are productive or useful. We may feel that our family loves us only for the money we make, rather than for ourselves.

Lying on the ground underneath the apprentice's bench is a lone pentacle. Out of sight of the apprentice, this pentacle represents thoughts that are below conscious awareness. Just as the pentacle is hidden beneath the bench, there are hidden beneath our actions many underlying beliefs about our work, our relationships, and ourselves.

The first of these beliefs is determinism, which is the belief that what we do directly determines the outcome of a situation rather than God or the Fates. In this world view, striking a metal plate with a chisel produces a pentacle without the need for divine intervention. There is a direct cause and effect that can be measured and controlled. However, when we carry this belief in determinism over into our personal lives, we find ourselves taking all the credit when things go right, and blaming ourselves every time things go terribly wrong. Not only does this way of thinking create an enormous sense of personal responsibility, it adds considerably to our burden of guilt. We may need to expand our belief in otherworldly influence, whether that influence is astrological, fatalistic, or divine.

The second underlying belief is that the future will be an endless repetition of our past. Just as the apprentice produces the same pentacle again and again, we may believe that past hurt or disappointment will be repeated in a bleak future. Because negative expectations tend to become self-fulfilling prophecies, we need to change this limiting belief. By viewing past problems as learning experiences which provide valuable insights for self-growth, we can expect a brighter future.

In this card's background is a golden path leading to a beautiful, walled city. This symbolizes our underlying belief in work as a path to success. If we work hard, we will be rewarded. This mechanistic premise fuels our work ethic and motivates us to go to work every morning. However, success in the workplace does not guarantee success as a human being. Professional or financial success is not the only yardstick by which we can measure the worth of our lives. Many of the most valuable things in life are intangible and are the true measure of success.

The Eight of Pentacles shows us the hard work we also have to do in the world of the psyche. Beneath our everyday concerns are important psychological problems that need to be hammered out. One of the most vexing of these problems is that of repetition. Any craft is, by its nature, repetitious, as raw materials are repeatedly fashioned into finished products. Just as the craftsman pictured must strike the same blows again and again to produce the pentacles, we often generate the same problems over and over to learn valuable lessons about ourselves. We may be attempting to carefully craft a new relationship to resemble an old one or repeating destructive behavior.

Whenever we find ourselves repeating the same pattern again and again, it is essential to recognize any underlying similarities in all the problems we have experienced. Recurrent themes such as fear of abandonment, the need for approval, or the fight for independence can run through our lives like replayed television dramas. Sometimes divorced persons have a tendency to choose a new partner who has the same faults as the original spouse, thus repeating the same problems. There may also be a compelling need to repeat the traumatic experiences of childhood. By unconsciously reproducing an identical situation to one we experienced in childhood, we are attempting to rectify the past by recreating it in the present. However, without insight into the repetitious nature of our problems, we are often destined to repeat the same frustrating or tragic outcome instead of reaching a resolution. One cannot change the past by repeating it. We can only learn from it and move on.

Once we recognize the repetitious basis of our problems, it becomes easier to find solutions. By realizing that our present problem is part of an unconscious pattern of poorly relating to others, we can eventually free ourselves from the mechanism of repetitive behavior. Like the craftsman who transforms cheap pieces of metal into valuable pentacles, we can assume the work of transforming unconscious energy into conscious awareness. Psychologists speak of this process as "working through" an emotional difficulty by repeatedly facing repressed feelings and experiences until healthier patterns of behavior are established. Change is possible only if we can face the same conflicts over and over again with insights into our habitual reactions. This is the work of the inner apprentice: to repeatedly approach the same difficult task in an insightful way.

When this card appears in a reading, be forewarned that this means there are no shortcuts or instantaneous answers to the current problem. This card indicates that hard work is necessary for a relationship to work. The labor of life cannot be easily avoided and, in the long run, it is far better to work through a particular problem than run away from it. This card clearly indicates that one should stay in a stormy relationship and work it through rather than going on to someone else who may initiate the same problems all over again. By choosing monogamy, we demonstrate a commitment to work on interpersonal problems, rather than avoid underlying issues by repeatedly changing partners. In time, it is often possible to better understand the nature of the relationship and master the difficulties just as the craftsman masters his trade.

THE NINE OF PENTACLES: WAITING

All things come round to him who will but wait.

—Henry Wadsworth Longfellow

A noble lady in a beautiful garden holds a hawk. She appears to be a woman of leisure who enjoys the pastime of falconry, the sport of kings and princes. Her comfortable inactivity is in sharp contrast to many of the other cards of this suit that reflect the struggle to survive. However, this lady of leisure's task is different, yet no less difficult: it is to wait. Just as the falconer must await the return of the falcon, this aristocratic woman must patiently wait for something or someone to return to her. In this respect she is like most women through the ages who have passively waited to be chosen, waited for their husbands to come home from the hunt, or simply waited for circumstances to change.

Historically, the vast majority of women have assumed a traditional, passive role, in which they were expected to remain at home while the men of the community ventured forth to find food. While the male of the species moves easily from one place or condition to another, the female is more inclined to remain in one place to provide a stable home for her dependent children. Summarily, it can be said that men quest while women wait. Interestingly, it has been theorized that through centuries of waiting, women developed the faculty of intuition. In order to survive, women in prehistoric times needed to develop their intuition to sense whether or not the hunter would return home with food. Those women who could accurately predict the arrival of sustenance were more likely to survive, and thus, intuition became an important tool for survival.

While waiting can be a positive experience, it can also be a part of a woman's passive pattern of inactivity and unresponsiveness. The passive woman is dependent, waiting for the actions of others for her own fulfillment. Unable to take action, she may vicariously live her life through the success of her husband or children. She is like the falconer, who stands still, allowing her hawk to sail forth to do her bidding for her. Because her success depends upon the achievements of others, she finds herself on the periphery, anxiously awaiting the fateful actions of others in the world outside her own.

While we usually think of waiting as a passive period in which nothing happens, waiting can also be a time of great inner activity. Although it appears to be an oxymoron, this special time is called active waiting. In contrast to the inactivity of passive waiting, active waiting is simply the postponement of any action until the arrival of the right moment. Timing is indeed everything, and any important action initiated either too soon or too late can result in failure. Like a hawk waiting for the right moment to strike his target, we need to wait for the perfect moment in which to act. Active waiting focuses our attention on obtaining a bird's-eye view of the situation and then using that lofty perspective to purposely choose the best time to connect with what we desire. Insight into the situation may even suggest that taking no action at all may be the best course. Active waiting teaches us that, paradoxically, when we choose to do nothing, we are actually doing something important.

Once we decide to act, we may find that our actions, like the hawk's circular flight, bring us back to where we started. This return of the falcon to the falconer reflects the importance of coming home. Many women venture forth into the world of work only to find a masculine realm of struggle and competition. The need to return home to the private sphere for intimacy and solace that are unattainable in the world of work is essential for a balanced life. While it is important for women to develop their masculine side, it is also vital for women to experience lives that are supportive of their feminine nature. This card symbolizes the need to return to a home in which emotions and creativity are honored. Like the hedge that creates a private space for nurturing and growth, we need to create a sheltered home life where we can return to ourselves.

Falconry has always symbolized control of our animal natures, as this medieval pastime required careful training of a ferocious bird of prey. Wearing its red hood of desire, the bird pictured represents our lofty ambitions and soaring desires that, for one reason or another, we have needed to control. Perhaps we've needed to abandon our adolescent aspirations and dreams in order to provide for our family. Like the hooded falcon, we can no longer see our earlier goals. We are unable to hunt down the fulfillment of our desires because we are blind to what we really want from life. The wild bird within us has been thoroughly domesticated, forgetting its original nature in order to serve the mistress of conformity. We may need to remember what our life goals were when we were adolescents in order to reassert what is important to us in the present.

Another way of looking at the relationship between the hawk and his mistress is to see it as an attempt of one person to control another. There may be a serious issue with a controlling type of woman in a man's life. Because it violates their own needs, controlling women are unable to allow men the freedom to be themselves. Consequently, a controlling wife or mother attempts to control a man's every move, sending him out only as far as her will dictates he should go. Surprisingly, he accepts this limitation because her love for him is the tether that keeps him tied to her. Although her domination may bring him great unhappiness, he will continue to live within her locus of control, just as the hooded bird lives within the restrictions imposed upon him. However, once he becomes aware of this tender entrapment, he can take steps to free himself and fly away.

In divination, this card could be a warning to be more aware of the hawkish qualities in others close to us. Human beings, like other animals, often have a predatory nature cleverly concealed beneath a mild exterior. Sometimes this results in an attack "from out of the blue" by someone we trust. In the business world that pentacles encompass, this card alerts us to ruthless ambition in someone nearby. Therefore, we should exercise caution lest we become an unsuspecting victim from this person's drive for power.

Unfortunately, not all predatory instincts are confined to the world of work. Falconry is a form of hunting which often has a hidden sexual meaning because it involves pursuing the object of desire until it is caught. We may need to be aware that there are those who play the game of love as a cruel sport, seeing each romantic encounter as an opportunity for conquest.

THE TEN OF PENTACLES: REVELATION

Yet all experience is an arch where through
Gleams that untraveled world.

—Alfred, Lord Tennyson

This card shows a familiar scene of pleasant socializing in the town square. Beneath an imposing archway, a man armed with a spear speaks with a woman who has a small child. Strangely, the couple completely ignores the old man in the foreground, whose only companions are a pair of dogs who seem to be inexplicably drawn to him. The dogs obviously sense something that the preoccupied couple fails to perceive, namely, that he is the Wise Old Man. Many cultures around the world have folk tales of a saint or wise man who comes into a community disguised as a humble beggar. Those fortunate few who befriend this pitiful old man eventually come to understand his true identity and are greatly rewarded for their charity. The moral of these tales is that the most holy phenomenon is often someone or something that is easily ignored because it is so commonplace.

In a similar fashion, this card tells us to look beyond outward appearances to perceive the extraordinary in the ordinary occurrences of everyday life. A belief that our spiritual goals can best be achieved by an arduous and distant spiritual quest can be deceptive. The true source of our spirituality is often where we are at the present moment, if only we have the courage to look around us. If we can see the significant in the seemingly insignificant pageant of life that surrounds us, then we will reach a true revelation. Mystical teachings proclaim that the material world is very much like the old man's intricately woven cloak that completely conceals what is underneath. By focusing attention on our present circumstances, we can find the wonder hidden beneath the commonplace.

Superimposed upon this familiar domestic scene is a Kabbalistic Tree of Life diagram formed by the card's ten pentacles. The Tree of

Life is a mystical gateway into the inner workings of the universe. As a guide to the many levels of existence, it forms a connection between the outer and inner worlds. This theme of a gateway from the known to the unknown is also shown by the card's two archways. The wide archway on the right leads to a courtyard beyond its confines and symbolizes an entranceway into the ordinary world of mundane experience. To the left of this large archway is a partially obscured entranceway into the magical world of the spirit. Exactly what is contained within its checkered borders is unclear, as if we are offered just a glimpse of this unfamiliar landscape. Most of us, like the couple on the card, ignore this gateway, believing it to be either nonexistent or a dead end. Many of us are afraid to pursue inner work for fear that our outer lives will suffer if we don't put all of our energy into the laborious responsibilities required of the material world. It is also difficult to relinquish the promised payoffs of the ordinary world such as money and power in order to enter an unknown world with ephemeral rewards. Like the child pictured, who clings to his mother, we may cling to our belief in the material world while ignoring the vast treasures of the spiritual realm. The suit of pentacles is concerned with what we value in life and, as the culmination of the suit, the Ten of Pentacles reflects the value of what we can actually see, hear, and touch. However, the inner world of dreams, prayer, or oracles such as the Tarot has intrinsic value as guideposts in the outer world. Without this inner guidance, we can easily lose our way in the "real world." We must remember that the inner world is real in its consequences. If we deny its reality we shall court the same disaster as if we ignored the perils of the material world.

To enter the world of the spirit is to have a heightened awareness of things that are hidden from ordinary consciousness. There is a knowledge contained within it that transcends time and space. While we are usually oriented to a definite past, present, and future (represented by the man, woman, and child beneath the archway of the ordinary world), esoteric knowledge alters this view of reality. Suddenly, the self is seen as an immortal soul transcending personal history and earthly location. The goal of existence then shifts from accumulation of material goods to accumulation of spiritual experience. We are no longer human beings having spiritual experiences, but rather spiritual beings having human experiences. Of course, once we visit the spiritual world through study, prayer, or meditation, we need to bring our experiences back into the real world in order to implement the lessons learned in the spiritual realm. Revelation has little relevance unless it can be used to better our earthly lives or the lives of others. In this card, the wise Hermit has come down from the mountaintop to re-enter ordinary life. He is then able to utilize metaphysical explanations to understand the world around him.

Revelation can also be found in the world of the psyche. In this case, the two doorways represent the psychological worlds of the conscious and the unconscious. Like the obscured, checkered entranceway on the card, our unconscious fears and motivations are always carefully hidden from our conscious minds. Often the only way to enter this forbidden world is through examining our dreams and fantasies. Dreams, as the voice of the unconscious, can lead to revelation only if we take our dreams seriously. Keeping a dream journal, discussing our dreams with a trusted friend or counselor, or dialoging with dream figures keeps the importance of dreams alive. By listening to the messages hidden in our dreams, we may come to realize that many of our worldly problems are reflections of unconscious emotional states. Keeping a balance between our conscious and unconscious lives is essential for our well-being. Like the Wise Man seated between the two archways, we can position ourselves between the conscious and unconscious worlds in order to fully benefit from both.

Because the background of this card is a public space, it represents collective opinion. As social animals, people often strive to fit in with the crowd. However, this card warns us to be aware of these social influences in our decision making. Social pressure to conform can often undermine our efforts to grow as individuals. Although we usually see ourselves in a society that advocates freedom of choice, in reality, our choices are severely limited by social convention. Therefore, we should be aware that the present problem may be related to exterior influences.

Public conversations, like the one pictured on this card, often contain a key to the solution of many problems. Attentively listening to what others say at the next table in a restaurant or overhearing a conversation while waiting in line can bring valuable insights. Many times the overheard conversation will provide a different perspective on a problem identical to ours, or contain a clear message as to what action we should take in the future. Listening to "accidentally" heard conversations often provides the advice we seek.

THE PAGE OF PENTACLES: FOCUSING

Wherever we go, whatever we do, self is the sole subject we study and learn.

—Ralph Waldo Emerson

Here we see a beautifully attired page intensely focused on a pentacle that he carefully holds aloft. Looking ahead at the other court cards in this suit, we find that they are also intently gazing at their pentacles as if they are looking for divine inspiration. The answers to all their questions seem to be contained within these small, yellow spheres. However, it is not the pentacles themselves that assume so much importance as it is the importance of the act of focusing attention on an object.

Clearly, what we focus on determines the quality of our lives. We focus on our social roles, businesses, creative endeavors, relationships, or a myriad of other subjects we deem to be important. When we choose to focus on one aspect of our lives to the detriment of others, we automatically determine the path our lives will take. We will follow the road illuminated by our focus, just as the headlights of a car concentrate light on the dark road ahead. Attentive focus is so important that it is often very helpful to objectively monitor exactly what we are focusing on. Determining what occupies our thoughts for most of the day will most likely determine our focus. We may be focusing on our jobs when we're at home or, conversely, focusing on what is happening at home when we're on the job. We can also spend much of our time focusing on television, computers, or sports. Once we've discerned our primary focus, we need to ask ourselves if this subject is worthy of our attention, or if we need to turn our attention to something more worthwhile instead. We also need to keep in mind that sometimes intensely focusing on entertainment or other people's problems acts as a distraction from personal issues we would rather not look at too clearly. In this case, it is necessary to turn our attention away from everyday concerns so that we can look within for answers.

Focusing on anything outside ourselves automatically transforms the thing focused upon into a separate object. Objects may be desired, pursued, controlled, owned, or contemplated. This is because we consider the observer and the object being observed as two separate entities. The object is seen as a passive thing that can be changed only by the application of some physical force. However, recent developments in physics, particularly Heisenberg's Uncertainty Principle, point to a reality in which the observer subtly influences the object merely by observing it. So, a mechanistic universe working independently of human desire seems to be nonexistent. We are slowly beginning to realize that when we expect certain results, we influence the actual outcome of the situation. Therefore, focusing on a positive result and having confident expectation that a situation will ultimately turn out well are the real keys to success in any endeavor.

An alternate explanation to the dualistic belief in observer and object is proposed by mysticism. In the mystic world-view, subject and object are one and the same thing; therefore, the objective world we live in becomes a mirror of our inner experience. So, we must look outward to see ourselves. This projection of ourselves into the environment transforms the world into a classroom in which we are constantly given the opportunity to learn about ourselves. Whether we are looking through either a microscope or a telescope, we are observing ourselves. This card shows us that the page's pursuit of knowledge of the outside world leads him to self-knowledge.

Traditionally, the Page of Pentacles has been seen as a young student. We are all students of life, but the first lesson we must learn is to trust our own senses and experience. Even if our experiences are fundamentally different from others, we must remain in touch with our own perception and trust the validity of our senses. The five-pointed star found on the suit of pentacles represents the five senses and is a daily reminder to pay attention to what we see, hear, smell, taste, and feel. The page elevates these five senses to a lofty position of reverence so he can acknowledge his unique perception of the world around him. The first step in learning to trust ourselves is to trust our own experience, and that of others. Experience is a great teacher, but only if we constantly ask ourselves what is the lesson we must learn from difficult experiences. Many times, once we understand the lesson to be learned, the distressing situation automatically disappears.

As students, we also need to learn the important lessons of the body. There is an interesting theory that proposes that unresolved issues travel downward from higher to lower levels. Spiritual dilemmas manifest as emotional problems, while emotional problems manifest as physical ailments. If we look closely, we can see the psychological nature of many of our illnesses. Asthma is often associated with a smothering mother, while digestive disorders are generated by a situation that we just can't stomach. By focusing on the secret symbolism of our diseases, we may be able to correct the underlying cause of our distress. As students of life, we need to connect with the hidden wisdom of our bodies in order to learn important lessons about ourselves.

In medieval times, pages were young men who attended to the daily needs of valiant knights. Like a page's dutiful attention to his knight, we need to serve our ideals and goals in order to succeed. By loyally serving a knight, a page fervently hoped to gain the necessary skills to become a knight someday. In this way, the pages represent our aspirations for a better job or a richer life. The pages exemplify daily devotion to higher aspirations and a higher purpose in life. Like the page holding the pentacle, it is always best to put these aspirations before us while we walk toward our goal.

The role of page was an important preparatory stage for becoming a knight, and many years of intensive training were necessary before an ambitious page acquired the requisite skills that would confer knighthood. Likewise, our own goals cannot be obtained without proper preparation. As the plowed field in the card's background suggests, laying the groundwork is essential before we can plant the seeds of future accomplishment. The fertile soil of experience must be carefully prepared before a new idea can take root. Sometimes this preparation will take the form of many seemingly insignificant steps toward our goal, as the page's mincing footsteps indicate. One small step is to set aside the necessary time and energy every day to further our goal. Devoting daily resources to our higher aspirations prepares the way for significant life changes.

THE KNIGHT OF PENTACLES: POTENTIAL

Events, circumstances, etc., have their origin in ourselves.
They spring from seeds which we have sown.

—Henry David Thoreau

A knight in shining armor sits astride a dark horse in the middle of a plowed field. Medieval knights embody the archetype of the hero because of their great strength and courage. Heroes fearlessly move toward accomplishment and change, confidently confronting their difficulties head-on. They seek solutions to their most challenging problems by realizing the need for assertive action. Heroes act in spite of their fears because their need for accomplishment far outweighs their apprehension. Moving steadily forward, the hero perceives problems as challenges, continues to take risks, and finally confronts his enemies both within and without. He is also an independent seeker who ventures into unfamiliar territory to find value in life. His search for answers usually involves a heroic quest in which his courage and virtue are severely tested.

Our own heroic journey is not to slay dragons or vanquish deadly enemies, but rather to integrate qualities of the opposite sex into our lives. The real heroic quest is to find the hidden, inner contrasexual parts of ourselves: women seek the masculine qualities within themselves, while men seek the feminine. For either sex, every step on this journey of finding the inner man or inner women brings them closer to realizing their full potential as whole human beings.

Men's heroic journey starts at the point in their lives when their drive for success is totally self-centered and, hopefully, ends in unselfish caring. Like a knight in full battle regalia, men see the world as a battle to be won and, consequently, are often preoccupied with competition and success. Fatherhood often helps them develop feminine characteristics such as nurturing, tenderness, and cooperation that eventually create a more balanced viewpoint. For women, the heroic journey begins with their submissiveness or powerlessness and ends in assertiveness and inner authority. Many women internalize their inferior role in society by developing a dependent or passive attitude. However, women who find challenges in the workplace or at home develop masculine characteristics such as courage and strength to counterbalance these feelings of inferiority.

Life experiences such as parenthood or promotion can catapult us into the foreign land of the opposite sex, where we must quickly develop unfamiliar characteristics in order to cope. The deep furrows of earth in the card's background are the result of this integration of masculine and feminine forces. The earth is the eternal feminine part of ourselves, receptive to the masculine plow digging beneath her surface. The resulting plowed earth forms a balance between activity and passivity that becomes fertile ground for new growth.

The four knights of the Tarot represent the heroism needed to transcend death. Although we must all return to our place of origin one day, our actions in this life can extend way beyond our tenure here on earth. Our good deeds can far outlast our bracketed existence, so that we can have a resounding impact on future generations. In fact, our socially sanctioned quest for fame and fortune is often a cleverly disguised attempt to simply be remembered for what we have accomplished in life. We all seek to transcend mortality by leaving something worthwhile behind while we continue our journey on the other side. This can be accomplished in a number of ways: through immortal love for another (the Knight of Cups); through immortal glory (the Knight of Swords); by building a monument to withstand the test of time (the Knight of Wands); or by passing on our genes to future generations (the Knight of Pentacles).

As the first of the four knights, the Knight of Pentacles seeks his own immortality through his children. By passing on his name and traditions to the next generation, he is assured that an important part of his existence will outlive his demise. To such a person, children are the embodiment of hope—hope for a continuance of life and hope for a better future. Children link us to future generations who may favorably remember their ancestors. As the progenitor of future generations, the Knight of Pentacles faces his fateful annihilation secure in the knowledge that the seeds of life he has sown will assure his own immortality on earth.

Like the knight, we can also envision the potential inherent in our present actions. The seeds we plant today through our thoughts, words, and deeds will blossom someday into fruit that will nourish others. The key is, of course, to focus on actions performed in the here and now, for what we do today produces future consequences. No matter what the past has brought or what the future may hold, we can fulfill our potential by concentrating on those things we can accomplish in the present moment. While the distant mountains may beckon to us, the seeds that we sow at this moment will produce the fruit that we will harvest later.

The divinatory aspects of this card are reflected in the knight's draft horse, a massive horse bred for work. These horses were used for plowing the fields, so they symbolize a need for the cultivation of new projects and personal growth. Plowing, as the most thankless and difficult phase of farming, reminds us of the hard work necessary to fulfill our potential. As this sturdy plow horse slowly works carving furrows in the field of limitless potential, we are likewise advised to make haste slowly in any new endeavor.

The knight's strong steed is harnessed to a heavy plow, even though this is not explicitly pictured on the card. As it is literally behind him, this burdensome plow represents the weight of the past that we drag behind us. While the personal histories we all carry with us are full of wonderful recollections, they can also contain traumatic memories and the burden of guilt. Nevertheless, it may help to remember that, like the massive horse that pulls his heavy plow, the heavy burdens of the past that we carry with us only make us stronger.

THE QUEEN OF PENTACLES: ACCEPTANCE

Nature to be commanded must be obeyed.

—Francis Bacon

In a scenic country setting, the Queen of Pentacles regally sits upon her stately throne. Unlike the previous court cards of this suit that were concerned with changing the landscape through agriculture, the Queen of Pentacles is surrounded by a wild, uncultivated garden. As Mother Nature, she is perfectly content with things exactly as they are, rather than as someone else would like them to be. Sitting amidst the wildflowers whose seeds have been sown haphazardly by wind and water, she seeks her fulfillment in being rather than in doing. The meandering river in the background is also a reminder to release our controlling ambitions and let life proceed on its own natural course. Sometimes we need to let go of our willful expectations and simply enjoy whatever happens. This peaceful acceptance of a sublime order in which all things naturally develop at their own time and pace can lead to a greater sense of contentment. As the English proverb states, "Contentment is natural wealth," wisely affirming that there is no greater bounty than a peaceful state of mind.

Acceptance of the natural world is fundamental to our well-being, but first we need to understand the origin of natural forces. The Kabbalists speak of the four worlds of existence progressing downward from the ethereal world of divine will to the material world in which we live. In the first world of Emanation (the dimension furthest from our own), God acts directly; however, in subsequent worlds he works through intermediaries. In the second world, the world of Creation, He acts through archangels. In the third world, that of Formation, He acts through angels. Finally, in the fourth world of Action, which is our own material plane, God acts through the elemental forces of nature.

THE MINOR ARCANA

The Queen of Pentacles, as the reigning monarch of her suit, finds her power by aligning herself with the vital forces of nature. She realizes that divine will acts through nature, whether it is in the form of bright sunshine or a hurricane, the birth of a new baby, or the death of a friend. She attains equanimity through the acceptance of natural laws that thoroughly dictate what she cannot change. The queen also understands that human beings are an integral part of the natural world; therefore, divine will usually manifests through the actions of others. God works through gardeners and bus drivers, children and their parents, employers and surgeons. The Queen of Pentacles is truly a woman of the world to whom everyone and everything is an integral part of her experience.

However, total immersion in the material world can create an estrangement from the world of intuition. All the queens of the Minor Arcana are personifications of Jung's four psychological types: the Queen of Swords is the thinking type; the Queen of Cups is the feeling type; the Queen of Wands is the intuitive type; and the Queen of Pentacles is the sensation type. In the Jungian scheme, the four types are polarized into two sets: thinking versus feeling and sensation versus intuitive. These dichotomies of personality represent the eternal conflict between reasoners and romantics, or pragmatists and dreamers. While most of us are born with the characteristics of one psychological type, we find it almost impossible to cultivate the qualities of our opposite type. For example, one cannot be ruled by the heart and the head simultaneously.

The queens in the Tarot exemplify this inability to connect with their opposite function. Although there is great strength in their particular viewpoints, there is also an inherent weakness in not being able to develop the opposing point of view. The Queen of Swords fails to connect with her feelings, while the Queen of Cups may be divorced from logical reasoning. As the pragmatist of her suit, the Queen of Pentacles is cut off from her own intuition. She sits beneath a rose arbor that effectively blocks her from the sun. Because the sun represents the elemental fire of intuition, she is effectively cut off from her intuition and creative imagination. Quietly gazing at her beautiful garden, the Queen of Pentacles limits her perception to what she can actually see, never extending her vision beyond the confines of her small world.

Like the nearsighted Queen, there are many times in our lives when we lack the intuitive ability to envision a different existence than the one we are currently living. Sometimes we are so preoccupied with the practical problems of day-to-day living that we fail to imaginatively project ourselves into a brighter future. Whether we desire a better place to live or a more fulfilling relationship, we will need to imaginatively visualize where we are going before we can get there. The Queen of Pentacles faces left, turning her back on this probable future. The inability to trust in a better future is actually an inability to trust ourselves. By utilizing the light of intuition to visualize exactly what we want, we can begin to trust in a better tomorrow.

In divination, as well as in the psychoanalytic interpretation of dreams, kings and queens represent the querent's father and mother, while knights and pages symbolize siblings. The Queen of Pentacles could easily be the querent's mother or someone in a maternal role. As a mother figure, the queen is naturally focused on the issues of fertility and pregnancy. Mothering can also be expanded to include nurturing any creative project or caring for the growing yet undeveloped parts of ourselves. There may also be an unconscious need for our mother's approval that subtly influences all of our decisions. Queens are powerful figures, and there may be no more powerful person in our lives than our mother.

THE KING OF PENTACLES: HARVEST

Live within your harvest.

—Pesius

The previous cards of this suit have shown the various stages of farming, from sowing the first seeds to anxiously waiting for the new crop to develop. In this card is the culmination of the suit of pentacles, the harvest of all the painstaking work that has been completed. The King of Pentacles, clothed in his grape-covered robes, represents the fruits of our labors. Enthroned in his lofty castle, he symbolizes the realization of our dreams and the fulfillment of desire.

The king is a middle-aged man, indicating that the hard work of personal growth eventually results in more mature outlook. All of the kings in the Tarot represent the important work of midlife. The challenge of middle age is to finally face our own mortality by reassessing our actions and beliefs in the shadow of death. This is a time in which we hold onto enduring values that sustain us and discard the unimportant aspects of our lives. While the youthful knights of the Tarot need to battle external adversaries, the kings, representing midlife, must confront the enemy within. Midlife is a time to examine the road we have traveled in the past, giving new meaning to the triumphs and failures along the way. Having developed a loftier perspective on our lives, we become the king of all we survey.

The King of Pentacles, as a symbol of earthly authority, also reminds us of our own power. We all either consciously or unconsciously strive for power within our careers or relationships. Men typically seek power in the workplace, where the attainment of success can confer superiority. Women seek power in the world either by emulating men or by being desired by men. Both sexes follow a masculine concept of authority in which power can only be conferred by those who hold power in the outside world.

However, there is another source of power that goes largely unrecognized by us. This is the authentic power of inner authority. It is the power of knowing what is right for us, of trusting our own experience, and finding our own truth. Inner authority is the small voice within that quietly tells us to love ourselves for who we are at the moment, rather than screaming that we should withhold self-love until we have earned it through achievement. By having inner authority, we can lay claim to our own sense of self-worth rather than believe in someone else's concept of self-respect.

Inner authority also encompasses the acceptance of responsibility for our actions. We often give most of our power to others simply by holding them responsible for our problems. When we blame our parents, our boss, or our spouse for our misbehavior, we give them undue authority in our lives. Blaming others for our misfortune gives power to those whom we see as somehow in charge of our fate. On the other hand, those with inner authority act like the King of Pentacles, having ultimate control over their domain. Because he is the reigning monarch, he can only blame himself for the fate of his nation. By fully accepting responsibility for his actions, he is able to govern wisely. If we can envision ourselves as resplendent kings whose only authority is our own, then we can successfully rule ourselves.

In divination, this card signifies the successful conclusion of a business matter or creative endeavor. The King of Pentacles sits upon his black throne of death, symbolizing the end of a cycle, project, or ambition. Although he has risen to the pinnacle of success, the king appears depressed at having no more worlds to conquer. There is always a period of deflation after the attainment of a crowning achievement, whether it takes the form of postpartum depression, or dispiritedness after winning the big game. Just as the cold winter season follows the time of harvest, we can naturally expect a barren period before it is time to plant new seeds again in the spring.

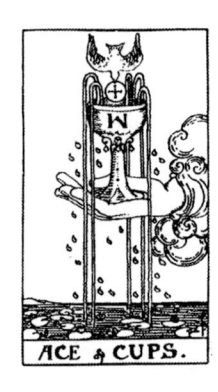

THE ACE OF CUPS: EMANATION

> If attention is directed to the unconscious, the unconscious will yield up its contents like a fountain of living water.
>
> —Carl Jung

The suit of cups in the Tarot is a magical place where there is a unity of opposites. Like many mythologies, the cup cards contain a recurring theme of reuniting two elements that had previously been separated by fate. In one of the cards, a rainbow traverses heaven and earth, uniting the sky with the land. In another, a mysterious gift brings a man and a woman together. A bridge connects the past with the future. An eclipse produces the celestial union of sun and moon. In each one of these cards, opposing forces are brought together to become one. Often this reunion is fleeting (the rainbow soon fades or the lover leaves), but while the opposites are briefly united, there is a special magic that tells us that anything is indeed possible.

In the Ace of Cups, a mysterious hand holding a beautiful golden chalice suddenly appears from inside a cloud. A fountain of water flows downward from the cup into a still pond below. The cup has become a wellspring of the cascading waters of life. These waters could well be the great waters of human experience or the waters of wisdom; however, they are most likely the waters of emotion.

The suit of cups represents Jung's feeling function, or what we commonly refer to as our emotions. Like an ancient fountain, our emotions seem to well up from inside ourselves, spilling over into every area of our lives. Like looking through either still or rippled water, emotions can either clarify or distort all of our experiences. Love and compassion can give greater meaning to our actions, while negative emotions such as fear, jealousy, or hatred can cloud our judgment, causing us to act against our best interests. However, whether we view our most profound emotions as either passages or blockages, we must always accept the fundamental truth of our feelings and honor them. This is reflected in the Tarot, as all the cups are sacred vessels containing the most vital parts of ourselves.

In this card, emotions are divine gifts that enrich our lives on many different levels. Our feelings determine what matters most to us and, therefore, are always a determining factor in making important decisions. The most important decision in our lives, that of choosing a mate, is usually made solely on the basis of emotion. Emotions are also an expression of our conscience because they are an accurate barometer of right and wrong. By carefully listening to our feelings we can have a truer understanding of who we are and master the situations in which we find ourselves.

When we respond to a situation with more feeling than is warranted by actual circumstances, we need to find the origin of this exaggerated emotional reaction. Like a river whose source is many miles distant, the source of our problematic feelings is to be found far from conscious awareness in the realm of the unconscious. The Ace of Cups is the golden chalice of the unconscious from which emotions flow forth. The unconscious is a container, a depository of forgotten memories and feelings that affects everything that we do. By working with symbols, dreams, and fantasies, it is possible to uncover this source of our deepest emotions.

The Ace of Cups, as a fountainhead of the waters of emotion, symbolizes the source of our deepest feelings. Like the fountain's source, many of our emotions originate in problems found in our parental home. The strong emotions of today are often triggered by something that unconsciously reminds us of a similar situation from childhood. A seemingly harmless event or casual remark can suddenly set off deep emotions that seem to bubble up from below. To understand the source of these emotional problems, we can mentally trace the unsettling event back to any incidents that resembled it in the past. Perhaps a heated argument with a coworker reminds us of similar clashes with our brothers or sisters. Likewise, current problems with authority figures may originate in teenage rebelliousness. Any emotional connections we can make between the past and the present will bring us closer to understanding and, hopefully, to surmounting our problems.

In divination, we can look to the symbols contained in the card for inner direction. The dove, which is so prominent on the Ace of Cups, is symbolic of peace. There may be a need to bring peace into a household or business through the art of compromise. If peace becomes a worthy goal in our lives, we will need to put personal considerations aside in favor of peaceful coexistence. Certainly, having peace of mind is more important than giving someone a piece of our mind.

The surging fountain of water represents overflowing emotion. There is a need to communicate our feelings to others, even if to do so entails some risk. The flowing water also symbolizes a renewal of hope and love. This may mean a new love interest or the opportunity to love again. Like an inexhaustible fountain, the archetypal wellspring of deep emotion is always present, for we never lose the capacity to love.

The overflowing chalice also reveals an important psychological truth. When we completely fill our minds with positive ideas, there is no longer any room in our psyches for negative thoughts. Repeating positive affirmations throughout the day will replenish the waters of positive emotion and dispel negativity. Just as a fountain contains its own waters, happiness can also spring from within ourselves.

THE TWO OF CUPS: ATTRACTION

Journeys end in lovers meeting.

—William Shakespeare

In this card, a man and a woman reach toward one another while a mysterious, winged lion gazes down upon them from above. The Two of Cups symbolizes the Law of Attraction in which each of us either attracts or is drawn to another. Although we usually think of attraction as either an unfathomable mystery or sexual chemistry, there are significant reasons why two people come together at a particular place and time. Usually, certain people enter our lives at particular junctures in order to teach us important lessons about ourselves.

Carl Jung said, "We meet ourselves in a thousand disguises along the path." Since it is often difficult or impossible to see ourselves clearly, our companions along the way mirror hidden aspects of our personalities which we may need to confront. This is particularly true of negative behavior that we easily perceive in others but have difficulty seeing in ourselves. Whether we recognize our potential greatness in the stunning achievements of others or realize our mistakes in a friend's misbehavior, the people we come into contact with offer us an important opportunity for self-awareness.

Surprisingly, attraction for someone always originates within ourselves, particularly from the undeveloped parts of our personalities. Underlying all of our seemingly chance encounters with other people is an unconscious wish to find these missing parts of ourselves. In this card, the man gently reaches out to the woman, showing his intimate connection to her. When we connect with another person, we are actually touching some incomplete element within ourselves. In discovering a lifetime companion, we find the Self contained within the Other. In the mutual give and take of partnership, we each bring to the relationship what the other person does not have. Like a drink from an offered cup, our companions contain needed qualities which we need to incorporate into ourselves.

To get a clearer picture of the missing qualities our partner represents, we can make a list of all the positive qualities that our beloved possesses. If we find our partner to be thrifty, nurturing, knowledgeable, or lighthearted, then we may have a clue to what we seem to be missing in ourselves. Many of these mirrored qualities are what Jung called the animus and anima: the hidden feminine qualities in a man or the hidden masculine qualities in a woman. Like the two figures in the card, walking toward each other, we will need to take positive steps toward integrating these contrasexual qualities into ourselves.

Unfortunately, if we fail to develop some of these hidden qualities, we will expect our significant other to express all the undeveloped aspects of our personalities. The relationship then assumes the heavy burden of hidden assumptions and unconscious contracts as we valiantly try to meet the other person's expectations. The love that we feel may make relentless demands upon its object of affection in order to fulfill our unspoken dreams.

Attraction can also be based upon mutual need. When two people meet, they bring along their personal pasts and their hopes for the future. Our dreams for a better tomorrow are often predicated on having our innermost needs met by a special person. In this card, the man and woman offer each other a drink that will quench the other's thirst, and by doing so, they fulfill each other's needs. We all have needs for love, companionship, sexual fulfillment, admiration, or financial support. We may also have an overwhelming need to escape from our family of origin or to start a family of our own. If we can find someone who can satisfy these important needs, the relationship will work. However, relationships based upon mutual need can quickly deteriorate if one of the partners suddenly becomes incapable of fulfilling the other's expectations. On the other hand, vowing to maintain the relationship during times when our needs are not being met indicates that the other person is valued for their inherent worth rather than for need fulfillment. By putting our partner's needs above our own, the relationship can evolve from self-interest to self-sacrificing love.

Attraction is also firmly rooted in our personal past. The little house in the card's background represents our parental home, in which we first learned about the nature of love. As adults, we are often compelled to recreate the events that took place in our childhood home in order either to relive it if it was idyllic, or to try to correct it if it was problematic.

In striving to reproduce the past in a current relationship, we seek to heal ourselves of childhood pain. The caduceus suspended above the two figures is an ancient symbol of healing which reflects the need to repair the damage inflicted upon us in our early years. An intimate relationship provides us with the opportunity to work through the unmet needs of childhood and, therefore, redeems the hurt inner child. The partner we are attracted to usually has certain aspects of his or her personality that are similar to that of a parent who has harmed us. For example, a little girl who was constantly chastised by her overbearing father may, in adulthood, seek a verbally abusive husband. Unconsciously vowing that this time things will be different (the husband/father will magically stop yelling), the inner child repeats the past in order to attempt to change it. Although we cannot change the past, we are driven to re-create it in order to confront our pain. Healing takes place when we finally realize that the mature love we long for must be based upon unreserved acceptance of our present partner rather than a doomed re-creation of the past.

In divination, this card introduces a magical third element into the bonding of two people. The winged lion above the figures acts as a catalyst that changes the chemistry between the man and woman. In our lives, this suggests the need for an intermediary of some type such as a counselor, matchmaker, or interpreter. This third party, by acting as a go-between, may hold the key to a successful relationship. The Two of Cups also shows us the need to reach out to those we love. If there has been a recent parting, we will have to meet our partner halfway in order to reconcile. If reconciliation is not possible, a karmic connection will still remain. Just as the snakes of the caduceus curl around each other, the life destinies of two people will continue to be intertwined.

THE THREE OF CUPS: GRATITUDE

Gratitude is a fruit of great cultivation.

—Samuel Johnson

The carefully tended trees found in the Seven of Pentacles have produced their fruit in this delightful card of harvest and celebration. With their cups raised to the heavens, the three women pictured partake in a jubilant celebration thanking God for a plentiful harvest. Here, the cups have become cornucopias overflowing with the ripened fruit found beneath the women's feet.

In our own lives, harvesting takes place when we successfully bring a process or project to fruition. Like the ripe fruit pictured, we can view our accomplishments as a natural outcome of all the hard work we have done in the past. It is time to gather the fruits of our labors as well as celebrate another level of growth that has been achieved. Even the small accomplishments found in our daily routines can be a cause for celebration and self-congratulation. By honoring this inner harvest, we are able to pay tribute to our accomplishments and ourselves.

This card, as a celebration of success, is a beautiful depiction of women's achievement. Many women find it difficult to openly proclaim their positive accomplishments in a culture that traditionally values women's self-sacrifice more than women's self-interest. This is reflected in the fact that, when we gather together, we are more than ready to divulge our weaknesses, failures, and suffering while neglecting to mention our inner strengths and outer accomplishments. We may be embarrassed to admit we are homemakers instead of feeling proud to follow the traditions of Hestia, goddess of the home. Likewise, while we can't all be CEOs of major corporations, we can be gratified in the way in which we have successfully managed our lives. The harvest shared in this card is the emotional nourishment we give to one another. We can each be an inspiration to our friends, daughters, and coworkers by being proud of our achievements. The bonds of friendship should extend to the support we give each other in times of triumph as well as in times of crisis.

This card is also the time of Thanksgiving, a period after the fall harvest in which we express our gratitude for the blessings we have received. Although we ritually give thanks once a year, cultivating feelings of gratitude daily can heal the many wounds carried by the discouraged spirit. Gratitude eventually triumphs over feelings of envy and loss by putting these potentially destructive emotions into perspective. Because envy is based upon the belief that others possess more than we do, we can nullify envious feelings by consciously focusing on the treasures we already possess. Gratitude is the emotional equalizer that we can use to generously share in each other's success without constantly comparing ourselves unfavorably to our friends or associates.

Loss can also be tempered with gratitude. While it is true that we naturally accumulate many losses during the course of our lives, we can also take time each day to remember the blessings we have received on the journey. In this way, gratitude automatically focuses our attention on what we have in the present rather than what we have either lost or failed to achieve in the past. Here, the emphasis lies in our present abilities, earned wisdom, and abundant opportunities. As the memory of the heart, gratitude reminds us of all the good things we still possess. The Three of Cups is a reminder to develop a positive outlook based upon the fruitfulness of the present moment.

In order to keep the virtue of gratitude alive in our hearts, it is helpful to keep a daily gratitude journal. At the end of the day, we can make a brief notation of all the things for which we are grateful. This can include all the positive people and situations in our lives, as well as the intangible blessings of love and encouragement we have received. Our positive inventory can also include our pets, homes, jobs, and books that enrich our lives. We can also include the blessings of our senses such as seeing a magnificent sunset or smelling a fragrant flower. It is also important to note the invisible energies that we normally take for granted such as electricity, sunshine, or vitality. By learning to appreciate the small blessings in life, we can become stronger and more positive in our daily outlook.

In divination, this card reflects a time of celebration: weddings, birthdays, anniversaries, and family reunions. The essence of celebration is to honor one another and value our relationships with friends and family. Like the three women's intertwined arms, we are intimately connected with our loved ones, sharing their joys and sorrows. The social support and bonds we form with one another is the basis of women's wisdom. The answer to the current problem may lie in these shared strengths and resources.

THE FOUR OF CUPS: REJECTION

Self-respect is the root of discipline: the sense of dignity grows with the ability to say no to oneself.

—Abraham J. Heschel

In this card, a mysterious cup emanating from a cloud is rejected by a young man sitting under a tree. The cup materializes out of thin air as if a wish had suddenly been granted. However, it is clear from the man's crossed arms that he has no intention of taking this heavenly gift. His defensive stance communicates that he is stubbornly rejecting his dream come true. Interestingly, Freud theorized that a conscience was a rejection of a particular wish operating within us. So, this picture is actually the inner working of a healthy conscience telling us that what we most wish for is clearly wrong.

Not everything offered to us in this life is necessarily good for our well-being, and there are times when we simply have to reject what we most desire. This is not an easy task, as addictions or compulsions may rule our thoughts. To break this addictive behavior, we valiantly try to resist the object of our desire. However, focusing exclusively on what we are attempting to reject only makes the desired object more powerful in our minds. To rise above this situation, it is necessary to replace what we don't want with something positive which we do want. The man pictured has three other cups representing these additional positive resources at his disposal.

Self-denial may also be in the form of rejecting undiscovered parts of ourselves. There are many hidden aspects to our personalities that we may have rejected due to either parental or societal disapproval. For hundreds of years, most women have had to repress their business acumen, artistic impulses, and assertiveness because these attributes did not conform to the expected behavior of a wife or mother. Likewise, men in our time often repress the ability to nurture themselves or others for fear of being effeminate. Because we have all internalized society's expectations in order to be accepted, we have had to reject some aspects of ourselves that endangered our sense of belonging. This also includes the hopes and dreams we had at one time, but that we rejected because we thought them to be too fanciful or impractical. This is symbolized by the way the man rejects the cup which suddenly materializes out of the air (a very potent symbol of our dreams and aspirations), while he accepts those cups which are firmly on the ground (symbolizing the importance of realism). It may be time to re-evaluate the rejected dreams of our youth and find ways of integrating some of our earlier aspirations into our present lives. By using all of our God-given gifts, we can evolve into more complete human beings who are capable of being all we can be.

Much of the time, the unacceptable parts of ourselves lie hidden beneath the surface of conscious awareness. However, by carefully observing what we are unwilling to accept in others' behavior, we can often discern what it is that we are unwilling to accept in ourselves. Basically, we reject in others what we unconsciously reject in ourselves. Therefore, when we react very critically to the behavior of our friends or family, their behavior becomes a mirror for the unseen parts of ourselves. For example, we may criticize a friend's preoccupation with her appearance only to realize that we have narcissistic tendencies too. By bringing this into conscious awareness, we bring ourselves closer to self-acceptance.

Of course, the part of ourselves that we most often deny is our feelings. The cups on this card are symbolic containers of emotion, yet the seated man rejects the cup holding his feelings. We often push away powerful emotions because we fear being carried away with them. Contrary to our thinking, unacknowledged emotions are the ones that often raise havoc in our lives, not those that we recognize. So, the realization that we are hurt, angry, or resentful is a necessary first step in learning to work with our emotions rather than rejecting them. By not trusting our emotions, we fail to benefit from the guidance of our deepest feelings. By spending a short period for emotional reflection each day, we can learn to stay in touch with our emotions and reap their wisdom.

In divination, we must consider every object pictured in a Tarot card to be a reflection of ourselves. In the case of the Four of Cups, we may wish to identify with the cup that is being rejected. Rejection from others has many disguises ranging from the rejection of being fired to unrequited love. It is very painful to graciously offer our energy and loyalty to someone only to be ignored or rebuked. This can lead to decreased self-esteem that, in turn, leads to the belief that we really don't deserve the beautiful gifts the universe offers us. Eventually, we may not want to invest any more of our energy into new relationships or career opportunities for fear of being rejected. However, we can view rejection objectively and realize that this may have been best for us in the long run. A terrible rejection has often turned out to be a great opportunity for something better to enter our lives.

One of the traditional meanings for this card is boredom with life. In the card, a sense of ennui has overtaken the man, and he naturally becomes totally indifferent to whatever is offered him. This indifference can affect long-term relationships where, over the years, we become bored with our partners. The sexual attraction that once overwhelmed us has waned, leaving us in a state of apathy. Some of us may go on to other partners in an effort to re-experience the desires of youth, only to find the whole cycle of interest/disinterest/apathy happening again. Before familiarity breeds contempt, it may be wise to try to rekindle desire with our present partner. Apathy is lethal to a long-term relationship only if we allow it.

THE FIVE OF CUPS: LOSS

It may serve as a comfort to us, in all our calamities and afflictions, that he who loses anything and gains wisdom for it is a gainer by the loss.

—Sir Robert L'Estrange

A cloaked figure looks down upon three overturned cups by a rushing river. The cups have lost their precious contents, having spilled over onto the thirsty ground. There is a finality in the scene because spilt water can never return to its container. What has been done cannot be undone. Something of great importance has been lost forever, spilled onto the sands of time.

We have all experienced serious losses in our lives. Loss is an important part of life as each stage of the life cycle requires us to relinquish something we cherish in order to grow. Growing up requires us to leave our original family so that we may find our place in the world. Later, we may give up a career or relationship so that we can move forward with our lives. Retirement forces us to leave the world of work in order to pursue our own interests. Loss is our constant companion through life that, like a wise friend, quietly tells us it is time to move on.

The woman pictured has gray streaks in her hair, and it is rare to find a person in middle age who has not experienced at least one of the terrible losses known as the three Ds: death, divorce, or disease. Each of the card's empty cups symbolizes one of these three major life losses. When someone we have loved has died, we have lost a relationship in a painful divorce, or we have lost our physical strength to disease, we deeply mourn these irretrievable losses. This card's central figure conveys this sense of grievous loss by wearing a black cloak of mourning. The stages of mourning require a gradual emotional withdrawal from the loved person or object so that life may go on. Without this period of mourning, we may immediately rush to replace the lost person with an inadequate substitute in an attempt to fill the emptiness inside. However, in the long run it is far better to face the void created by loss. A wise person knows that "only the empty cup can be filled."

Mourning is a time of transition, and this is symbolized by the bridge in the background linking the past with the future. During the process of mourning, we gradually come to realize that life without the beloved is bearable if we can turn our grief into a positive memory of the lost person. Resolving our loss also requires us to value what we presently have left, as well as what we've lost. During the period of mourning, we may neglect important areas of our lives that once gave us a sense of satisfaction, accomplishment, or joy. These positive activities should be reawakened because they can provide the bridge across the chasm of loss. The mourner pictured has not lost everything, because there are still two cups left standing. These two cups close at hand reflect the French proverb that states, "When we cannot get what we love, we must love what is within our reach." We need to hold onto the precious parts of our lives that remain, because an empty cup cannot quench our thirst.

Loss requires us to re-evaluate our lives, for it is only by seeing where we have gone that we will know where we are going. Our first reaction to loss is usually a feeling of regret. Like the wasted fluid spilled from the cups, our efforts seem to have been wasted because a large part of our lives is gone forever. We may even feel foolish for having spent our time and energy on something that failed to last. Regardless of our feelings, we must learn to accept the transience of life and the inevitability of change. As the river of life sweeps us away from one situation to another, we can trust the process of change. In the card's background is a ruined castle, symbolizing the impermanence of all the supporting structures in our lives. Like a crumbling ruin, our marriages or careers may have failed to withstand the test of time, leaving us to gaze upon the remnants of our former lives.

As we see our chances for happiness ruined, it may be difficult to explore the positive side of loss, although it does exist. First, loss forces us to rebuild the decaying structure of our lives to create a more solid future. However, in order to do this, we will need the remaining two cups containing hope and faith. These two important virtues reflect our perceptual shift to a present or future orientation instead of focusing on the bleakness of the past. By remaining in the present moment, we can dispel the ghosts of the past and, hopefully, keep past failures from spilling over into future projects. Another positive result from loss is our passage through an identity crisis. Because we no longer know who we are without the thing or person we have lost, we can lose our identity as an employee or spouse. Loss gives us the opportunity to discard past selves and create a new identity based upon our self-worth rather than the worth bestowed upon us by others. The real paradox of this card is that we often gain through loss, just as spilled water nourishes the new growth of plants.

In ancient times, the covenants between God and man were ratified with a blood sacrifice, be it an animal, a human being, or circumcision. Blood represents vital life energy, and the loss of it through sacrifice symbolized a deep commitment to a divine contract in which humans received God's protection in exchange for blood.

The overturned cups pictured on this card spill out a blood red effluent that is symbolic of the nature of women's sacrifices through the ages. Every major rite of passage in a woman's life is marked by blood. From menarche to menopause, blood is a sign of fertility. It also marks a covenant with Mother Nature in which there are certain intrinsic gains and losses. The onset of menses at puberty marks the end of childhood, but the gain of womanhood. The blood of childbirth means the loss of certain freedoms, but there is a child to hold. Finally, menopause marks lost youth, but there is the gain of worldly wisdom. In each of these life stages, we need to mourn our losses but remind ourselves of all the gains that far outweigh what we have lost along the way.

In divination, this card reflects the loss of important elements in our lives. Missed opportunities, lost time, lost childbearing potential, or lost youth may cause us to wrap ourselves in a cloak of grief. There is also a possibility of lost energy symbolized by the spilled cups. Someone may be draining our vital energy or, like spilled water, our energy may be scattered instead of focused. The spilled blood is also indicative of excessive self-sacrifice. Energy must be contained in order to be effectively utilized, and it is important for us to halt any dissipation of our vital resources.

THE SIX OF CUPS: GIVING

The best thing to give your enemy is forgiveness; to an opponent, tolerance; to a friend, your heart; to your child, a good example; to a father, deference; to your mother, conduct that will make her proud of you; to yourself, respect; to all men, charity.

—Francis Maitland Balfour

In this card, two beautiful children play inside a fortified castle. An enchanted castle is the perfect setting for many fairy tales and childhood fantasies because it represents a time long ago when we were all Mommy and Daddy's little princes or princesses, living inside the mighty fortress of our parents' love. Childhood is the most vulnerable time in a person's life, and children living inside a strong family are given the protection of caring parents. A solid family gives the child a protected place to grow where he can be nurtured until he matures. The important security issues raised in childhood influence how secure we feel as adults. Those who are overly concerned about their health or financial security can often trace these concerns back to childhood fears. An insecure childhood often produces feelings of uncertainty about the future in an adult. So, the security of childhood, or the lack of it, can never be overemphasized.

The children playing inside the great castle symbolize the inner child of our past playing inside our adult selves. Childhood is a formative time when many of our fears and expectations are formed. Many childhood experiences leave a lasting impression upon us and, ultimately, influence adult behavior. Most adult desires center upon satisfying the needs of our inner child, particularly those needs for security and love that may have gone unmet in our early years. Also, many adult situations unconsciously remind us of similar situations in childhood in which we were ignored or mistreated in some way. When this happens, we usually find ourselves reacting childishly. In this card, the white mittens worn by the little girl show us that we sometimes handle situations in a childish manner instead of our customary maturity. When a current problem causes us to act as we did when we were much younger, we need to go back in time to find out the reason for our actions.

In order to gain some perspective on our immature behavior, we must first ask ourselves if the current situation reminds us of a similar situation in childhood. Once recognized, the old hurts or longing will have to be relived. This is a vital step because the feelings of the inner child cannot be denied but rather need to be recognized and respected. Second, we need to be a compassionate yet firm parent to our inner child by patiently explaining in an inner dialogue the significant differences between the present situation and the hurtful situation in the past. Furthermore, we need to tell ourselves that, as adults, we are now in a position of power and authority rather than the vulnerable and helpless position we experienced as children. This helps to create a strong adult perception in which we view problems in their own light rather than as re-creations of the past. By slowly recognizing the influence of the past in the present, we can, like the male figure walking away in the background of the card, finally move away from childhood to create a better future.

Although this card shows a happy childhood scene, there are subtle clues in the picture that indicate that our youthful past may have been far from idyllic. Hidden in the background of the card is a man carrying a long spear. He is purposefully walking away from the children, leaving them defenseless. This can be seen as the failure of a parent to properly protect his or her child from the dangers inherent in the world. Every parent knows that it is not possible to protect children from all the evil in society, but some parents are unable or unwilling to safeguard their children from harm. When this happens, the child must learn to protect himself.

A child left unprotected must create psychological defenses in order to protect himself from further injury. Unfortunately, these defenses are often carried over into adulthood where they are inappropriate. As children, we erect castle walls of psychological defense to protect us, but as adults these defenses usually isolate us from others. Withdrawal or inappropriate anger usually keeps others far enough away so we can't be hurt; however, the strength of our defenses keeps friends and family from knowing us intimately. It may be time to tear down the castle walls, for they are protecting us from an enemy who has long since disappeared.

As children, we have also learned to protect ourselves from emotional pain by suppressing our feelings. Like the potted flowers pictured, we have carefully contained our feelings for fear that they may have gotten beyond our control. However, we should remember that flowerpots not only protect growing plants, they also restrict their growth. A flowering plant left in a container will have to either break out of its constrictive environment or have its growth permanently thwarted. Likewise, we need to move beyond our carefully contained feelings if we are to grow emotionally.

Like the little boy giving flowers to his friend, we need to take emotional risks by reaching out to others and expressing our love. The children on the Six of Cups embody the innocence and trust of childhood, for it is in childhood that we learn whether or not to trust. If we have learned to trust implicitly, we may be far too trusting of others with either our hearts or our finances. When we enter into a relationship, trust is vital, but it cannot be the blind trust of a child. To trust too readily is to be as defenseless as a small child who has been abandoned by his protector. In the adult world, we may require others to prove their trustworthiness before we commit to a relationship. In this way, we can be assured of our partner's true motives and protect ourselves from harm.

Because it deals with childhood issues, this card has many divinatory meanings including regression, avoiding the responsibility of adulthood, or trying to heal sibling rivalry. However, the Six of Cups is basically about giving to others. When we offer flowers or any other gift, it is a tangible expression of our love. Most gift giving is actually the giving of ourselves to others, and we all give according to our particular God-given talents. For example, a man who isn't particularly demonstrative may give a handcrafted gift to show his affection. In generously receiving whatever we are given by others or by fate, we learn to be appreciative of all gifts. As a wise man was heard to say, "Success is getting what you want; happiness is wanting what you get."

THE SEVEN OF CUPS: DESIRE

In the light of eternity, we shall see that what we desired would have been fatal to us, and that what we would have avoided was essential to our well-being.

—Francois de Salignac de La Mothe-Fenelon

In this card, a man in the shadows reaches toward a mysterious cloud containing seven cups. Contained within the cups are an array of riches, alluring figures, and mythical creatures. Although these objects can have many meanings, a clue to their hidden significance lies in their relation to the seven deadly sins.

Of medieval origin, the seven deadly sins are listed historically by the church as pride, sloth, lust, anger, greed, envy, and gluttony. Each of these seven sins is symbolized by each of the cups on the card. While the word sin usually conjures up images of self-righteous clergymen sermonizing about hellfire and eternal damnation, sin can simply be viewed as the negative side of human nature. However, because we don't usually want to see the worst in ourselves, we rarely acknowledge our sins. The materialistic society in which we live also fails to recognize most sin. In fact, we could conclude that modern society, in all its triumph and disaster, has decreed the seven deadly sins to be fundamental values that its citizens should strive for daily. Greed is seen as inherently good, anger as a perfectly acceptable form of self-expression, and envy as a necessary stimulus for conspicuous consumption. Nevertheless, if we look beyond society's expectations for our behavior, we find what the Buddhists call "wrong desire." The seven deadly sins are actually a reflection of man's baser desires to possess wealth, other people, or others' esteem. Because they don't take into account others' needs, these desires for our own self-gratification are obviously the wrong path. Like the man on the card, it is very easy to be completely overshadowed by our own self-centered desires. These negative character traits need to be recognized in ourselves so that we may hopefully have some control over them. Recognition of the seven deadly sins is of inestimable value because while each of the sins is harmful to either ourselves or others, each one also has an antidote in particular virtues which we can deliberately cultivate. The Seven of Cups shows us how we can transform vice into virtue and, therefore, lead better lives.

The first of the seven deadly sins is pride, which is depicted by the large head floating in one of the cups. Man's ego is most often associated with his head (hence, the well-known phrase, "having a swelled head"). This head's disconnection from the body is indicative of the inflated ego's disconnection from reality. While pride makes us feel vastly superior to others, it also disconnects us from meaningful relationships. Those with an inflated sense of self-worth frequently boast of their exploits, alienating those around them. When we hear ourselves bragging about our latest victory or acquisition, it is advisable to cultivate this vice's antidotal virtue: humility. Humility is not a lack of self-esteem, but rather is an acknowledgment of our shortcomings and handicaps that keeps our own self-importance in perspective. Developing humility can also have a practical application, because when "pride goeth before the fall," a more humble attitude can save us from potential disaster.

The second deadly sin is sloth, portrayed by the shrouded figure in the center of the card. Sloth is not constitutional laziness on our part, but rather is the inability to take any action. The shrouded figure that is unable to see or hear, is not able to do anything and is, therefore, slothful. Sloth is related to the medieval concept of melancholia, or what we today would call depression. Like the figure pictured, depressed people feel they are shrouded in a terrible darkness they are unable to escape. Overwhelmed by sadness, they no longer have the desire to partake in any activities they previously found pleasurable. The solution to the vice of sloth is the virtue of fortitude. Fortitude is the inner strength to keep moving forward even when we feel discouraged, for it is only by forcing ourselves to advance that we can leave the world of sloth.

The third deadly sin is lust, symbolized by the hissing snake. The phallic snake emanating from the hollow cup implies intercourse, but the sin of lust is more than the sexual act. Lust is the need to have one's desires fulfilled at others' expense, thus reducing all partners to sexual objects. To control lust requires us to develop the antithetical virtue of chastity. Although chastity traditionally means celibacy, the virtue of chastity encompasses respect, restraint, and modesty when dealing with others. It is an opportunity to see past our own desires in order to recognize the needs of other people.

The fourth deadly sin is anger, which is illustrated by the medieval castle in the clouds. Our anger, like a fortified castle, is often our first line of defense against injury from those who would hurt us. When we have been hurt by someone, our initial reaction is usually an angry outburst directed at the offender. In contrast, developing the virtue of empathy helps us to see where the other person is coming from and thereby assists us in cultivating a compassionate attitude toward those who have hurt us either in the present or in the past.

The fifth deadly sin, greed, is symbolized by the glittering jewels that are overflowing from one of the cups. Greed forces us to accumulate money and a vast array of material objects that we believe to be wealth. In actuality, real wealth is the lasting inner change we develop in this lifetime. Practicing the opposite virtue of charity quickly dissipates our greedy impulses because in giving, we finally come to understand that the reason we receive wealth is so that we may give it to others.

The sixth deadly sin is envy, which is represented by the laurel wreath. This noble laurel wreath symbolizes the victories and accomplishments of others whom we secretly envy. However, like the skull cryptically engraved on this cup, envy is poisonous to our relationships. Envy causes us to make derogatory remarks and spread gossip about those whom we believe have received unmerited laurels. Rather then focusing on others' affluence, we might want to count our blessings. The virtue of gratitude quickly eliminates the distress caused by envy because a grateful heart is always happy.

The last sin is gluttony, symbolized by the bloodthirsty dragon. Being true gluttons, dragons are monsters that ravenously devour everything within their taloned grasp. Although we often associate overeating with gluttony, any situation in which we find ourselves consuming things in extraordinary amounts is considered gluttonous. This includes overspending, drinking to excess, and compulsive gambling, to name a few. The antidote to gluttony is temperance. As in the Temperance card, carefully meting out a small portion of whatever satisfies us produces a more balanced lifestyle so we are not consumed by what we consume.

In divination, this card can have many meanings including delusion, idealization, or unrealistic expectations. This may include the wish for a partner who can fulfill all our desires, whether they are financial, sexual, emotional, or egotistical. As it is rare to find a person who can satisfy all of our needs, we need to focus exclusively on the fulfillment of those desires that are essential to our well-being.

THE EIGHT OF CUPS: SEARCHING

No matter how much we seek, we never find anything but ourselves.

—Anatole France

In this card, a lone figure wanders through a darkened landscape, leaving behind a set of eight cups. This scene reflects one of life's greatest decisions: when to stay in a situation or when to leave it. Clearly, this card is telling us it is time to go. There seems to be nothing left to keep us in our present circumstances, so we must, however reluctantly, move on.

There are many reasons why we make the fateful decision to leave. Sometimes we leave in order to fulfill a dream; sometimes we leave just to survive. Whatever our conscious motivation appears to be, the underlying reason for leaving is always to further our growth and development. This is because leaving often entails finding a personal purpose in life independent of others' needs or expectations. In this card, there is no path for the traveler to follow. He must make his own path, his own destiny down a road no one else has traveled before. This can be an arduous, rocky journey as we search for ourselves. When we leave in order to search for a better job, we are actually seeking contact with the undiscovered part of ourselves that can learn and grow in a new work environment. The improvement we seek in the outside world is actually self-improvement.

We most often leave a situation in order to find our own autonomy. Leaving may require us to experience abandonment and deprivation so that we can discover the hidden strength needed to stand on our own without the help or support of others. The inner fortitude we develop on the difficult journey of self-discovery is the real goal of our constant striving. As we walk through the moonlit landscape, we become stronger and more determined. The journey becomes the destination.

Because the seeker always moves from the known to the unknown, fear is a constant companion to those who venture forth into unfamiliar territory. Having little of the emotional or financial security that once sustained us, fear becomes an understandable part of the journey. Less understood are the feelings of anger that usually accompany our decision to leave. Anger is a necessary stage in the process of leaving because it is only through anger that we can gather enough energy to make an emotional separation from a relationship that previously nourished us. It is often only through our anger that we can find the necessary determination to break away from ingrained attachments so that we can find a new career, partner, or place in the world.

On the other hand, there are times in our lives in which a situation leaves us before we have the opportunity to leave it. In the case of divorce or sudden unemployment, we are involuntarily cast out of the place that we called home. In this situation, we may feel like the abandoned cups on the card. If we find that things we are greatly attached to are leaving our lives, we should let them go. Loss awakens us to the inevitable truth that what we lost is not a part of our true destiny. It lies elsewhere.

The man in the Eight of Cups walks in darkness, but this is an artificial night created by a solar eclipse. The sun's brilliant rays have been overshadowed by the serene face of the moon. This very unusual celestial event symbolizes the direction we take in mid-life. During the middle years, we are guided along our chosen path by the light of the unconscious (symbolized by the moon) rather than by our previous conscious awareness (symbolized by the sun). We find ourselves guided more by dreams and intuition than by family values or the marketplace. The profound changes of mid-life bring about a quest for self-knowledge as we begin to detach ourselves from societal definitions of success in order to align ourselves with a more personal and meaningful lifestyle. This card shows a necessary step on the way toward this new, meaningful life: the need to abandon the false cups of others' expectations before seeking personal fulfillment within ourselves. Interestingly, as soon as we decide to leave behind those attitudes and beliefs that are no longer needed in our lives, the universe sends our own inner truth to meet us in unexpected ways. A book found serendipitously or a fateful encounter can change the course of our lives forever. However, it is only by relinquishing the old that we can find the new.

This is also a card about ambition and the sacrifices needed to satisfy our lofty aspirations. The man using his staff to climb upward represents our ascent either spiritually or materially. Never looking back, we continue on our journey unimpeded. However, once we have reached the pinnacle of success, we find that the sacrifices we have made have created a gaping hole in our lives. Like the pattern of stacked cups on the card, in which one cup seems to be missing, we find our lives to be incomplete. We may have to search further for what is missing, whether it is for a long-lost parent, a child, or a partner.

In divination, this is usually a positive card denoting new opportunities on the horizon. There is also a negative side, particularly if the card appears frequently in different readings. In this case, the card reflects our inability to commit. The Seeker becomes the Drifter, who goes from one job, relationship, or religion to another in the constant hope of finding something better. When confronted by a serious problem, the Drifter literally moves away. However, seeking a geographical solution to one's problems is rarely a viable option. Rather, it points to a habitual pattern of handling interpersonal conflicts by leaving. As we can never really leave ourselves, nothing is really solved.

THE NINE OF CUPS: GRATIFICATION

He that feasts everyday, feasts no day.

—Charles Simmons

In this card, a jovial man is seated before a table laden with nine cups. This bounteous table is reminiscent of medieval banquets in which autumnal feasting was an enjoyable counterpoint to the imposed fasting of the winter season. The Middle Ages were truly times of either feast or famine, depending upon the season. During the harsh northern winter, food was naturally in short supply, causing many to endure long periods of desperate hunger. With spring came the promise of better times, and by fall there was usually a bountiful crop to be harvested. Fall was the annual time of celebration in which the villagers could feast upon a banquet of foods found in abundance. If we look back upon our lives, we can also see alternating periods of feast or famine in which we either endured deprivation or celebrated bountifulness. We have all had to do without companionship or employment at times only to find wealth or love a little farther down the road. However, it is the lean times that make the good things in life sweeter when we finally find them.

There are certainly times when we experience life as an abundant harvest of good fortune. Traditionally, the Nine of Cups has been the "wish card" of the Tarot because the man pictured resembles a genie ready to make the querent's fondest wishes come true. While we all have dreams of having our wishes immediately granted, some of us have an irrational belief in instant gratification, and this becomes the foundation of our lives. Overindulged children often grow up to be adults who expect their desires to be anticipated and fulfilled automatically by others. They wholeheartedly believe that all their desires should be fulfilled easily, comfortably, and, most of all, quickly.

THE MINOR ARCANA

Many of our greatest goals in life require us to postpone gratification until we've earned it. Higher education or job training, in particular, requires us to work many years before we can start to reap the benefits of all our hard work. In contrast, those who need instant gratification believe that sacrifice isn't necessary to obtain what they want out of life, or, if it is necessary, that the goal is not worth the price. Because these unrealistic expectations of how the world works are rarely met, those who believe in instant gratification lead very discontented lives. They constantly complain how life is unfair or how they've been dealt a poor hand. Disappointment and anger are their constant companions because the people surrounding them naturally fail to provide for their every need. Only by recognizing and challenging this underlying belief in instant gratification can the chronically discontented find happiness in an uncompromising world.

Another problem brought about by the belief in instant gratification is gluttony. As one of the seven deadly sins, gluttony is simply an excess of anything, be it food, wine, or television. Anything we take into ourselves can lead to overindulgence. Food addiction, drug addiction, and alcoholism are just a few of the gluttonous behaviors plaguing modern society. We are encouraged to want more than we need and need more than we want. Although we may not all suffer from addiction, it would be wise to be aware of the appearance of gluttony in our lives. Any situation in which there may be too much of a good thing is open to suspicion. We may need to be constantly vigilant in choosing what we take into ourselves, either physically or mentally. We have to keep in mind that modern life is very much like the buffet table pictured on this card, with its many choices and opportunities. Discrimination in our choice of food, drink, or friends is essential to our well-being. Although affluence creates the freedom to have what we want, we also have the freedom to refuse what is not best for us.

A key to avoiding overindulgence is to find satisfaction in what we already possess. The man on this card has a complacent and self-satisfied outlook on life because he is content in his circumstances. Likewise, we can find happiness in the pleasures of the present moment. Fulfillment can be found close at hand using resources that are already available to us. With a positive attitude and a little imagination, we can discover that the banquet of life is always within our reach.

In divination, this card personifies a friend or relative who is friendly, but who may become overly defensive about certain issues. The man's crossed arms are a defensive posture designed to keep others away from vulnerable areas. There may also be possible duplicity on this person's part. The table in the background is completely covered with a drape, obscuring it from view. Perhaps this person has something to hide that he would prefer was not exposed. With a large hat concealing his true thoughts, he can easily deceive others by pretending to be something he is not. A final clue to this person's deceptive nature is the nine cups proudly displayed on the table, indicating a grand display of emotion solely for others' benefit. It has been said that all of us lead public, private, and secret lives. If we look beyond the surface joviality of the man on this card, we find dark secrets that we expose at our own risk. In this card, all is not what it seems.

THE TEN OF CUPS: HOPE

It is the rainbow—Hope, shining upon the tears of grief.

—Robert G. Ingersoll

This lovely pastoral scene shows a happy family enjoying the splendor of a shimmering rainbow. Historically, the rainbow has always been a symbol of hope for mankind. In the Old Testament, the rainbow was a sign of God's promise not to re-enact the biblical flood that destroyed the world. The small stream of water in this card may reflect this divine promise that the earth should never be inundated with water again. As part of the Judeo-Christian tradition, the rainbow symbolizes our heartfelt hope that previous disasters will not reoccur. Psychologically, we have all been sensitized to the particular tragedies that have befallen us in the past. This card gives us some reassurance that our catastrophic past will not repeat itself in the future, and therefore there is hope for a better tomorrow.

Hope is one of the three theological virtues (the other two being faith and charity) that need to be cultivated in our daily lives. Like the rainbow, hope is ephemeral, yet its momentary appearance fills us with great joy. Although the rainbow's vivid spectrum of colors suggests a wide range of emotions from the fiery red of anger to the blue of depression, it is the yellow band of hope that can brighten our darkest days. Just like the rainbow that holds the ten cups aloft, hope sustains our emotional lives in turbulent times. Hope, as the passion for the possible, gives us the strength to visualize a better future and the confidence to meet it with a song in our hearts.

Because it spans great distances, the rainbow has also been seen as a vital connection between two distant points. In many cultures, the rainbow is a supernatural bridge between God and man that holds the hope of redemption. Synchronistic events and oracles such as the Tarot also serve to connect heaven and earth in our lives.

Divination brings divine guidance so that we may feel a connection to something greater than ourselves.

The rainbow's theme of connection can also be seen in the strong connection we have with our parents. In the Ten of Cups, the dancing little boy and girl are wearing the same colored clothes as their parents. This seemingly coincidental similarity in dress shows us that the children reflect their parents' behavior and values. The children have unconsciously repeated their parents' positive behavior or destructive patterns. We often identify with the parent of the same sex by either choosing the same career or following the parents' lifestyle. Our attempt to emulate our parents may even be carried over into the choice of disease symptoms we develop. To be or not to be like our parents is a question which plagues us all of our lives. We may secretly fear that we will have the same tragic fate as our parents and, therefore, spend our entire adult lives rebelling against any similarity between ourselves and the people who raised us. On the other hand, we may wish to emulate our parents' success at the cost of our own individuality. Whatever path we choose, we need to appreciate the ways in which we are either similar or dissimilar to our parents so that we may be fully conscious of the choices we make in life.

There is also a subtle connection between the relationship we had with our parents and the relationship we presently have with our spouse. As adults, we often have an unconscious need to re-experience the familiar feelings of home. So, when we choose a companion for life, we often choose a person who resembles one or both of our parents. Unfortunately, we usually choose someone who personifies the worst qualities of a problematical parent. We do this because we want to symbolically repeat the past in order to rectify it. There is always an unconscious hope that this time things will be different: the father/husband will stop drinking; the mother/wife will nurture our self-esteem instead of constantly belittling us. We valiantly hold on to the great hope that the difficult person we live with presently is redeemable and that their redemption can rectify the pain of the past. However, the attempt to re-create the past often meets with disappointment, as the chosen spouse usually fails to change into our idealized version of the perfect, nurturing parent.

Rather than becoming bitter at this state of affairs, we need to remember that hope is often unrealistic, for such is its nature. The hope we had as children of living happily ever after with indulgent parents can never be realized, but our awareness of our adult need for what we never experienced in childhood can help us make healthier choices in life. Paradoxically, this may include avoiding what we think will make us happy. Sometimes we need to consciously stay away from the familiar places of the heart that blithely promise us a rainbow made up of tears and light.

In divination, this card represents a golden window of opportunity. This is a favorable time in which to take full advantage of any opportunity that presents itself. However, like the transitory rainbow, this window will quickly disappear. So, it is best to immediately commit to this once-in-a-lifetime chance while it is still within view. Sometimes the opportunity that presents itself may seem to be a small, insignificant event (like the small cottage in the background), but even small beginnings can be a rainbow bridge to life-altering events. If we continue to see all opportunities as bridges leading to bigger and better things, we will find all our cups filled with success.

THE PAGE OF CUPS: INSIGHT

Unless you expect the unexpected, you will never find truth.

—Heraclitus

In this card, a young page makes a startling discovery: there is a fish emerging from the cup he is holding. This is one of the truly magical images in the Tarot, showing us that life is full of unexpected surprises and miracles. Life sometimes seems like a series of surprises, some judged to be good and others bad, but which are always challenging. Surprise, with its apparent incongruity, forces us to re-evaluate our expectations and view of reality. We are often taken aback by new developments simply because we expected that life would continue to go on exactly as we had planned. Surprise quickly shakes us out of our complacency as we unexpectedly find ourselves in a hospital, in Cairo, or in love.

Sudden change on the outside also has its corresponding reaction on the inside of our psyches. We find ourselves in psychological conflict when new information contradicts beliefs that we hold to be sacred. Parental dictates (the psychological "thou shalt nots") and societal expectations may be surprisingly different than our present reality. Dreams, psychological breakthroughs, Tarot readings, or synchronistic events can also undermine our previously held beliefs about ourselves and our world. It can come as quite a shock to our rational way of thinking when pictures on pieces of cardboard accurately predict future events in our lives. Psychological insights also take us by surprise by exposing unconscious beliefs and memories that have been hidden for many years. The fish that naturally makes its home deep in the ocean of the unconscious has been brought up to conscious awareness so that we may examine it. Dreams, like the displaced fish, also offer us images from a fathomless, unseen world. All these subtle connections to the future, the unconscious, and the dream world leave us amazed at the tremendous depth of human experience. As we realize that everyday events have intimate connections with levels of awareness beyond our conscious comprehension, we begin to see the magic contained in ordinary events.

Another surprising event that opens the door into magical consciousness is synchronicity. Carl Jung coined the term synchronicity to explain coincidences that seemed to directly connect matter with the psyche. His most famous example of this phenomenon was of a female patient who, while recounting her dream of a golden scarab to Dr. Jung, actually saw a beetle outside the window. These types of experiences make us feel connected to the world and foster a belief in the unification of all things. We are no longer separate individuals trapped inside isolated bodies and minds, but rather are part of an ever-expanding, connected universe of possibilities.

Synchronicity often acts as a surprising revelation, very much like the astonishment felt by the Page of Cups. It is the unusualness of an incident that is the key to a synchronistic event. For example, any object that is suddenly found after being missing for many years has a hidden symbolic significance connecting it to a current problem. To dream of someone we have not thought about in years, only to hear from them the next day, emphasizes their importance in our lives. When we answer the telephone to hear a strange caller say, "It's good that you're leaving," we have unexpected confirmation that it is time to move on.

Synchronicity is a form of divine guidance, but it is up to us to decipher the underlying meaning of these strange coincidences. While the unusualness of a synchronistic event quickly gets our attention, it may take a long period of time to discern the event's hidden message. This is the experience of insight. The synchronicity causes us to look inside ourselves for a personal meaning by using our intuition. We intuitively sense that the universe is either trying to encourage or discourage us. For example, we can immediately sense the warning that was evident in the dream of the locked door when we lose our keys the next day. On the other hand, our spirits soar when we learn that our new promotion magically coincides with our birthday. Whether they are gentle reminders or a red flag, synchronicities provide valuable insights into our careers, relationships, and ourselves.

When this card appears in a reading, it is often helpful to review any unusual occurrences that have happened in the last few days. A sighting of a peculiar animal or an animal that is behaving peculiarly is often an omen of things to come. It is always the unnatural, unusual, or peculiar image that contains the most value for personal insight. This is particularly true of someone or something that seems out of place. Like the fish emerging from the waters of a cup instead of the sea, a person can be at the wrong place at the wrong time, with disastrous results. Any disruption of the established order of things can be a very significant message that we need to address.

THE KNIGHT OF CUPS: HESITATION

.The advantage of the emotions is that they lead us astray.

—Oscar Wilde

In this card, a knight on horseback is on the verge of crossing a river. All knights have a heroic task in life, whether it is to find the Holy Grail or save the damsel in distress. In this case, we may need to be our own knight in shining armor. Dissatisfied with the way we are, we set out on a quest for self-improvement. Unfortunately, as anyone who has tried to break a bad habit or tried to stay on a diet can attest, this journey can often be cut short. This is due in large part to our failure to make a good beginning.

At the start of every journey, whether it is a cross-country trip or a voyage of self-discovery, there are obstacles of one sort or another. We may encounter bad weather, illness, prejudice, or bad timing, to name a few. These formidable problems are often symbolic of what are termed "threshold guardians," those demons that block our way along the path. These unforeseen obstacles take the form of unrealistic fears, emotional scars, or dependencies rooted in our past. These unresolved issues hold back our growth and progress, similar to the way in which the Knight of Cups reins in his horse beside the river. On the threshold of a new life, we want to pull back, finding the obstacles too great to surmount or the river too wide to cross. At this point, in order to keep going forward, we need to keep our destination clearly in view. As the knight attempts to cross the river, he scans the distant riverbank for a safe place to arrive. Likewise, we should clearly envision our goal of better health or a better relationship while crossing the rushing river of emotional turmoil.

We all want to be better people, but sometimes, we just can't seem to break through our own emotional barriers in order to change. Like the hesitant knight, we cannot go forward yet find it impossible to retreat. Distrust, anger, or fear can be like a mighty river that stands in our way. When we are confronted with emotional obstacles, the best course of action is often to take it one step at a time. In this card, the horse is taking small, prancing steps leading him closer to the river's edge. By breaking down the long, perilous journey into smaller, more manageable steps, we can make remarkable progress. As each interim step is completed, we can congratulate ourselves on having the necessary fortitude to continue toward our chosen goal. However, we also need to keep in mind that all these steps may not be taken in a straight line toward our destination. Like the serpentine river, our path may have many twists and turns before it ends.

Crossing a river is also symbolic of the afterlife because mythologies around the world explain death as a journey across water. The most famous of these myths is that of the ancient Greeks, who told stories of the dead being ferried across the river Styx. Interestingly, the Knight of Cups bears a striking resemblance to the Death card found in the Major Arcana. Both cards feature riders on pale horses posing in the same stance. This is not coincidental. As all the other knights in the Tarot, the Knight of Cups attempts to transcend death. While most men seek immortality through their courageous deeds, women seek immortality through love. It is through the loving relationships with our family and friends that we transcend our earthly existence to live forever in the minds of those we have loved. The Knight of Cups holds her cup of love before her like a compass to direct her journey. She is following her heart.

Following our hearts, though, entails some risk. There is always the possibility that if we are guided solely by our emotions, that they will lead us astray like an unbridled horse. Emotions can lead us to safety or danger, to the heights of ecstasy or to the depths of despair. One of the greatest skills in life is to accurately predict where we are headed should our emotions continue to be aroused. If we continually become angry at work, we can accurately foresee unemployment. Repeatedly becoming emotionally involved with the wrong type of man predictably results in another tragic ending. Like a rider who uses his reins to carefully guide his horse past certain hazards, we can learn to steer clear of the major emotional pitfalls in life. However, like a recalcitrant horse, our emotions have a will of their own, which is not easily subdued. We will need to work with our strong feelings if we are to lead them instead of letting them lead us.

In divination, the Knight of Cups is the embodiment of an emotional quest. This card reflects an emotional journey soon to be undertaken such as finding a new love, reuniting with old friends, or even entering therapy. Understandably, there may be some hesitation on our part when beginning something new. When confronted with any life-transforming event, whether it is marriage, buying a new home, or becoming pregnant, there is always a moment of hesitation when we question our decision. This is perfectly normal. Not only is it unwise to make major commitments in haste, but also the extra time we give ourselves provides us with an opportunity to adjust to the new possibilities in our lives.

THE QUEEN OF CUPS: REPRESSION

Water lends itself to the shape of the vessel that contains it.

—Japanese Proverb

Sitting on a beautiful, carved throne at the water's edge, the Queen of Cups silently contemplates her elaborate chalice. The cup she holds is very different from all the others in the suit of cups. This large chalice is lavishly decorated and encrusted with glittering jewels. This cup also appears to be a sacred receptacle, as it is adorned with angels and is crowned with a cross. While the queen sits mesmerized by this extraordinary piece of art, the contents of the cup appear to be a mystery. Yet, here is the perfect vessel to contain the intricacy and complexity of human emotion. While they are both sacred and profane, the emotions are truly what make us human. It is our love or hate which defines us, and often our hope or despair which forms our character. The Queen of Cups naturally rules over these passions of life because the realm of the emotions is woman's true domain.

Whether or not we rule wisely is another matter. Though we can easily get caught up in our emotions, it is quite difficult to understand the language of the heart. Just like the Queen of Cups, who stares at her beautiful cup, most women focus their energy on things that have emotional value. Feelings always deserve our careful attention because emotions largely determine our quality of life. Gaining an understanding of our deepest emotions is vital to our well-being, both physically and psychologically. Whether we choose self-help methods, lengthy analysis, or simple introspection, the rewards of getting in touch with our feelings can never be overestimated.

Of course, some of us have difficulty exploring our feelings, and this is reflected in the covered chalice held by the queen. Of all the cups pictured in the Tarot, only the cup held by the Queen of Cups is covered, keeping the contents inside. In order to keep our distressing emotions contained, we cover over our emotional problems with a preoccupation with our work, our health, or our family. Feelings that are contained within the cup are not allowed to escape, and so become repressed. Overwhelmingly painful experiences such as assault or the death of a loved one can become locked away from conscious awareness like a dangerous Pandora's Box that we are terrified to open. Because acknowledging these painful emotions creates extreme anxiety, feelings of anger or grief continue to be contained in the unconscious like the contained contents of the covered cup. Although we deeply believe that it would be dangerous to let these repressed feelings escape, the real danger lies in locking them away. Repressed emotion, if it is not released, can erupt in self-destructive behavior. To correct this situation, it would be wise to carefully look at our dreams, since repressed emotion can escape briefly in the symbolism of the dream world.

The covered cup can also be seen as a tendency to be overprotective, particularly a mother's overprotective feelings. Parents naturally want to protect and shelter their children, but women who are too protective keep their children from becoming independent. Constantly warning a child of hidden dangers lurking in every corner or obsessing over the child's health increases the child's feelings of insecurity. Adults with overprotective parents consider the world unsafe and, hence, never wish to leave the apparent safety of the parental home. While most mothers wish to see their children safely traverse the world, overprotective mothering can result in an adult who is afraid to venture forth on his own.

The cup's cover prevents the contents from escaping, but it also prevents any air from entering the cup. Since air is associated with thinking, we could conclude that there is a lack of reasoning pictured on this card. Just as the Queen of Pentacles is divorced from her intuition, the Queen of Cups is cut off from her capacity to carefully think things through. The queen sits too closely to the changing tide of her feelings, forgetting the rational objectivity that could solve her problems. Like the queen, we can become so enmeshed in our feelings about an issue that we lose sight of a rational solution. Instead of focusing on how we feel about a problem, we should focus on trying to solve the problem. We can make a detailed list of possible solutions to our most pressing problems and then gather the necessary courage to begin implementing those solutions. Solving problems is very rewarding because it builds our confidence while giving us the opportunity to learn and grow. Taking appropriate action usually produces a far better outcome than constantly contemplating how we feel.

In divination, the closed cup is symbolic of a love that cannot be shared. Therefore, this card can represent unrequited love, or a relationship that is socially unacceptable. If the relationship is out in the open, the elaborate handles on the cup imply that we are holding onto someone because we are afraid of losing them. There may also be a tendency to become so involved with the emotional problems of the moment that we forget the larger issues we may have to confront in the future. In this card, the queen is so transfixed by her beautiful cup that she fails to notice the incoming tide encroaching upon her throne. As the Japanese proverb states, "One who attaches no importance to far-off things will certainly have near troubles."

THE KING OF CUPS: DRIFTING

I find the great thing in this world is not so much where we stand, as in what direction we are moving. To reach the port of heaven, we must sail sometimes with the wind and sometimes against it—but we must sail, and not drift, nor lie at anchor.

—Oliver Wendell Holmes

Each of the court cards in the suit of cups have ventured closer and closer to the water until, in the King, we see a royal figure floating upon the ocean. Adrift on the sea, the King of Cups sits regally upon his throne while overseeing his watery domain. The ocean upon which he travels is the waters of the unconscious. Being afloat on the surface of the unconscious implies that we are unable to delve into its mysterious depths. Fearing what we may find hidden below, we often skim the surface of a serious problem rather than analyze it in greater depth. Furthermore, the more we ignore the urging and symbolism of the unconscious, the more power it has to rule our lives. To reclaim our power, we must recognize this vast source of emotional energy and be willing to thoroughly navigate it. Writing down our dreams and consulting a dream dictionary are positive steps in this direction. Tarot readings also help us explore our unconscious desires and fears in a divinatory context.

While on this voyage of self-exploration, we may feel like the King of Cups, adrift in perilous seas. It is reassuring to note that, like the fish leaping out of the water, the unconscious can provide us with vital nourishment in the form of insights. When we analyze our dreams or a Tarot reading, we symbolically eat the fish; therefore, integrating unconscious desires into consciousness. The result is the same as that achieved by good nutrition: a healthier outlook.

The clueless king floating on the open sea is drifting without direction. At the mercy of the ocean's currents and being without oar or rudder, he has virtually no control over where he is going.

Like the king, we sometimes drift through life without motivation or concrete goals. However, those who go wherever the seas of change take them often find themselves washed up on the shore of a very harsh reality. We need to develop a clear direction in life instead of constantly drifting wherever the current takes us. If we are concerned that the direction we choose may not be our true destiny, we can always change course at a later time. Nevertheless, it is important to choose an initial destination and deliberately head toward it.

Drifting may also refer to our inclination to go along with the status quo. It is very easy to get caught up in others' expectations for us. We may be expected to do more than our fair share of work at home or in the office. These implied expectations may be more subtle when, for example, our family always expects us to be the nurturing and supportive person in the household no matter what happens. When we automatically go along with these constant expectations, we eventually feel resentful and victimized. Periodically re-evaluating others' expectations to see if they are realistic can help us feel better about ourselves and create better relationships.

Many times we fail to act in our own best interest because we desperately want to please those who are close to us. Like the drifting king, we passively go along with what others want for fear of displeasing them. However, we can reclaim the power to say no. This can be accomplished by developing assertive communication skills. Assertiveness is neither a defensive position nor an angry outburst. It is simply expressing our feelings in a confident, straightforward way. In a calm voice we can succinctly state how we feel such as, "I feel that I need to spend more time with my family, so I will be unable to attend the meeting." By making positive, declarative statements instead of getting angry, we become more like the empowered king reigning over his emotions. By making our wishes perfectly clear, we can prevent others from maneuvering us into doing things we would rather not do. Instead of passively drifting with the tide of others' expectations, we are able to chart our own course through life.

This card shows that even a king can be literally carried away by the waters of emotion. When this card appears in a reading, it points toward the querent being emotionally overwhelmed by some disturbing circumstance. Important decisions should be postponed until the flood waters recede. Nevertheless, there is hope. This is one of the truly magical cards in the Tarot, as it depicts a heavy, stone throne floating magically upon the water. Here is the positive realization that we can ride out our sea of troubles rather than sink into the abyss of despondency.

THE ACE OF SWORDS: THINKING

Reason rules all things.

—English Proverb

The suit of swords has traditionally been one of conflict and pain. Although it may be true that human beings learn best from the lessons provided by life's hardships, we all want to avoid pain whenever possible. The swords are present in the Tarot to remind us that it is not possible to avoid pain in this earthly existence. Pain must be acknowledged and confronted so that we can move through distressing experiences rather than be stuck in them. Most of the sword cards are real or thinly disguised scenes of painful death, but these predictions should not be taken literally. Rather, they represent the way in which painful experiences change us forever. They may make us more mature, or cause us to regress or become more compassionate or embittered. Pain is a conduit to our becoming someone else, for pain never leaves us where it finds us.

Swords also represent the thinking function. Under this heading we find logic, reason, rationalization, and the tendency to overintellectualize. While we may need a rational explanation for bad experiences, this is not always possible. Sometimes the most we can hope for is to gain some wisdom from our pain and then consciously decide to leave it behind. As for reason, most of our so-called reasoning actually consists of finding justification for continuing to maintain what we already believe. Our entrenched beliefs, like a long-held sword, are difficult to relinquish. Letting go of our old beliefs may make us feel unprotected and vulnerable, so we hold onto them much longer than necessary.

Swords are primarily defensive weapons used to protect the wielder from injury. Interestingly, thinking can actually be a very effective defense against feeling. When we overintellectualize, we lose sight of the valuable insights that emotions generate.

Overintellectualization keeps seemingly dangerous feelings at a safe distance where they can be carefully observed and dissected instead of being felt. Men, in particular, seem to have a tendency to overanalyze a problem at the expense of their feelings. Readings in which there are many sword cards reflect this inclination toward too much thinking and provide a warning to carefully consider our feelings as well as the feelings of others.

Our greatest conflict is often between our heart and our head. Nevertheless, in the eternal battle between the emotions and the intellect, there can only be one victor. Whenever an important decision has to be made, we are torn between logical considerations and emotional needs. Choosing a mate, choosing whether or not to return to work after the birth of a baby, or choosing to place an aging parent in a nursing home are just a few dilemmas which cause considerable conflict between our heart's desire and a rational solution. The Ace of Swords in a reading clearly shows that, in the present situation, logic must prevail. Although painful, the rational course of action is the only path we should consider at this time.

Although we can depend upon logic to solve problems, thinking can also be a double-edged sword. The Ace of Swords has both a light and a dark edge. On one side are all the positive thoughts that support our greatest potential. On the other side are all the negative thoughts that feed low self-esteem and result in self-defeating behavior. Positive thoughts such as, "I can do it," or "I am healthy," affirm our belief in ourselves and help us achieve our goals. On the other hand, negative thoughts such as, "I'll never be able to do that," or "I'm afraid of what might happen," erode our self-confidence to the point that we won't attempt to try anything new. Our own negative thoughts have the ability to wound us just as surely as a razor-edged sword. However, instead of being constantly victimized by our own thoughts, we can consciously change the way in which we think. When a negative thought arises, we simply acknowledge it and then transform it into a positive statement. "I'll never get the job" becomes "I can successfully get the job." While positive thinking does not guarantee that all of life's experiences will be pleasant, it does help to alleviate the depression and anxiety caused by negative thinking.

In divination, swords are instruments of separation. Therefore, the Ace of Swords can reflect the need to cut someone out of our lives, or even the need to cut the umbilical cord. Marital separation is another unwelcome possibility. Also, because the sword is such a powerful symbol, we may be well advised to take aggressive and forceful action in the present matter. This power may also be used inappropriately by others resulting in implied threats or possible victimization. Finally, the Ace of Swords shows a sword inserted into a crown, and this has obvious sexual connotations. Therefore, this card could be a warning that someone is using sex as a weapon or that a present relationship is a dangerous liaison.

THE TWO OF SWORDS: AVOIDANCE

A man who fears suffering is already suffering from what he fears.

—Michel de Montaigne

On a moonlit night, a blindfolded woman sits with her back to the sea, holding two swords. This enigmatic figure holds the key to the pain and suffering found in the remainder of the suit of swords because she personifies denial and emotional conflict.

The two swords that this woman holds point in opposite directions, reflecting her ambivalent nature. Like this undecided woman, we may be simultaneously holding two conflicting feelings such as love and hate. We may also be drawn in two directions such as desiring two different careers or two different partners. These contradictory desires often produce guilt because we have an unrealistic expectation that we must be totally committed to only one thing. Unresolved conflicts produce stress, but resolution often requires sacrifices that we are never eager to make. For example, anyone on a diet can attest to the conflict produced by the choice between a piece of chocolate cake or a carrot. To sacrifice the cake for the carrot breeds dissatisfaction, while choosing the cake leads to guilt. Another common situation is when the man in our life is a dream come true, but has serious problems. In this case we "can't live with him and can't live without him." This card reflects how easily we can become stuck in no-win situations in which choosing the lesser of two evils is the only viable option.

Other themes expressed in this card are avoidance and denial. The blindfolded woman clearly does not want to see the reality of her predicament. She is blind to her situation and to her own emotional nature. Not wishing to see reality, she uses denial to block out anything that may cause too much anxiety or pain. This avoidance may take the form of conscious denial, alcohol abuse, or even oversleeping. However, if we totally deny that a situation or feeling exists, it will merely be mirrored in the external world. If we become angry with ourselves, but avoid feeling our rage, we will see that anger mirrored in the people around us. If we deny our failings, then we will meet someone who exhibits those same failings. The world becomes a mirror of all the unconscious feelings, hopes, and problems that lie buried deep inside our psyches. In this card, this is symbolized by the reflective moon above, which constantly influences the changing tides of the mind. Although denial can temporarily shut out painful experiences, problems cannot be completely resolved until they are confronted. It is only by removing the blindfold of denial and finally facing our problems that we will be able to see a better future.

The woman's blindfold also symbolizes our blind spots: those areas in our lives that we fail to see clearly. For some, it is their mother's emotional manipulation, while for others it may be their children's misbehavior. Infatuation will always blind us to our lover's shortcomings. Our love often overpowers our ability to objectively see those we love, causing constant problems. Like a blindfolded woman trying to defend herself, we are unable to protect ourselves when we fervently believe that the other person can do no wrong. This tenderhearted delusion can lead to our being taken advantage of in many cases. To avoid being victimized by loved ones, we need to ask a trusted friend or relative for their honest evaluation of the troubled relationship. While we may never be able to clearly see those we love, a friend's objectivity can alert us to our blind spots.

The Two of Swords shows a woman who also wishes to avoid serious conflict with others at all costs. Blindfolded and seated, her passive stance conveys her desire to avoid confrontation. Although she holds defensive weapons, she seems unwilling to use them. Even the calm waters in the card's background communicate the unspoken message, "Do not make waves." This avoidance of conflict with family, friends, or coworkers usually stems from childhood fears. If a child is frightened of a raging parent or fears being abandoned, he will learn to avoid conflict as a way of ensuring his safety or security. If this lesson is well-learned, the child will mature into an adult who will placate others rather than confront them. Unfortunately, the price that has to be paid for avoiding confrontation is usually smoldering anger or deep resentment. However, this hidden rage is never expressed, because to do so might provoke someone.

There are also times when we need to avoid conflict. There is a woman pictured on this card precisely because most women are taught from an early age that to get what they want in life, they must placate rather than confront others. We tend to pacify our children by giving pacifiers to them to keep them from crying, and we naturally assume an accommodating attitude with our spouses to keep them calm. Many times we will express our agreement with someone else's views while silently disagreeing, preferring a peaceful household to a chaotic one. This card is a reminder that keeping the peace can be regarded as a victory hard won.

In a reading, the two swords pictured imply that we are of two minds about something. Because indecisiveness can result in missed opportunities, it is important to make a firm decision about the present problem. A choice clearly needs to be made. Like the two swords pictured, this choice may be between hurting ourselves or hurting others. If our desires can only be fulfilled at the expense of hurting someone else, then it would be better to inflict the pain of deprivation upon ourselves rather than cause another to needlessly suffer.

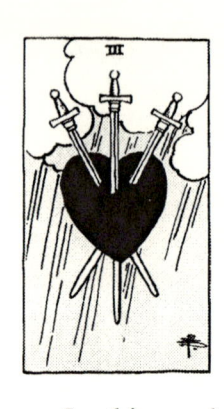

THE THREE OF SWORDS: PAIN

Yet each man kills the thing he loves . . .
The coward does it with a kiss,
The brave man with a sword.

—Oscar Wilde

In this card, a heart suspended in the clouds is gruesomely pierced by three swords. This Christian symbol of the sacred heart has been a traditional representation of the essential pain of human existence. While all the explanations in the world cannot adequately address the suffering inherent in life, we still need to attempt to understand the origins and consequences of our pain. Pain is seldom meaningless. It provides important lessons ranging from not getting burned again by a hot stove to not getting burned by an old lover. Although these lessons can be hard won, pain can be a source of wisdom and strength to those who know how to use it.

There are no people pictured on this card, which suggests the card's most important lesson: we must attend to the reasons why we are hurt, not to those who hurt us. If we focus all of our energy on blaming others for our pain, we will fail to understand our role in creating our own suffering. Although it may be difficult, it is important to view the hurtful person as a catalyst for pain instead of the cause of pain. Instead of asking the age-old question, "Why did you do this to me?" we should be asking, "Why do I feel so hurt by this?" or "What did I do to contribute to this situation?" Honest answers to these last questions can provide valuable insights into the root causes of our pain and may prevent future suffering.

There are many reactions to suffering: self-pity, helplessness, determination, depression, anger, stoicism, denial, or acceptance. How we react usually depends upon our religious upbringing, since most traditions address the meaning of suffering and we, in turn, internalize those beliefs. In Eastern religions such as Buddhism or Hinduism, pain is seen as a direct result of bad karma. Islamic tradition views suffering as a test sent by Allah, while the Chinese

THE MINOR ARCANA

believe pain is generated from an imbalance between the universal forces of yin and yang. The Judeo-Christian tradition has difficulty explaining how an all-loving God could possibly create a world in which there is so much suffering. However, the biblical explanation is that humanity suffers God's wrath because of its flagrant disobedience. There are also differences in the way the sexes view suffering. Men endure their pain as an undeserved punishment, whereas women accept it as their natural heritage. Although we can never explain away our pain, these underlying beliefs about the nature of pain affect our experience of it. Whether we view our pain as a punishment or a pathway will determine our response to suffering.

Like the three swords, there are three primary reasons for pain: to warn of danger, to give a life lesson, or to correct past karma. Physical pain can be a warning sign of serious illness, while emotional pain may be warning us of a potentially dangerous involvement. If it has been determined that there is no immediate threat, it is best to consider pain as a valuable life lesson. This is particularly true if, like the heart pierced by three swords; we have been hurt repeatedly in the same way. Then our task becomes figuring out how we set ourselves up for this wounding situation again and again. When we learn from our mistakes, pain can be transformed into a positive lesson for growth. Finally, if we can find no personal responsibility for our pain, then we may want to attribute it to bad karma. For example, a reckless driver goes through a red light and crashes into our car, causing injury. On the surface, this accident seems like a quirk of fate, as we were simply in the wrong place at the wrong time. However, it is possible that we have hurt someone in the past in a similar fashion, and this "accident" is merely a balancing of universal forces. Even if we don't believe in the concept of karma, our pain may help us to understand the particular kind of pain we have inflicted upon others.

Each of the three swords also symbolizes how we can resolve the pain of the past, effectively deal with pain in the present and, hopefully, avoid similar pain in the future. In the past are broken promises, childhood traumas, sibling rivalries, and bitter resentments buried in the memory of the heart. The pain that we experience in the present is often an opening of these old wounds by a situation that unconsciously reminds us of a painful past experience. Because what wounded us also sensitized us, we need to explore the parallels between past and present situations to get a clearer understanding of where our sensitivities lie. In the present is also our belief in whether pain should be experienced or repressed. Those who repress emotional pain believe that pain is overwhelming and never-ending, but this may be far from the truth. Repressed emotional pain may surface as a physical pain or bizarre symptom, particularly when we can't acknowledge to ourselves how much someone has hurt us. In the future, our beliefs and expectations can produce disappointment. When we have unrealistic expectations of ourselves or others, it usually leads to the pain of disappointment. However, expecting more of someone than they are able to give is not only unrealistic but often heartbreaking.

If we are heartbroken, it takes tremendous courage to make the heart vulnerable a second or third time by exposing it to another chance of being broken. The Three of Swords shows a heart which is totally exposed and vulnerable, yet it is this vulnerability that makes love possible. The word vulnerable derives from the Latin word vulnerare, which means to wound. When we love, we have exposed our innermost selves to another person, and we can easily be wounded. To risk the multiple injuries shown on this card or to be hurt repeatedly without withdrawing is to rejoice in our heart's resiliency.

In a reading, the Three of Swords is the death of love. The card shows love being killed by three things: jealousy, neglect, and dishonesty. Jealousy is an attempt to hold on too tightly to someone we love. Neglect is present when we ignore another person's needs, while dishonesty ranges from small lies to the betrayal of infidelity. All three of these problems emanate from selfishness that can destroy a relationship. When this card appears in a reading, there will definitely be injury inflicted by someone. Our task is to determine whether we are the wounded or the wounding.

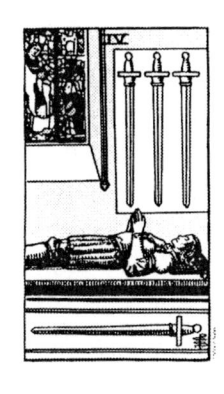

THE FOUR OF SWORDS: PERMANENCE

The more the marble wastes, the more the statue grows.

—Michelangelo

In this card, a gallant knight's sarcophagus lies under a brilliant, stained glass window. This is a portrayal of untimely death and martyrdom, for eternal rest has come too soon for a proud knight on a failed quest. The enclosed walls of his tomb echo the words unspoken, the deeds left undone. However, this does not have to be our fate. If we can find the courage to act and the heroism needed to change, we may be able to escape a similar destiny.

The knight's stone sarcophagus is an enduring monument to the fallen hero within us all. Here lies the valiant effort to succeed that ended in failure, or the years of hard work that only resulted in loss. While it is important to pay homage to our failed heroic efforts, we must be very careful not to stay too long in this place of mourning. To do so is to enshrine our defects, losses, and pain in a psychological space from which we cannot exit. Like the knight entombed for eternity, we can become trapped in our own self-pity. Although it is tempting to see ourselves as sacrificial victims, we need to treat the failures of the past as learning experiences from which we can emerge as stronger, more capable individuals. It is time to bury the wounded parts of ourselves in a forgotten crypt.

It is also clear from looking at this card that an important part of us has died in battle. Like a valiant knight, we have fought the good fight either in divorce court, the hospital, or the workplace. After the dust settles, we realize that while we may have won the battle, we have lost part of ourselves in the process. Perhaps we've replaced enthusiasm with cynicism or love with hate. Life's battles, both small and large, demand that we sacrifice certain emotions that do not lead to victory. For example, sometimes it is necessary to relinquish depression or anger in order to recover from serious illness. As the traditional meaning for this card is recovery from illness, it is important to recognize the impact of our emotions on our malady and be willing to let go of negative emotions that may be damaging our health. Like the stone coffin, we may also need to develop a more hardened attitude toward ourselves or others. Practicing "tough love" or developing discipline requires that we effectively kill off our feelings of complacency in order to obtain positive results.

Another theme found in this card is that of living in the past. To be inside this card is to reside in a mausoleum where we are still living with dead issues such as jobs we've left behind or failed relationships we have outgrown. At mid-life, we may still be reliving the triumphs of youth. This card of death and endings is very reflective of mid-life, a time when men symbolically put down their swords of competition while women typically end their childrearing duties. Since we have already fought the battles necessary to make our place in the world during the first half of our lives, the second half of life can be a welcome opportunity for personal growth. This inward direction is reflected in the enclosed interior of the mausoleum. Mid-life is a time to go inside. This can be a very rewarding period when we can truly get in touch with the essence of ourselves. By discovering new parts of ourselves, we can confidently move forward instead of living in the past.

The figure carved in stone is trapped for eternity in a place from which he is unable to move; therefore, he symbolizes our inability to act. The stained glass window above the sarcophagus focuses the light of understanding, illuminating one of the primary reasons why some of us fail to take action. The window shows a young man kneeling in front of a maternal figure. This symbolizes his submission to his mother's will, and some mothers willfully decree their offspring should remain children forever. By trying to please our mother, we may become fixated at an early stage of development. A childlike dependence on our parents leads to regression, helplessness, and the paralyzing inactivity found in the womb-like coffin below. In true knightly fashion, this intense longing for dependency must be bitterly fought against if we wish to mature.

There are many reasons for our inability to move forward in our lives, and each of the four swords on the card represents a different cause of this inactivity. Inability to act can be caused by fear of failure, fear of the cost (either financial or emotional), fear of criticism, or fear of imperfection. Basically, all of these hindrances are negative projections into the future of what might happen if we took a particular action. We believe we won't be able to succeed or, if we do, that the cost will be too great. We envision other people criticizing our efforts, or our unrelenting perfectionism causes us to become our own worst critic. All these negative beliefs keep us from acting in our best interests. When we fail to act, we effectively bury our talents in a crypt marked "fear of the future." To overcome these fears, we have only to look at the stained glass window on the card. Stained glass windows found in churches have always been a visual beacon for the faithful and reflect the faith we must have in ourselves, knowing that our best effort is always good enough for God.

In a reading, this card supports our hope that, even though we may be paralyzed by fear or unresolved conflict, we can find the courage to move forward. Although the card's enclosed tomb may reflect our deepest fears of being eternally trapped inside a distressing situation, we do possess the necessary tools to break free. We first need to practice detachment from the situation by removing ourselves from it either physically or psychologically. Meditation, prayer, or spiritual retreat can become important sanctuaries in troubling times. When we strive to develop the peacefulness of eternal rest reflected on this card, we can change our circumstances by changing ourselves.

THE FIVE OF SWORDS: VICTORY

He who conquers others is strong; he who conquers himself is mighty.

—Lao-Tzu

At the water's edge, a lone warrior has taken several swords from two other men, leaving them defeated. An ill wind whips against the strong and the weak, the tyrant and his victims. However, all is not as it seems, for in this card there is victory in defeat. Swords represent our thoughts, but not all of our thoughts are healthy or positive. Negative thoughts such as self-criticism or victimization can have a negative impact upon our lives and our health. These erroneous beliefs must be confronted and defeated if we are to make any progress. In this card, we are both the conqueror and the vanquished, for the enemy we have so cleverly defeated is ourselves.

The Five of Swords shows the familiar battlefield of self-defeating behavior, where our negative thoughts triumph over positive ones. It is here that we are our own worst enemy, sabotaging our efforts at every turn while convincing ourselves that we are unworthy of success. On this card, the victor with the contemptuous smirk on his face is also our own inner critic, who constantly reminds us of our previous failures or finds potential problems in every new venture. He sends us self-defeating messages such as, "I can't," "I'm not good enough," or "I know I'll fail miserably." Although this type of negative thinking is a worthy opponent, self-defeatist thinking can be effectively defeated. When we become aware of a counterproductive thought ("I can't"), we can restate it positively ("I can"). By changing a negative thought into a positive affirmation, we can make negativity work for us rather than against us.

There are other enemies lurking within our psyches that need to be defeated. Two of the most threatening are the opposite extremes of healthy self-esteem: inferiority and superiority. In this card, the giant victor looms over the two smaller, defeated men. Likewise, our beliefs about ourselves can distort our self-image. We may see ourselves as either ineffectual losers or domineering winners. Interestingly, those people who act as if they are superior to others are usually overcompensating for feelings of inferiority, while those who publicly denigrate themselves often secretly feel superior to everyone else. Feelings of inferiority or superiority can best be overcome by separating our sense of personal worth from our attractiveness, wealth, or intelligence. We are not our jobs, our bank accounts, or our marital status. Our happiness depends upon the development of a realistic appraisal of our inner worth without emphasizing an abundance or deficiency of socially approved characteristics. Unlike the defeated men pictured, when we divorce ourselves from society's expectations of success, our self-esteem can never be taken away from us.

Both inferiority and superiority can also be responses to real or imagined hostility from others. Like the three men on this card, we feel it is necessary to either conquer or submit in order to disarm the other person. Those who wish to dominate may do so in subtle ways such as telling offensive jokes or showing contempt for others' weaknesses. While submissive behavior is motivated by a fear of abandonment, dominant behavior usually stems from an abusive childhood. Sadly, the victimized grow up to victimize others. Many of our social systems also support the belief that power can only be acquired through dominance. While this male-oriented world-view of "the strong survive while the weak perish" dominates our culture, it totally disregards alternate ways to acquire authentic power such as prayer or knowledge.

Another inner enemy we need to become aware of is projection. When we become preoccupied with the misbehavior of others (their chronic lateness, untidiness, insensitivity, etc.), we may be unconsciously attributing our unrecognized faults to other people. If we are deeply disturbed by someone else's offensive behavior, it is very likely that we tend to act in a similar fashion, but fail to realize it. Because projection is very difficult to detect in ourselves, it is necessary to take a simple test to see if the anger we have for others should be redirected toward ourselves. When we catch ourselves constantly criticizing someone else, we merely substitute the pronoun "I" for the person's name in our inner tirade. So, "Harold is never on time" becomes, "I am never on time." Then we must honestly evaluate whether the amended statement is accurate. In this way, what we usually perceive as other people's problems can be turned into constructive self-criticism.

The Five of Swords explores the ways in which we deal with aggression stemming either from others or ourselves. When someone has hurt us, we would naturally like to respond in kind, but this is seldom advisable. On the other hand, if we totally suppress our anger, it can easily turn into depression or helplessness. These aggressive feelings can also become split off when we project our belligerence onto an enemy while we view ourselves as their helpless victims. A better approach is to take an assertive stance. At the bottom of this card is a line demarcating the place where the sea meets the shore. We may need to draw our own line in the sand that clearly tells others that they may proceed only so far, but no further. Telling others where we draw the line on their disrespectful behavior reclaims our personal power and self-respect, just as the figure on the card reclaims his swords.

In divination, it should be remembered that this card focuses on power in relationships, particularly how power is acquired or taken. Those who do not have power are often jealous of those who lay claim to it. Whether it is sibling rivalry or business rivalry, jealousy is based upon the belief in limited resources that seem to be unfairly distributed. Instead of getting caught up in poisonous feelings of jealousy, it is better to view the world as full of abundance. By focusing on our ability to obtain all things, we will always emerge victorious.

THE SIX OF SWORDS: CIRCUMSTANCE

Few men progress, except as they are pushed along by events.

—E.W. Howe

    In this card, a man silently ferries two people across still waters toward a distant shore. The woman and her child seem to be reluctant passengers on this voyage across the waters of time. Perhaps they are refugees from a broken family or war, trying to successfully navigate through a major crisis in their lives. Alternatively, they might be steering a safe passage away from some unknown danger. Wherever they have come from, it is clear that these three figures symbolize our own journey of discovery. The small child in the boat is our inner child, who always comes along with us on our journey through life. He is also a reminder that each time we more forward, there is always an urgent wish to regress to an earlier stage in our lives when life seemed easier. The mother on the boat is our inner nurturer, who needs to reassure the inner child that they will be able to safely get through the rough waters ahead. Finally, the ferryman pushing the boat through the water is symbolic of the uncontrollable circumstances that push us forward in life.

    Like a ferryman guiding a boat to shore, circumstance often determines our destination in life. The family into which we were born, a job offer from a distant city, or an unfortunate accident can change the course of our lives. Fateful circumstances propel us across an unknown sea toward a foreign land, for difficulties rarely leave us where they found us. Events can carry us to places where we would not normally go and to unfamiliar places of the heart. Hopefully, when we reach our destination, we will have changed for the better. We may be stronger or, perhaps, just grateful for having survived the arduous journey.

    While circumstances may dictate where we are in our lives, we still have the power to choose peace of mind. When we lose a job or a loved one, we can trust in a higher plan even though this divine plan is not revealed to us. To trust in divine providence is to be content in all circumstances, and we can be secure in the knowledge that we are always in the right place at the right time. As long as we travel along with the constant belief that God's plan is what is best for us, we will know that our ship is headed in the right direction.

Like the six swords on the boat, we can carry the belief in divine providence along with us on our journey. If our journey is particularly arduous, we can pray for our dire circumstances to change so that we may be magically transported to a better place. Nevertheless, our circumstances will not change until we do. The spiritual purpose of fortunate or unfortunate circumstances is to put us in a learning situation where we have the opportunity to change ourselves. The circumstances in which we find ourselves propel us to become better human beings.

The black pole used by the ferryman to propel the boat represents the motivation we need to propel ourselves forward. Fear and anger are usually prime motivators, but financial need is also an excellent incentive. Inner drives such as the need for recognition or the need for our parents' acceptance can motivate us to succeed, but we need to be fully aware of these motivations before they push us toward a destiny determined by someone else.

Just as the ferryman's pole disappears beneath the water, our motivations may also be hidden beneath conscious awareness. These unconscious motivations may be cleverly hidden underneath socially acceptable behavior. For example, philanthropy can become self-serving, and collecting can be a form of socially recognized greed. Ulterior motives abound in relationships in which helping someone else ultimately results in helping ourselves. While unconscious motivations are usually hidden, they satisfy some desire either for sympathy, dependence, or domination, which can be exposed. A desire for sympathy (symbolized by the sympathetic-looking woman on the boat) could be an unconscious motivation beneath an illness, while a desire for dependence (symbolized by the small child) could be an underlying motivation for a teen-ager failing to pass his driving test. The desire for domination (symbolized by the ferryman) could be the motivation for vicious gossip or constant criticism.

These unconscious motivations are as difficult to see as a pole underwater; however, we only have to ask one important question to find our elusive ulterior motives, "What positive things am I getting out of this problem?" There may be some hidden payoff to our problems of which we are totally unaware. Perhaps the problem satisfies a need for drama in our lives, or helps us avoid conflict. Honestly answering this difficult question can expose the secondary gains that we have carefully hidden from ourselves, and help us move forward on our journey.

Between departure and arrival lie the waters of transition, that perilous passage which separates the old life from the new. It is during this time that we are most susceptible to losing our momentum. In a reading, this card indicates a need to keep moving forward, even if it means we must leave someone or something behind. Independence is not achieved without cost. Whether we are leaving our family of origin to establish our own family or leaving a large corporation to start our own business, some sacrifices will have to be made. Nevertheless, if we just keep putting one foot in front of the other, we will finally reach our destination.

THE SEVEN OF SWORDS: CONSCIENCE

The efforts which we make to escape from our destiny only serve to lead us to it.

—Ralph Waldo Emerson

On this card, a thief furtively runs away with five swords while leaving two swords behind. However, his focus is on what is behind him rather than his destination because he is in danger of being caught in the act of stealing. Actually, the pursuer that the thief fears will quickly catch up with him is an aspect of the thief himself. The thief's pursuer is unseen and, therefore, represents an unconscious part of his personality that has yet to be integrated into conscious awareness. Any part of ourselves that we cannot accept is relegated to the unconscious, where it can pursue us in our dreams and phobias. Only by confronting the rejected aspects of ourselves can we free ourselves from being pursued.

The thief is also being relentlessly pursued by his guilty conscience, which threatens to overtake him at any moment. Like the fleeing thief, the road we take and the decisions we make are often influenced by an irrational fear that some misdeed in our past will someday catch up with us. In many ways, we are like the thief with a guilty conscience who is eternally looking over his shoulder with the expectation of being caught. However, no matter how fast we run, we can never escape from ourselves. Our conscience will pursue us, filling our lives with mysterious illnesses, strange accidents, and deep depression until we surrender to our own inner judgment.

On the other hand, the thief may represent a fervent wish for something prohibited which we have never actually acted upon. In this case, care must be taken that we don't blame ourselves for something we never did. Swords represent our thoughts, but thoughts themselves are not wrongdoing. Like the deceptive thief, there are some situations in which our conscience can trick us into believing we are to blame when we are actually blameless. For example, blaming ourselves when we've been victimized, or feeling guilt when someone has died, may give us some sense of control (after all, someone is to blame, even if it is ourselves), but these feelings can be very damaging over time.

The thief sneaking away with his swords is also symbolic of one of the greatest crimes committed against the individual: self-deception. We seem to have an almost infinite capacity to mislead ourselves. As long as we get what we want, we can easily convince ourselves that the ends have justified the means. We can also deceive ourselves into thinking that our circumstances will automatically change in our favor. For example, a husband will naturally leave his wife for his mistress. When we become obsessed with the objects of our desire, we can easily become victims of our own self-deception. However, like a thief who runs away from the authorities, those who deceive themselves are always pursued by reality. Sooner or later, reality catches up with us, and we must face the consequences of our self-deception.

The five swords that the thief manages to take away with him represent five essential qualities of a successful thief, which may either help or hinder us on our journey through life. These characteristics are impulsiveness, rebelliousness, evasiveness, risk taking, and resourcefulness. First and foremost, stealing is usually an impulsive act carried out without thought to the potential consequences of breaking the law. Without thought to the future, the thief pictured does not look ahead to where he is going or to where his actions might lead him. Similarly, we may need to carefully consider the negative consequences of any major decisions we make in the present, particularly important decisions that could affect our future. Second, there is always an element of rebelliousness in any criminal activity. There is a rebel inside all of us who enjoys breaking the rules, whether they are self-imposed or dictated by others. While adolescent rebellion against authority is a normal stage of development, it can become a destructive lifestyle when carried over into adulthood. Clearly, the choices we make as adults must be based upon our best interests rather than willful disobedience.

The third quality of any good thief is evasiveness, but a thief who wishes to get something for nothing seeks to evade responsibility as well as capture. Likewise, some of us try to avoid the responsibility of employment or relationships by constantly changing jobs or partners. The background of this card shows a group of tents, reflecting the temporary nature of many relationships. Many of us seek to avoid capture in marriage simply by pulling up our stakes and moving on again and again.

The last two qualities of a good thief, risk taking and resourcefulness, are actually positive attributes. Some situations require that we take risks in order to make progress. Nothing worthwhile is without risk on some level, whether it is financial, emotional, or physical. Therefore, it may be advisable to take some risks in seeking what we need in life. Lastly, we may need to be more resourceful by going around the accepted way of doing things in order to find workable solutions to our problems.

In a reading, we may see ourselves as victims of thievery rather than the perpetrator. What are stolen from us may not necessarily be valued possessions. There are many intangible things that can be taken from us in life: our self-respect, time, trust, or peace of mind. However, no one can take away our ability to love or trust again after we have been hurt except ourselves. Similarly, no one can negate our self-respect after we have been dishonored except ourselves. In order to lose these intrinsic qualities, we must give our express permission for them to be stolen from us. It may be time to stop the important people in our lives from stealing what has always been ours.

This card can also represent someone whom we should distrust, perhaps someone who is intent on stealing our ideas. The card's thief also mirrors a wish to escape. There may be a desire to escape a repressive home environment or an unfulfilling job. Ultimately, we might even try to escape our destiny, only to find that our plan to run away from our fate only leads us closer to it.

THE EIGHT OF SWORDS: LIMITATION

. . . the many prisons of life—prisons of stone, prisons of passions, prisons of intellect, prisons of morality and the rest—all limitations, external or internal, all prisons, really. All life is a limitation.

—Oscar Wilde

A bound and blindfolded woman stands at the shoreline surrounded by eight swords. She is imprisoned by the swords around her and unable to extricate herself from her bonds. This is the place in which we find ourselves much of the time, the place of limitation. We find ourselves in a situation in which all our actions are thwarted, and we can't seem to free ourselves from a fateful confinement. Our plans are cancelled; our dreams perish. Frustrated at every turn, we just can't seem to make any progress, no matter how hard we try. Bound by circumstances beyond our control and blindfolded by unseen forces that conspire against us, we can only passively stand by while accepting our fate.

Limitation can be either self-imposed or forced upon us by others. Like the woman bound by an unknown assailant, we are all products of societal constraints, genetic limitations, and parental controls. We can also become our own jailers by holding onto self-limiting beliefs which keep our personalities restricted and our potential imprisoned. We can be imprisoned by what we love or by what we hate; by marital bonds or divorce decrees; by religious belief or atheism. If the human condition is basically one of limitation, then we must find a way to free ourselves from ourselves.

The first step toward freedom is to acknowledge and fully understand our limitations. Krishnamurti said, "Freedom is when bondage is understood." Many times, we blame a difficult person for our limitations in life when we should be examining our underlying beliefs for the source of our restriction. For example, a single woman may forego buying her own home because she has an underlying belief that owning her own home would betray her future dream of marrying someday and starting a family. In this example, we can see that our beliefs often keep us immobilized, while they blind us to positive alternatives that could enrich our lives.

To discover the limiting beliefs that hold us hostage, we need to develop objectivity. In the background of this card is a beautiful castle sitting on top of a mountain. We will need to climb that faraway mountain to obtain an objective view of everything below. Keeping a journal or consulting a trusted friend about our difficulties can often give us the detachment needed to see our situation from an objective vantage point.

After uncovering the hidden beliefs which act as jailers in our inner prison, we can attempt to rise above them. Carl Jung said, "Problems are not solved, they are transcended." In order for us to go beyond our limited way of thinking, social conditioning, or parental dictates, we will have to change ourselves. There are many paths to transformation including psychotherapy, loving relationships, or even disease. However, one of the most effective paths is that of meditation. If we are stuck in a situation from which we cannot extricate ourselves, then meditation may provide a way to spiritually transcend our problems. The Eight of Swords shows us the problem of limitation as well as its solution through meditation. The woman pictured is a representation of the meditative state because meditation requires that we remain perfectly still, just like the bound woman. Like a spiritual blindfold, meditation also forces us to close our eyes to the outside world so that we can look within ourselves. A daily meditative practice can help us get in touch with our essential being and transcend the limitations of earthly existence.

The eight swords surrounding the woman on this card are symbolic of all her negative beliefs and desires. On the right side are five beliefs which effectively hold her hostage: victimization, powerlessness, helplessness, self-blame, and passivity. This woman appears to be the eternal sacrificial victim, awaiting her cruel fate; however, it is only when we identify with being a victim that we can be victimized. Instead of viewing every painful experience as a justification of our victimization, we could make a conscious decision to view distressful situations as learning experiences. This simple reframing of experience can free us from the perpetual role of victim.

Bondage is also symbolic of our feelings of powerlessness and helplessness. While we have little power to change many external events, we certainly have the power to change our reaction to those events. Self-blame is also very limiting. It is not coincidental that a woman is pictured on this card, as women have a tendency to constantly blame themselves for their loved one's difficulties. We blame ourselves for our husband's failures and our children's problems. In this case, it is vitally important that we distinguish between our own responsibilities and the responsibilities of others. Like the bound woman, we can also become very passive by surrendering our personal will to others. Unfortunately, as long as femininity continues to be identified with passivity, we will continue to idealize a passive nature. In the meantime, we need to remind ourselves that not taking any action is in itself an act.

On the left side of the woman are the three swords of unconscious desire that imprison her: the wish to be desired, the wish to be rescued, and the wish to suffer. The wish to be desired is instilled in every girl at a young age and is reflected in our culture in the popularity of romance novels and seductive rock stars. In this card, the woman's seductive appearance may have made her a victim of her own attractiveness. Unfortunately, the wish to be desired is very self-limiting simply because, when this dream is fulfilled, we become a sexual object in someone else's life rather than a subject of our own.

The woman waiting for someone to free her from her bonds is symbolic of the unconscious wish to be rescued. Like a damsel in distress, we often wait patiently for someone (usually a man) to save us from our latest predicament. Sometimes we even purposely sabotage ourselves in order to be rescued. In this way, we can avoid responsibility while the rescuer tries to help us by taking responsibility for us. A more mature attitude is to accept personal responsibility and rescue ourselves.

The last sword imprisoning us is our belief in suffering. Freud believed women to be inherently masochistic in nature, but this has proven to be a myth born of the Victorian culture in which he lived.

However, some of us do suffer but fail to take any constructive action, in the mistaken belief that suffering is somehow ennobling. Victimization and its attendant suffering do not guarantee transformation or sainthood. The woman eternally stuck on the shoreline shows us by negative example that suffering is a place we need to move through rather than a place we wish to dwell in for the rest of our lives.

THE NINE OF SWORDS: AWAKENING

You will wake, and remember, and understand.

—Robert Browning

In this card, a woman suddenly sits up in bed after being awakened by a terrible nightmare. Unlike many of the other Tarot cards that take place outdoors, this scene takes place inside a darkened bedroom. Historically, the bed is an archetypal place where we are born, have sex, give birth, and often die. The bedroom is also our refuge, where we can relax as well as find security and warmth. Although the bedroom can be a place of relationship, it is also where we go to be alone. The bedroom represents the most intimate parts of our lives and, therefore, mirrors the darkest recesses of our psyches. It is here that our greatest desires and fears reside.

The woman pictured seems to be completely alone in her night terror. To experience a nightmare is to feel helpless terror by being plunged into a threatening situation from which there is no escape. The disturbance and fear caused by a nightmare can haunt us for days afterward, causing us to wonder why our mind would want to frighten us half to death. There are many theories as to why we have nightmares, ranging from simple emotional catharsis to self-punishment. However, many theorists agree that nightmares are eruptions of repressed impulses, particularly dangerous impulses. On this card, one side of the bed shows an obscure engraving of what appears to be two men fighting. This unconscious hostility appearing below the woman's conscious awareness may be the dreamer's repressed rage. Often when we dream of being attacked, the assailant is simply our own unexpressed aggression pursuing us into our dreams. Nightmares are clues to aggressive impulses that have been repressed, but which are still breeding resentment in the depths of the unconscious. Acknowledgment of our hidden anger can often dispel our terrors in the night.

Anger that is unacknowledged can also cause depression. The woman pictured is in the depths of despair, unable to get out of bed. Because this anguish takes place in the bedroom, the depression she experiences may be caused by the tremendous rage generated by sexual rejection, infertility, or sexual abuse. This scene does provide some hope, however, because the nine swords hanging above the woman also form a ladder that can be used to climb out of her depressive state.

The quilt on the woman's bed points to another antidote for depression. Quilts are naturally associated with our mothers, as they provide warmth and security in their womblike envelopment. Because quilts were often made by our grandmothers and passed down through generations, they are also symbolic of the great strength of women through time. We can gain a valuable perspective when we consider that previous generations of women had to struggle to survive and persevere in a prejudiced society. Yet, they still made the effort to create magnificent quilts of lasting beauty. Patchwork quilts, like the one on the card, are made from useless remnants that have been combined to create a pleasing design. Likewise, we all have certain gifts and abilities that may be taken for granted but can, nonetheless, create a beautiful life. To follow our gifts and do what we love is often the best prescription for depression.

Making a quilt, or any other craft, can be very therapeutic. Artists and craftspeople have a positive, constructive outlook even though they may be suffering through hardships in life. When life becomes a nightmare, we can momentarily escape the pain by working on a creative project every day. When the circumstances of our lives are out of control, we can control what we create. When our lives are shattered, we can sew the pieces back together, if only in symbolic form. The folk wisdom of our grandparents remains the same today as it was in days past: it is far better to be creating than crying.

When we channel our feelings into the receptacle of art, we create something of beauty out of suffering. On a spiritual level, we need to view the intense suffering portrayed on this card as a necessary stage in our spiritual development—a stage that can transform us into beautiful people. Physical or emotional pain can make us better people if it awakens our compassion. To realize that we are not alone in our suffering because others have also experienced the same devastating losses is to realize our compassion. Unfortunately, the path of compassion pictured on this card is the most difficult path in the Tarot because it requires us to understand someone else's pain through our own suffering. It is only through our painful experience that we can feel others' sorrow. To be compassionate is to know that the darkness of despair is an integral part of the human condition.

The woman who suddenly awakens from a deep sleep may also parallel our inner awakening. Psychological awakening causes us to wake up to the realization that we have suddenly become conscious of an action that was previously not recognized. For example, we realize that the disparaging words coming of our mouths echo our mother's words. Spiritual awakening, on the other hand, is almost indescribable to those who have experienced it. Awakening has been compared to going from the darkness into the light or waking up from a bad dream. To turn on this light of awareness requires tremendous faith and spiritual practice. Nevertheless, even after all our effort, sometimes all we can hope for is that spiritual awareness will somehow find us.

In a reading, the Nine of Swords is a problematic card foretelling of possible disaster. We could find ourselves being suddenly thrown into a medical or financial nightmare from which we desperately want to wake up. Also, a dream come true could turn into a nightmare such as when a dream vacation is ruined or a new home needs extensive repairs. In this case, the swords suspended above the bed are symbolic of a potential disaster hanging over our heads, and we spend our days anxiously awaiting the axe to fall.

The reasons for such a disaster are to be found on the quilt covering the bed. This is a magical quilt embroidered with signs of the zodiac. The woman sleeps under this blanket of stars, accepting celestial influence in her life. Likewise, we may need to consider that our fate may be written in the stars. When things go badly, we can consult an astrologer who can hopefully give us an astrological explanation for our run of bad luck. Not only does this fateful information counteract our belief that everything must be our fault, it also gives us hope that when the celestial positions change, things will get better.

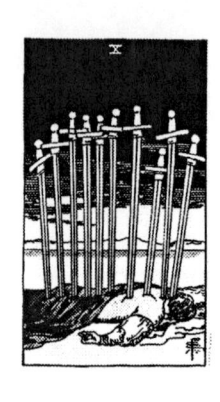

THE TEN OF SWORDS: FORGIVENESS

And dying, bless the hand that gave the blow.

—John Dryden

Under ominous skies, a man lies murdered by an unknown assailant. He has been stabbed in the back not once, but ten times. To be stabbed in the back is to be betrayed, a wound that cuts deeply into our consciousness. Betrayal has many forms including infidelity, embezzlement, or simply the betrayal of a confidence. However, all these emotional betrayals are made possible by misplaced trust. By explicitly trusting another, we open the door to the dark place of betrayal and, once inside, we are unlikely to trust again. The real victim of betrayal is our trust, which we voluntarily kill in an effort to protect ourselves from being victimized again in the future.

In many ways, we directly contribute to others' betrayal of ourselves by handing them the swords of their deception. Long before any action was taken against us, we either trusted too completely, expected too much, or ignored the perilous situation around us until it was too late.

Although betrayal may not be directly our fault, we often have a larger role in the drama than that of victim. For example, by withholding affection from their spouse, a husband or wife can create a situation in which the injured party may be tempted by the betrayal of infidelity. Likewise, we may believe that an untrustworthy friend will not take advantage of us as he has in the past. Like a strong sword that has been tempered by heating and cooling, we must temper desire with caution if we are to survive.

There are also many ways in which we betray ourselves. Disease and disability are the twin betrayals of the body. When the body that we have either carefully cared for or taken for granted is struck down by disease, we feel betrayal in the deepest sense. Suddenly, our focus is severely narrowed to our body's pain or distressing symptoms. Disease can make us feel just as severely limited as someone impaled upon the ground. Any type of disability, either temporary or permanent, relegates us to a lower level of awareness and prevents us from exercising free will. Personal will is symbolized by the Magician card in the Tarot, and in the Ten of Swords it is this same magician who lies prostrate on the ground. He has been slain by the betrayal of his body, by the disease that controls him. Disease can also quickly kill off our determination, desires, and dreams. Certainly, no external enemy could do more harm to us than this.

Another inner enemy is the betrayal of the mind. Each time we proclaim we should be slimmer, wealthier, better organized, etc., we stab ourselves in the back. "Shoulds" only contribute to our growing storehouse of guilt. They also kill off our self-esteem when we cannot live up to our own impossible expectations. Another subtle betrayal is the belief in victimhood or bad luck, which can ruin our lives. Believing in ill fortune can easily become a self-fulfilling prophecy. For example, some of us believe we were born unlucky and spend the rest of our lives proving ourselves right. These crimes against the self can be professional suicide if we let them. We need to replace the negative thoughts that are hurting us with positive thoughts about our professional abilities.

Because this card usually predicts ruin or death, it is unlikely that we can find any positive meaning contained in this card; however, in the Tarot there are always surprises. The murder victim portrayed on the card has left us a cryptic message that is positively reassuring. As a final act of communication, the dying man has formed the sign of blessing with his outstretched hand. This is also the same sign of benediction used by the Hierophant. The hidden message from the dying man is that the terrible things that befall us are actually blessings in disguise. For example, sometimes the ending of a career or relationship gives us the opportunity to find someone or something better. If we can find the hidden positive value in our problems, we can transform them into opportunities for growth. The painful wounds we must endure may be what we need to develop virtuous qualities such as fortitude, sensitivity, self-reliance, or empathy. By making a list of all the ways in which a negative experience has changed our lives for the better, we can transform every curse into a blessing.

If we can wisely understand the pain that has been inflicted upon us as a blessing in disguise, then we should be able to forgive those who have betrayed us. Like the fallen hero pictured, we may at some future date be able to bless our enemies. Realistically, this step may not be possible for many of us in every major hurtful situation, but we can all make an effort to forgive the small transgressions of daily life. Instead of screaming at the driver of the car that has just cut us off, it is far wiser to forgive the other driver so that we may proceed peacefully. Although it may be very difficult to accept, whatever happens to us may ultimately be for the best in the grand scheme of things. If we can accept the premise that misfortune at the hand of another is a strangely disguised form of divine guidance, then we can find it in our hearts to forgive those who have hurt us.

In this card, pain, betrayal, and death are all dark forces that shed light on everything around them. Unlike all the other cards in the deck, in this card there is a sharp contrast between the darkness of night and the light of dawn. This reflects our ability to turn the blackest night into a sunny day simply by changing our attitude. The Ten of Swords shows us that our task is not to battle the darkness, but rather to shed more light. Just as night must surrender to the day, we need only create light and the darkness will fade away.

THE PAGE OF SWORDS: INFLUENCE

The wind sways the willow.

—Chinese Proverb

A young man stands on a bluff buffeted by the wind. Holding his gleaming sword aloft in an aggressive stance, he is prepared to do battle. Yet, his only enemy is the wind. Just like the page battling the wind, we must confront our invisible enemies and eventually conquer them. The enemies we seek are the imperceptible influences that subtly control our lives. These social and psychological influences are like a strong wind; we can't see them, but we can feel their powerful effect. When we suddenly feel depressed for no apparent reason or panic over a trivial incident, then we must search for these invisible enemies lurking inside and outside ourselves.

First, there are many external influences that have become so familiar to us that we barely notice them. The strongest of these outside influences is probably that of drugs and alcohol. When we are "under the influence" we can no longer be true to ourselves and may wind up hurting others. Another external authority is the considerable influence of our family and friends. Like the tree in this card's background which sways in the wind, we may be too easily swayed by others' opinions and lose our sense of inner direction. While others may think they know what is best for us, their advice is based upon their own perspective and life experience. It is not our own. Like the direction of the wind, it is always wise to know where the other person is coming from in order to correctly evaluate their suggestion as to what direction our lives should take.

The Page of Swords is a young man and, therefore, he embodies the most important influence during adolescence: peer pressure. In the time between childhood and adulthood is adolescence, that period in which we all strive to belong. In order to fit into a group, it is necessary to go along with what everyone else is doing. A deck of Tarot cards is not needed to predict that this can have a disastrous outcome. However, this isn't only a problem of adolescence. Adults can easily be swayed by the subtle messages of conformity found in advertising and the media. Usually these messages define success as wealth or fame. Although these subliminal messages appeal to our inner adolescent, maturity comes with the knowledge that life does not come with a price tag, nor is it a popularity contest. We need to emulate the Page of Swords and take a defensive stance against these outside influences that lead us in the wrong direction.

Of course, there are also positive influences in our lives as well. Mentors, spiritual guides, and teachers can be instrumental in the fulfillment of our true potential. When we find ourselves as neophytes in the business world or novices on the spiritual path, we need the help of an experienced teacher to guide us. When a teacher isn't available, we can always ask for the guidance of the cards. Tarot can be one of the most positive influences in our lives because it gives us encouragement while it teaches. While guidance can come from almost anyone we meet, the Tarot specifically guides us toward realizing our latent potential.

In order to fulfill this potential, we need to battle the negative internal influences in our lives. Our hidden fears and complexes can hold us back from becoming the person we were meant to be. These invisible enemies hide in the unconscious, where they are difficult to find, much less defeat. It is only through analyzing our dreams and fantasies that we can bring these hidden motivations into conscious awareness. Working with the Tarot is also helpful, as it provides us with a magic mirror in which we can clearly see the distortions of our mind. Reoccurring cards in consecutive readings force us to confront those parts of our interior lives we would rather not examine. However, once exposed, these internal complexes can become allies rather than enemies.

The most important influence in our lives is not found in our family, society, or our complexes. Rather, it is our innate nature, otherwise known as our personality type. Our personality type is the compass that determines our direction in life, because character determines destiny. Of course, some people would argue that we are all born a blank slate on which environmental factors make the only

THE MINOR ARCANA

marks. Yet, there are temperamental differences in newborn babies that cannot be explained. Some are naturally curious, others afraid, and still others cry incessantly. Obviously, we are all born with different types of personalities that manifest in different behaviors.

The study of these innate differences in human nature usually results in some form of typology. There are astrological types, psychological types, numerical types, goddess types, and color types, to name just a few. Most of these typologies have lists of characteristics that conform to each type in their system. For example, those born under the astrological sign of Libra usually appreciate art, but have difficulty making decisions. Knowing one's type, no matter which system is used, is very important because it categorizes each of us according to our different gifts. By understanding our type, we better understand ourselves. Because there are no good or bad types, we can accept ourselves as a typical Pisces or a typical thinking type without judging our innate inclinations. Most importantly, once we have deduced our particular type, we can work with our nature instead of against it.

The Page of Swords is fighting the wind, trying in vain to battle nature. Often in life we try unsuccessfully to fight against our own nature with disastrous results. A feeling type who becomes a financial analyst or an introvert who becomes a social director are just two extreme examples of ways in which we valiantly try to be someone other than ourselves. Battling our own natures can also be exhausting. Like the Page of Swords eternally holding up his sword, we find it very tiring to always be at war with ourselves, constantly trying to outmaneuver all the unfulfilled desires within us. It is only through self-acceptance that we will finally be able to achieve peace.

Because wind symbolizes a change in circumstances, the Page of Swords in a reading signifies a change of some kind. Unlike the page, we should be prepared to accept these changes rather than fight them. A strong wind can also clear the air, so we should expect arguments that will get certain issues out into the open where they can be cleared up.

THE KNIGHT OF SWORDS: OVERREACTION

A man in a passion rides a wild horse.

—Benjamin Franklin

    A knight on horseback charges into a storm. He is caught up in a storm of emotion, rushing into the unknown. This card mirrors the impulsiveness that surfaces when we are suddenly carried away by strong emotion. With little thought to the consequences of our behavior, we act without thinking. The loose reins on the horse's neck suggest we have no rein on our emotions and no self-control to hold back the momentum of our passions. Rash behavior is carrying us toward an unknown destination or, possibly, a fall.

    Nevertheless, there are certain skills we can develop to stop this wild ride of emotional overreaction. The first step is to honestly acknowledge whatever emotion we are caught up in at the moment. Simply saying, "I am angry, jealous, depressed, anxious, etc.," gives us permission to have these feelings while simultaneously lending some objectivity to the emotions we feel. This initial step should be immediately followed by substitution of a positive affirmation or positive emotion for the original distressing feeling. For instance, overwhelming feelings of anger that quickly get out of control can be completely transformed by feelings of empathy. Instead of being infuriated because someone has made an offensive remark, we can engender empathetic feelings by mentally saying to ourselves that this person has probably had a very bad day or isn't feeling well. Although this does not excuse their behavior, it can immediately subdue our anger.

    One of the strongest emotions is that of vengeance, and the Knight of Swords perfectly personifies this lust for revenge. He charges off to the left, indicating that he is riding toward some injury done to him in the past. The memory of previous injury fuels his determination to avenge any wrongdoing that was done to him or his loved ones. Leaping over the sands of time, his only desire is to change the past by seeking vengeance in the present.

Becoming bitter from what we perceive as a past injustice, we often feel the need for vengeance. Somehow, we believe that evening the score will automatically erase the pain we've experienced. Unfortunately, this is far from the truth. In actuality, vengeance only creates more chaos and guilt. Ultimately, it brings us down to the same level as our persecutors, where we become the people we love to hate. Truly, the best vengeance is simply refusing to resemble the person who has injured us.

Although the urge for vengeance is usually fleeting, some people have a constant need to avenge themselves. They use any small slight as ample justification for hurting others. The source of their unforgiving nature lies in a childhood filled with unrelenting pain. Tragically, it is a well-known axiom that abused children usually grow up to become vengeful adults. The driving force in their lives is a deep desire to take revenge on the parents who severely punished them in the past. This rage is then extended to friends and coworkers whom they perceive as worthy objects of retaliation. Holding tightly onto their sword of vengeance, they also view most interactions as potentially injurious and, therefore, never hesitate to verbally defend themselves. Although the burning anger of abuse can never be completely extinguished, the vengeful person can be taught anger management techniques in order to let go of retaliation. By refusing to act on their angry feelings, they can regain a measure of control in their lives.

On a more positive note, the Knight of Swords can also personify the rescuer. As the knight in shining armor who dashes off to save the damsel in distress, the Knight of Swords uses his anger constructively to help others. In our lives, there are doctors, lawyers, policemen, firemen, and even plumbers who come to our rescue without a moment's hesitation. There are also those who valiantly try to save the world in their own way, or simply try to save their company from financial ruin. Having an overwhelming need to help others, rescuers are courageous and dependable in times of personal crisis. However, they may also have an unconscious need to rescue themselves. Because they are constantly busy rescuing others, they have little time to attend to their own needs and problems. In this way, they can avoid facing painful issues in their lives while being a hero to others. Like the knight dashing off on his steed, heroic pursuits may disguise our flight from an unknown enemy: self-knowledge.

Like all the other knights in the Tarot, the Knight of Swords wishes to transcend death. This knight seeks immortality by fighting for an important cause that will be remembered after he is gone. By supporting activities much greater than himself, this valiant warrior fights for immortal glory. We can all transcend our limitations by believing in something greater than ourselves. When we attach ourselves to a self-sacrificing ideal (motherhood, caring for the elderly, working for peace, volunteering), we can ascend to greater glory.

In a reading, the Knight of Swords represents a difficult person in our lives. This knight's sharp spurs show he does not mind hurting others in order to get ahead in life. Undoubtedly, we have met people who routinely hurt their friends or family to get what they want. In this case, getting out of their destructive path is probably the best course of action.

The knight also mirrors our inclination to charge off somewhere without thinking. The knight's galloping adventure is like the desperate quest we get caught up in when we are searching for just the right home, a great job, or a perfect spouse. Hurrying to meet some internal deadline, we may quickly pass by the right opportunity. It may be time to slow down and wait for the dream to find us rather then zealously trying to pursue it.

THE QUEEN OF SWORDS: TRANSFORMATION

Great men are they who see that spiritual is stronger than any material force, that thoughts rule the world.

—Ralph Waldo Emerson

The Queen of Swords sits on her elaborately carved throne and quietly surveys her domain. The magical land she commands is the vast territory known as transformation. Both her crown and throne, symbols of her power, are adorned with butterflies. Because caterpillars metamorphosize into butterflies, beautiful butterflies are a universal symbol of transformation and life after death. Although this card does reassure us that we have the power to transform ourselves, it often seems a Herculean task. There is often such a gaping chasm between who we are and who we want to be that we frequently give up in despair. Nevertheless, the path of transformation can be followed if we start from where we are, continue on the right road, and never arrive at a final destination.

The first step in the transformative process is often the most difficult. In order to change, we must first totally accept where we are in the present moment. If we spend most of our time blaming ourselves for our misfortune (we are in debt, overweight, addicted, etc.), then we're just putting more energy into those things we are attempting to change. By withdrawing that negative energy and replacing it with total acceptance of ourselves, we can move forward.

The second step is to recognize any new quality that, like a butterfly breaking free from its cocoon, is trying to emerge. Perhaps we've become more patient or stronger because of the problem we've experienced. By reframing our view of ourselves, we may come to realize that problems are not punishments for our transgressions, but are lessons that we need to learn to further our growth. By treasuring the positive qualities that emerge on our journey of transformation, we can replace self-pity with self-appreciation.

The key to transformation is consistency, which is the third step in the process. Staying on the right road when we are confronted by constant detours can be very difficult. Nevertheless, it is the consistent daily commitment to transformation that will assure victory. When the phrases, "Just do it" or "Just don't do it" become our daily mantra, we can accomplish great things. As we put an X on the calendar at the end of each day to mark our abstinence from some negative activity or the performance of a positive action, we record each small step on our road to transformation. To develop a consistent daily practice takes courage and self-mastery. Like the dour-looking Queen of Swords, we need to become our own stern taskmasters in order to effectively rule over ourselves.

Even after we have accomplished our goal, transformation is never complete. There are always new worlds to conquer. Like a queen ruling over all she surveys, we can objectively observe the inner landscape of the mind to find our next transformative experience. Because swords are associated with thinking, this transformation would most likely include taking classes, learning a new skill, or becoming more organized. Any task that sharpens our intellectual skills will help us to cut through our most vexing problems like a finely sharpened sword cuts through wood.

The traditional meaning for the Queen of Swords is a woman who has greatly suffered due to widowhood or divorce. Beyond this limited meaning, she represents our reaction to suffering in general. In fact, there are many different reactions to suffering including depression, self-pity, anger, stoicism, surrender, and denial. We can choose any one of these forms of coping depending upon our temperament. Because suffering changes us and the way in which we see the world around us, it is very important that we become aware of how we react to the pain we must endure. Becoming conscious of our reaction to suffering will eventually help us transcend it.

In a reading, the Queen of Swords is usually someone who is rational, impersonal, and self-controlled. In other words, she is the epitome of the male model of success. Unfortunately, embracing masculine values does not necessarily lead a woman to happiness. On the contrary, identification with masculine ideals can produce a joyless woman who focuses on the facts without considering others' feelings. The queen is shown in profile to emphasize this one-sided dimension of her personality. Lacking wholeness, she can only make decisions based upon her intellect, rather than incorporating input from her heart. In our lives, we can easily make the same mistake by becoming too dependent upon logic and reasoning. One way to counter this tendency is to always consider the impact of our actions upon others. By being considerate of others' feelings, we will be less likely to rule from reason alone.

THE KING OF SWORDS: RATIONALIZATION

Love rules his kingdom without a sword.

—George Herbert

The King of Swords sits regally upon his throne in a beautiful garden. His sword, tilted to the right, shows his basic alignment with the right side or masculine point of view. He is the ruler of male-oriented attitudes while he shuns feminine values. Emotionally reserved, the king does not express his feelings easily and may see certain feelings as a sign of weakness. There is also a tendency to sanitize experiences of their feeling content in order to cope with unpleasant events.

The King of Swords tightly holds onto his sword of intellect, trying to rationalize the irrational. Like the king wearing his cloak of reasonableness, we often give our unacceptable behavior a convenient cover story of logical explanation in order to hide the real reasons behind our terrible actions. More importantly, a rational explanation provides excellent camouflage for the unconscious impulses that cause us to act so dishonorably. Repressed wishes for revenge on our enemies or for sex with a forbidden lover generate rationalizations as self-serving explanations for corrupt behavior. These unconscious impulses are symbolically carved into the back of the king's throne where he cannot see them. The two crescent moons at the top of the throne point to unconscious desires for the woman located below them, while the butterflies symbolize the libidinal wish to fly from flower to flower. Whenever we have the need to provide an explanation for our actions to ourselves or others, it may be a clue to a rationalization. Carefully examining the actions themselves rather than the reason for our actions can lead us to a better understanding of our wrongdoing.

Another hidden meaning for this card is to be found in the Law of Polarity. The two butterflies and the pair of crescent moons behind the king symbolize the polarization naturally contained in consciousness. Every person with a negative characteristic also carries an opposing positive quality. A greedy person, for example, also has the potential to be charitable, although it may be unexpressed. Like the butterflies on the throne, this Law of Polarity can be used to create constructive change and transformation. We all have negative qualities we would like to change; however, attacking them directly is usually ineffective. Fighting problems of addiction, anxiety, or obesity is difficult because our inner enemy becomes stronger the harder we fight against it. We incessantly think about our seemingly insurmountable problems until we use up all of our available energy.

A better alternative is to consciously cultivate an opposing positive attribute. Once we acknowledge that we have a particular problem, we forget it. Instead of focusing on the problem, we use the Law of Polarity to diligently work on developing an opposing characteristic. For instance, suppose we spend a great deal of time having envious thoughts about our friends and neighbors. When they acquire something we feel we should be entitled to, we become extremely angry. Because the antidote to the poison of envy is gratitude, we decide to develop a grateful attitude every day. As we put more effort into consciously being grateful for everything in our lives, the energy of envy becomes smaller until it is no longer a significant factor. Similarly, feelings of security triumph over anxiety, feelings of hope can defeat depression, feelings of empathy can triumph over anger, and feelings of humility defeat pride. In this way, we can transform destructive attitudes into positive attributes. Just as two kings cannot rule the same kingdom, two polarized attributes cannot reside in our consciousness at the same time. When we consciously cultivate a positive attribute, the corresponding negative quality must leave our minds. Eventually, we may find that the problem that took up so much of our time and energy is no longer an issue. We have learned to effectively rule ourselves.

Unlike the other kings in the Tarot, the King of Swords holds a defensive weapon in his hand. Like the well-armed monarch, we all want to defend our kingdoms, whether it is our workplace or our home. Traditionally, the role of protector was assumed by an authoritarian father figure who guarded his family against outsiders. Today, we may need to ardently defend our personal authority by taking a firm stance against those who would take our power from us. This can be accomplished by taking a stand in the workplace or by disciplining our children at home. The King of Swords personifies rule by force, and we may be required to take aggressive action to maintain order in our kingdom. Although we may have been brought up to relinquish or deny our power, we must learn to utilize our sword of power before it is turned against us.

The King of Swords is also the protector of our most vital asset: our minds. We may need to guard against harmful influences such as well-meaning relatives who constantly undermine our confidence, or television programs that glorify violence. Because swords symbolize communication, we also need to protect ourselves from misinformation, lies, and gossip spread by those around us. The desire to think independently and stay true to our deepest-held beliefs in the face of conflicting information is the secret strength contained in this card.

In a reading, the King of Swords may represent a problematic person in our lives. This person, man or woman, is a petty tyrant who rules by threats and intimidation rather than by love and respect. This may be someone in authority who misuses their power or has a corporate mentality which calculates the bottom line in every relationship.

THE ACE OF WANDS: OPPORTUNITY

To improve the golden moment of opportunity and catch the good that is within our reach, is the great art of life.

—Samuel Johnson

In this card, a magical hand holding a flowering wand suddenly materializes from out of a cloud. The Ace of Wands initiates new ideas and creative energy. Wands are symbolic of the invisible energy that fuels our world and psyches. It is the unseen energy that causes plants to blossom, sparks the creativity that inspires the artist, creates the boundless enthusiasm that propels us to start a new project, and provides the vision to see a better future. It has been called the Muse, intuition, or divine intervention. The mystic seeks it in a vision, the artist in a blank canvas. We firmly believe that this elusive energy emanates from within ourselves, but we are only a humble receptacle for it. This otherworldly energy works through us, providing the impetus for change.

The Ace of Wands illustrates that we cannot contact this sublime energy; it must contact us. The energy appears abruptly, like a mysterious hand suddenly appearing from nowhere. When this intense energy comes to us from out of the blue, we must be prepared to follow our inspiration wherever it leads us. Sometimes this requires us to give up previous notions of what we want in favor of what it wants from us. We may have to change the direction of our lives or move to a different location, even though it may not make any sense to us. However, by being the faithful servants of intuition, we will always arrive at the right time and place.

The conventional way for spiritual energy to manifest in our lives is through opportunity. Whether it is travel, relocation, starting a new business, or pursuing a degree, we must seize the golden opportunities that present themselves. Because magical apparitions like the one pictured on the Ace of Wands tend to disappear quickly, it is important to take decisive action before our window of opportunity closes. Just as the delicate shape of a cloud can suddenly dissipate with a gust of wind, our enthusiasm can also prove transitory. If we fail to follow through while we still possess the necessary enthusiasm, the fleeting opportunity will be missed. Like a wand tightly grasped, we must seize opportunities before they get away.

Where there is opportunity, there are also obstacles. In the background of the Ace of Wands is a beautiful castle situated on a grassy knoll. This castle represents a wonderful opportunity to fulfill our dreams, but to get to the castle we will have to cross the serpentine river below. The river, like many other formidable obstacles in life, stands directly in our way. While it is not possible to circumvent most of the obstacles that stand in the way of our fulfillment, we can learn to view them as helpful assistants rather than hurtful barriers. Initially, when we are confronted by an obstacle to our progress, we see it as a negative, external blockage which needs to be removed as quickly as possible. When the car breaks down, the money we needed to start a business disappears, or we fail to get a scholarship, it seems like the end of the world. Furthermore, we wholeheartedly believe that the apparent obstacle is an enemy that must be defeated before we can make any progress.

A better approach is to view the obstacle as a growth opportunity. The wands in the Tarot are budding branches alive with new growth. Similarly, every obstacle contains the potential for growth, if we understand its purpose. Obstacles contain meaningful information about ourselves, because they are a projection of our internal beliefs. For example, if the obstacle is an obstinate person who always blocks our progress, the person may symbolize our parents' negative attitude, which we have unconsciously internalized. When we realize that our parents' disapproval is actually our own, the person blocking our path will suddenly relinquish his position. Obstacles are usually projections of our own misgivings or fears that we must confront in order to make progress. If we feel we are unworthy of success, a roadblock will appear on our path to personal achievement. It is only when we contact the limiting beliefs within us that we can circumvent the obstacles outside ourselves.

The Ace of Wands also symbolizes the inherent ability to realize our full potential. Just as a seed contains the hidden potential necessary for the future growth of a plant, we all have sparks of energy within us that direct us toward the person we are destined to become. We can often get in touch with our latent potential through fantasy or daydreaming. Our reveries are an important source of creativity because, by playing with ideas, we can discover a world of possibilities. Then it is only a matter of time until we can realize the undiscovered potentials hidden within our imagination.

In divination, this card's advice is to heed the voice of intuition. Whether it is a shout of encouragement or a whispered warning, we need to follow our inner advisor. Because this card also represents the element of fire, it could be a valid warning that we are playing with fire. A new love that sparks our interest may unintentionally set fire to the life we have established. While intuition tries to encompass the greatest possibilities, it can also be blind to its own intrinsic dangers. We may need to prioritize our activities so we can use our energy wisely. Having too many ideas or projects can quickly deplete our inner resources.

Lastly, we need to find something to be enthusiastic about. Enthusiasm has been called the engine of life because it provides the impetus to get us started and the energy needed to keep going. Sometimes all we really need in life is to have something that captures our intense interest. By following our enthusiasm and doing what we love, we can cure many of life's miseries.

THE TWO OF WANDS: OBJECTIVITY

The world in which a man lives shapes itself chiefly by the way in which he looks at it.

—Arthur Schopenhauer

    A nobleman stands on a castle's battlement high above a beautiful harbor. The small globe he holds in his hand symbolizes our current understanding of the world. In the modern world-view, matter and mind are fundamentally different. The mind is an interior space that defines our sense of self, whereas the material world we inhabit is an exterior space governed by mechanistic laws. Like the nobleman pictured, we believe the mind to be a self-contained entity gazing out upon a world that is fundamentally separate from us. To hold the world in one's hand is to illustrate a belief in the eternal duality between consciousness and matter, between subject and object. As long as we see ourselves divorced from the world around us, we will feel alienated from nature and isolated from our fellow human beings. However, the synchronicities provided by a Tarot reading can bridge this gap between matter and mind. When we see our personal experiences accurately reflected in the cards, there is an immediate connection between our thoughts and the world around us. These meaningful coincidences teach us that there is a fundamental unity between psyche and matter. In this way, Tarot readings can change our consciousness as we feel intimately connected to the world around us.

    The Two of Wands also represents our Weltanschauung or world-view. As the nobleman gazes at the world, he forms a philosophy of the world and his place in it. Our outlook on the world around us is one of most important yet overlooked belief systems, for how we view the world can determine our destiny. For example, if we believe the essential nature of the world is nurturing, then we will perceive ourselves as fortunate and believe good things will always happen to us. On the other hand, those who have had many painful experiences may view the world as a malevolent place where brute force is essential for survival. If we see the world as essentially controllable, we may feel very safe. However, if we see only chaos around us, we will constantly feel threatened by the unpredictability of events. If we view our existence as essentially meaningless, then we will probably try to find what little pleasure we can without any thought to moral consequences. When we view life as an experience imbued with spiritual meaning, we can find great satisfaction in even the most trivial tasks. Clearly, our outlook on the world can affect our health, happiness, and our relationships with others. In order to make progress in these important areas, we may need to challenge the basic assumptions we have about the world.

Like the nobleman holding his globe, we usually tightly hold onto our world outlook. In fact, we may spend our entire lives searching for experiences that validate our world-view: gamblers gamble because they believe life is based upon luck, while soldiers go to war because they believe in a deadly enemy. Furthermore, we often unconsciously censor the truth if we feel it threatens our established viewpoint. Like a nobleman defending his castle, we are quick to dismiss any idea that threatens our conceptual system. As we grow older, there is also a tendency to become overly attached to our viewpoint, just as one of the wands is firmly attached to the castle's stone wall. In order to change our view of reality, we first have to recognize that there are alternate ways of looking at events rather than the habitual way in which we have viewed them in the past. Then, we must understand that conflicting viewpoints do not necessarily threaten our way of seeing things. It is possible to integrate others' beliefs without negating what we already believe. Repeating the affirmation, "I can assimilate new experiences in life without threatening those things which are important to me," can help us change the vantage point from which we view the world.

The nobleman in this card represents our ability to objectively observe our behavior in order to better understand ourselves. By holding the world in our hands and looking down upon it, we automatically become objective observers. To have a totally objective viewpoint is to see our lives dispassionately without interjecting our thoughts or feelings into the situations in which we find ourselves.

This important concept of the observing self who can gain a better perspective on life is the key to spiritual growth and peace of mind. When we can develop the detachment necessary to objectively view our lives without judgment or regret, we can become truly noble.

In a reading, this card signals a return to a secure place, just as a ship returns to a safe harbor. Moving back with our parents or returning to the safe haven of work can give us a feeling of greater security. However, we can overemphasize safety to such a great extent that we fail to venture out of our enclosed environment. Some risk is necessary, for as the ancient proverb dictates, "A ship in a harbor is always safe, but that is not what a ship was built for." This card also reflects our tendency to constantly look to the outer world for answers to our problems instead of using introspection to discover the solutions that lie within ourselves.

THE THREE OF WANDS: VISION

The eye seems to demand a horizon. We are never unhappy as long as we can see far enough.

—Ralph Waldo Emerson

A robed figure stands on a bluff overlooking the sea while three ships sail into the sunset. Setting forth on a voyage of self-discovery, these three ships symbolize the exploration of our desires, fears, and needs. While on this voyage, we will be driven by the wind of intellect and carried by the waters of emotion to a destination we may never reach. Like a ship in pursuit of the endless horizon, the closer we get to our destination, the farther it will recede. This voyage of self-discovery is never complete because we must traverse the vast sea of the unconscious. Just as the man on the hill courageously faces the immense ocean before him, we must be prepared to face the vastness of our unconscious. Like good sailors, we will need to work with the inner tides of emotion if we are to set forth on our inner journey.

To begin any journey requires vision. The figure on the hilltop looks far out to sea, beyond the horizon. The ability to see beyond our present circumstances into a distant future is essential for our growth. Just as early explorers envisioned a wondrous destination before they ever set sail, we need to set our sights on a far-off goal. By imagining our ultimate destination, we can successfully chart our course into the unknown. Even though we may have no idea what lies ahead, we can have faith in ourselves and our singular vision. Even if we fail to reach our original destination, we cannot fail to discover the belief we have in ourselves.

If we look at this card from another perspective, it also symbolizes abandonment. In this case, we see the ships sailing away, leaving the man alone and deserted on the shore. There is often no greater threat in life than abandonment, for to be left alone to struggle with life's burdens is very frightening. Spouses die, children leave home, and friends unexpectedly move far away, leaving us behind. The ships have set sail without us and, suddenly, there is a terrible distance between our loved ones and ourselves. Even the remote possibility of being abandoned can, in some people, trigger separation anxiety. They need constant reassurance from their partner that they will not leave. Those of us who have lost family members early in life can easily become angry or depressed when their partner leaves for a business trip, fearing they will never return. Fears of abandonment also lie at the heart of our erroneous expectation that the people closest to us will always leave one way or another. Tragically, without faith in someone else's commitment, we may be reluctant to invest our energy in caring for anyone. Although we can view our life as a series of abandonment episodes, it is best to focus on the happiness the relationships brought us rather than their fateful conclusion.

There is also a basic conflict reflected in this card's foreground and background. The man situated on the hill stays on the land while the ships travel far out to sea. While we all fervently wish to move forward with our lives, there is always a part of us that wants us to stay where we are. In other words, we cannot cross the sea by staring at the water. This natural reluctance on our part can be traced back to a time in our childhood when we were trying to establish our own separate identity. Like the departing ships, a child's pursuit of personal development is the ability to gradually move away from his parents, psychologically and then physically. The ambivalence we feel when we leave a situation or venture forth into a new project often originates in this critical stage of childhood development. We may need to contact our inner child and reassure them that they will continue to be safe in the new circumstances we have chosen.

Not only does the man pictured on the Three of Wands fail to leave, he also fails to act. The man's inactive stance reflects his passivity as he fails to utilize his wands. Instead of venturing forth or completing his tasks, he chooses to do nothing. In our lives, this may manifest as a stubborn refusal to do what is expected of us. Like the man standing alone, we may take an inflexible stance against the demands of authority figures. Because we resent being told what to do, we naturally become very angry. However, we may also fear reprisals for expressing our anger, so we use passive-aggression to effectively avoid the demands of others. For example, we conveniently forget to perform some task, or we procrastinate until the task is forgotten. If we finally perform the work we've been given, it is usually done with a minimum of effort and a maximum of complaint. Other symptoms of passive-aggressive behavior are being constantly late and failing to return phone calls. In all these ways, we seek to communicate our displeasure while avoiding confrontation. Unfortunately, these tactics are not very effective and usually lead to rejection. A better alternative is to constructively express our anger without resorting to avoidance behaviors.

In a reading, there are various interpretations for this card. Because the figure on the card has literally missed the boat, there will be missed opportunities in our future. This card can also reflect our vicarious nature. When we watch from the shoreline as friends and family sail forth to pursue their destinies, we are living vicariously. We must be careful not to live through others, because our partner's achievements and knowledge can easily replace our own development. While we can certainly applaud others' accomplishments, we need to remind ourselves that no one can sail our ship for us.

THE FOUR OF WANDS: SECURITY

He that is too secure is not safe.

—Thomas Fuller

This is a celebratory scene heralding the coming of spring. Like the Greek goddess Persephone, who was only allowed to leave her imprisonment in Hades in the springtime, the two women pictured have finally come out of their dark castle into the brilliant sunshine. The Four of Wands shows our emergence from winter's confinement into the warm, welcoming embrace of spring. Springtime always awakens the possibility of self-renewal. If we have recently experienced dark days resulting from loss or separation, we can make a new start. No matter how dismal our circumstances, we can envision every day as a unique opportunity for a new beginning.

In this card, there are two contrasting architectural elements: the formidable castle in the background and the delicate arbor formed by the four standing wands in the foreground. While the castle is impenetrable, the arbor offers little protection from either the elements or attack. Like the women who are poised between a fortress and a leafy shelter, we are constantly vacillating between security and risk. When we depart for college or marriage, we leave the security of our family to pursue the risky business of independence. When we embark on a new career or move to a new city, we leave the security of the known for the unknown. Nevertheless, on all these new adventures we can bring along an inner sense of security, for security is not found in a particular place or in another person; it is in ourselves.

Sometimes on our journey toward independence, we can become temporarily lost. This happens when we believe in a secure future and permanent order to life, but are surprised to find neither in our world. Like being ejected from a castle, we have suddenly lost the framework that gave us a solid structure to our lives. Divorce, unemployment, or life-threatening illnesses are just a few of the many situations that cause instant insecurity and make us lose faith in ourselves.

However, this card reflects our hope that whatever happens to us is always for the best. The four vertical wands, although offering less protection than a fortified castle, are beautifully decorated with colorful flowers and festive ribbons to celebrate the possibilities that lie ahead. Just as the wands are in the foreground of the card, we need to constantly keep the possibility of a better future in the forefront of our consciousness. When we create an optimistic outlook, we realize that we can move beyond the confinement of our inner castle into an unrestricted place of openness and freedom. Like the unenclosed structure of the wands, we can obtain a state of mind in which we can keep all of our options open.

The two structures on the card also reflect those things that are either temporary or permanent in our lives. While the impenetrable castle of stone will withstand the ravages of time, the flowering arbor can quickly be destroyed by a strong wind. It is our task in life to choose between the important things that are enduring and the things that are impermanent. Fleeting pleasure and passionate emotions may offer us a temporary dwelling place, but commitment and spirituality will give us a more secure refuge. Blind faith and romance may seem eternal, but in reality may prove transitory. We must judge whether our new partner will be strong enough to endure future hardships or will leave at the first sign of a problem. On the other hand, the family and friends this card celebrates are always permanent fixtures in our lives, although we may have temporary problems with them. When we can fully distinguish between the important and the unimportant, the lasting and the fleeting, we will have gained great wisdom.

The castle and the arbor also reflect those parts of ourselves that can be changed, and those that cannot be altered. Castles are permanent structures, while arbors can be easily changed or dismantled. Likewise, if we wish to change some aspect of ourselves, we need to know which parts are resistant to change and which parts can be easily modified. This is vitally important, because many of us spend our entire lives trying to change an immutable aspect of our personalities or bodies. Genetics, biology, and social conditioning, once thought of as our unalterable destiny, have proven more changeable in recent times. Still, qualities such as intelligence or sexual orientation seem to be firmly etched into the stone of our being. Any attempt at self-improvement should be undertaken with the caveat that certain parts of us are not alterable.

Something we can change is our mood, but this also depends upon whether we view a situation as either temporary or permanent. We can either tell ourselves that we are in a hopeless situation that will never improve, or that tomorrow things will get better. If we lose money in the stock market, we can either blame ourselves for being stupid (something we may view as a permanent condition), or we can blame a falling stock market (something temporary which will improve with time). Accurately assessing whether a situation is permanent or temporary can put us in either a pessimistic or optimistic mood. Just as the women rejoice upon entering their temporary dwelling, our belief in the temporary nature of misfortune can create a joyful place in our hearts.

In divination, the Four of Wands shows us that a good friendship, like a strong building, is supportive. The two women pictured support each other's goals and dreams. They stand side by side celebrating each other's achievements. Although we dearly love our friends, we often have a love/hate relationship with them. This is because our friends represent the shadow or undeveloped side of our personality. Our friends can do those things that, for one reason or another, we cannot do. So, we wind up envying the friend who is talented, graceful, or spontaneous. Their negative qualities fascinate us as well, as we find friends who are always expressing their anger or their passion. Although they may be well-hidden, we too have these qualities. When we realize that our friends are mirrors of our shadow side, we can unconditionally accept and support our friends.

The arbor, as the most prominent feature in this card, is central to its meaning. As a very simple structure, the arbor sends us a message to simplify our lives. When life becomes too complicated and hectic, there is little time for self-development or spiritual reflection. By removing many of the extraneous activities from our lives, we can give ourselves the space to renew our love affair with life.

THE FIVE OF WANDS: CONFLICT

Have the courage to act instead of react.

—Earlene Larson Jenks

In this card, five young men wage a gallant battle by brandishing upraised wands. Their conflict is eternal, for it symbolizes all the internal conflicts that have plagued mankind through the ages. An internal conflict arises when two or more contradictory desires oppose each other in a person's mind. An inner battle ensues in which conflicting passions fight each other for control of our behavior. Unfortunately, in this inner conflict, the victor and the vanquished are one and the same: ourselves. When we make a conscious decision to choose one desire over another, we win and lose at the same time. A part of us must go unsatisfied so that we may reach our long-term goal, and that part will remain unhappy as long as its desires are not being met. For example, suppose we want to stop eating chocolate cake in order to lose weight. The nature of the internal conflict is that although we want both the cake and the weight loss, it is impossible to have both. Like a battle, there can be no compromise, only victory or defeat. If we choose the cake, our taste buds will be satisfied, but we may lose our positive self-image. This is the classic win/lose situation in which we get what we want, but have to forfeit an important part of ourselves in order to obtain it.

Another conflict scenario is the lose/lose situation, also known as choosing the lesser of two evils. The youths engaged in mock combat are a perfect example of this no-win predicament because their actions are a type of warfare. In war, no matter how glorious the victory, everyone loses. We have all sustained losses from our conflicts with others because not all wars take place in distant battlefields. On the home front, children become casualties of divorce wars, and unemployment results from corporate battles.

When antagonism escalates into harmful action, someone is going to get hurt. Whether we are playing war games in the home or in the office, we must realize the potential consequences of our actions. The urgent message of this card is that we should choose our battles wisely because conflict is not worth the enormous cost to ourselves and others.

Like the five combatants pictured, there are five parts of ourselves that are in constant conflict with each other: the body, the mind, the heart, the spirit, and the memory. The body wants its desires satisfied immediately, regardless of the consequences. Biological desires for food, water, sex, or sleep, if deprived, will loom in our consciousness until they are fulfilled. The mind's desires may also go largely unsatisfied because we desire logic in an illogical world. Our hearts want the emotional fulfillment of love, hate, compassion, or anger. The spirit deep within us wants to learn from our earthbound existence so it can grow. Lastly, our memory desires that we act solely upon the basis of our previous experience.

Each of these warring factions within us wants to annihilate the others so it can have complete control over our behavior. For example, we want to start an exercise program. Our body wants to rest, our mind knows that exercise is beneficial, our heart doesn't feel any great passion for exercise, our spirit wants to experience exertion, and our memory relives the pain of the pulled muscle, which occurred when we last attempted to work out. The countless decisions we make each day are controlled by one or more of these battling parts of ourselves. There have always been classic battles between the heart and the mind or the body and the spirit that each individual has had to quietly endure. Nevertheless, the inner struggle between the best and worst within us only makes us stronger. The interior battle each day between warring parts of our personalities must be waged not to win, but rather to understand ourselves. These inner conflicts force us to focus on what is most important in our lives so we can prioritize our activities. If health is a priority, then the opposing factions of our personalities will have to support our new exercise program. By confronting our inner objections and then prioritizing our goals, we learn about ourselves so we can emerge victorious.

Inner conflicts can usually be resolved by consciously sacrificing our desires for a higher purpose. If it is necessary to give up a basic desire (food, sex, money, status), we will sacrifice it gladly if doing so will satisfy a higher ideal. Some of these noble ideals are marriage, moral virtue, justice, self-respect, or our children's happiness. For example, our conflicting desires for rest and money are easily resolved when we realize that working double shifts will allow us to buy Christmas presents for our children. When we keep our ideals uppermost in our minds, we can transcend many desires and resolve most of our conflicts. When we are wedded to an ideal, conflicting suitors are quickly rejected.

Another theme present in this card is reaction. The young men in combat must quickly react in order to fend off each other's swift blows. In the battle of life, we are constantly responding to other people's actions. When our family or friends "push our buttons," we automatically react by bursting into tears, going into a rage, or becoming depressed. However, the wise person within us would say that our response is much more important than the event which triggered it. By focusing on our response instead of the instigative person, we can stop our negative reaction. In this way, we consciously choose to act rather than react to others' actions. Furthermore, when we stop getting caught up in incitement and decide not to react to it, very often the people around us will cease to react as well. The end result is usually a more harmonious environment for all concerned.

In divination, this card represents some type of competition. The most common competition is sibling rivalry in which each child competes for its parents' attention. There is also unrecognized competition between mothers and daughters or fathers and sons as each tries to be more successful than their rival. When we habitually view another family member as a domestic rival, it forces us to constantly prove ourselves as adults. This is very much like the young men trying to prove their skills on the battlefield. There can also be professional rivalries that can poison the workplace and create an atmosphere of distrust. While competition can fuel the marketplace, it can be very destructive in interpersonal relationships. If we are very competitive by nature, it is preferable to focus our competitive instincts wholly on ourselves. By competing with ourselves and constantly striving to better our performance, we can only succeed.

THE SIX OF WANDS: APPROVAL

The real merit is not in the success but in the endeavor; and win or lose, he will be honored and crowned.

—William Morley Punshon

In this card, the conquering hero arrives on horseback to be warmly welcomed home and applauded for his wartime exploits. He is the personification of success as he triumphantly parades past the jubilant crowd. Of course, everyone defines success differently because there are societal as well as personal standards that constitute success. Most of us see success in terms of fame and fortune, and so we fail to feel successful in life when we fail to achieve the wealth and adulation which we feel should be rightly ours. Even if we do achieve worldly success, it will not magically eliminate all of our problems. Superficial success, like the horse's voluminous blanket, may cover over our inner conflicts temporarily, but cannot hide our problems indefinitely. At some point, even the most successful people realize that their achievements cannot guarantee happiness. External success, like the wreath held atop the warrior's wand, is a hollow victory.

When we view success as an inner state instead of an outer reward, we have a better understanding of the true nature of achievement. True success can be measured by our personal triumph over addiction, anger, fear, rejection, or any number of negative states that have controlled our lives. Our private victories will probably go largely unnoticed by others, but are nonetheless, very rewarding. We can also define success as cultivating positive behavior. Attaining inner peace, tolerance, and compassion are major achievements that should be applauded. Developing masculine or feminine virtues is another hallmark of success. For men, these include courage, loyalty, and devotion to duty. Women's virtues are very dissimilar, although no less important, and include connection, cooperation, and nurturing. These six virtues, like the six wands pictured, can be developed by either sex to achieve a truly successful life.

There are also six false virtues of modern life, which we pursue at our own peril: wealth, beauty, celebrity, competition, freedom, and acceleration. When we define success as the acquisition of any of these so-called virtues, our success will be an illusion. We soon come to realize that the attainment of wealth cannot increase our self-worth; becoming beautiful will not raise our self-esteem; celebrity cannot replace the need to applaud ourselves; winning a competition does not make us better than everyone else; freedom does not release us from our obligation to help others; and accelerating the pace of our lives means we do things faster, not better. Focusing our attention exclusively on these false gods of the modern era will usually bring ruin rather than success.

Most of these false virtues are based upon the need for approval. Just as the returning hero relishes the approval of the crowd, our lives are spent in the pursuit of admiration. When we've invested most of our energy in achieving socially sanctioned goals, we need other people to recognize our success and assure us of the validity of those goals. Hence, we desire other people's admiration or envy to reinforce our inflated view of ourselves. Ultimately, our entire self-image may depend upon what others think about us. When we see ourselves through the reflected approval of others, we view a distorted picture. External validation can never be a substitute for self-esteem, no matter how successful we become.

Like the self-important rider in the Six of Wands, our need for approval can lead to excessive pride and a preoccupation with status. We may have a need to feel special because we have achieved more, suffered more, or risked more than others. Like the man on horseback looking down at the crowd below, we may secretly feel superior to those who we see as more ordinary. This desire for status can result from a childhood in which we received love from our parents only when we excelled in some activity. This conditional love created a belief that we have to constantly earn the love we want. Just as the crowd only loves the hero after his great victory, we may feel the need for constant accomplishment in order to love ourselves. Instead, we should believe in our inherent self-worth, regardless of our success or failure.

This card also encourages self-improvement. While the Five of Wands shows disharmony and competition amongst the various parts of the personality, the Six of Wands shows all the different elements united against a common enemy. Self-improvement is a form of inner warfare in which we must rally the divergent parts of ourselves to defeat the bad habits, addictions, or compulsive behaviors that control our lives like an invading army. We must all become conquering heroes, because the goal of self-improvement is self-conquest.

Because this is a scene of approval conferred by a group, it also depicts the importance of collective values. In a reading, this card symbolizes a conditional relationship in which one person must go along with prescribed behavior in order to receive love and approval from others. Any deviation from the rules usually results in immediate rejection. However, we usually go along with the group dynamic so we can gain acceptance or keep our jobs. In this card, we could be one of the many followers, following a particular religion, political candidate, or business leader. However, if we are going to play follow the leader, we must make certain that we are being led in the right direction.

THE SEVEN OF WANDS: RESISTANCE

May God defend me from myself.

—Michel Montaigne

In this card, an angry man uses his wand to protect himself from the approaching enemies looming far below. He has taken up a defensive position in which he must protect his territory from an unknown threat. We can also become very territorial if we perceive ourselves or our family to be in jeopardy. Of course, the threats we experience are more likely to be to our self-esteem or reputation than to our physical bodies. Nonetheless, these threats are perceived to be just as real as physical danger, so our reactions to them are immediate. The most frequent reaction to any type of threat is fierce anger. When we perceive a psychological threat to our well-being, we become very defensive and angry in an attempt to protect ourselves from further injury. Anger can also be a response to feelings of powerlessness. Becoming infuriated can create a false sense of power that, like a defensive wand, we can hold onto momentarily. Furthermore, underneath our bravado, we fear that the anger we experience is actually a defensive reaction to our fear of being unworthy. We interpret the bad treatment we have received from others as confirmation of our own feelings of unworthiness. It is only by feeling worthy of others' respect that we can finally release our anger and take a less defensive stance.

We also use our anger to purposely distance ourselves from others. Just as the man uses his wand to warn his assailants not to come any closer, we can use our anger as a defensive weapon to purposely push people away from us. This stems from an underlying fear of being emotionally hurt from someone close to us. A resistance to emotional attachment is also a common defense against the expectation of abandonment. Unfortunately, when we project our worst fears about a loving relationship into an unknown future (we will be hurt, abandoned, or rejected), we never give the relationship a fighting chance. Instead of letting down our defenses, we become angry and verbally lash out at the other person. In response, our partner backs away, leaving us depressed until we repeat the same performance the next time. This vicious cycle never reaches the source of our anger, nor does it quiet our underlying fears. The only way to change this angry behavior is to let down our defenses and trust that no harm will come to us if we allow ourselves to become vulnerable.

Psychologically, this card also symbolizes repression. Like the warrior who offers armed resistance against anyone who would attack him from below, our mind tries to keep unacceptable feelings or memories from surfacing from the depths of the unconscious. Freud theorized that repression was a mechanism designed to keep unacceptable thoughts a safe distance from conscious awareness, and this is very similar to the way in which the warrior warns his enemies to keep a safe distance from him. This common defense mechanism keeps us from confronting the hidden desires and motivations that, if brought into consciousness, would threaten the positive image we have of ourselves. Our selective memory often erases terrible misdeeds in our past because our previous behavior does not favorably align with our present self-concept. A great deal of energy is expended to keep these terrible memories and feelings at bay because of the serious threat they pose. However, the great paradox contained in this card is that we are actually most threatened by what we have repressed. Repressed emotions often build up to a point at which, when they are finally released, they can become very volatile or even self-destructive. It is only by accepting our unacceptable impulses that we can hope to conquer them.

Resistance can also be a conscious process when we purposely choose to refrain from engaging in a harmful activity. We can heroically resist temptation by taking a firm stand against anything that has the potential to harm us. Like a warrior defending his position, we need to take the high ground morally in order to repel the enemy of temptation. Resistance to change is another conscious decision that certainly has an impact on our lives. Sometimes, change descends upon us like a conquering army that threatens to take us prisoner. Whether it is the change of menopause or changes in the workplace, most of us dislike having to adapt to new circumstances. So, we try to resist the new changes as long as possible by defending the status quo. When this fails and change threatens to overwhelm us, we should realize that our battle against change is with ourselves, not with the world. Patience and understanding are twin allies that help us cope with the inevitable changes that surround us. If we can assist change rather than resist it, we can win the battle.

Change is only one of the many opposing forces we must face during our lives. Criticism from family and friends produces an almost palpable force that we must constantly fight against. When well-meaning friends tell us the reasons why they think we will fail, or family members actively oppose the life changes we have in mind, we need to properly understand the value of their opposition. Criticism can actually be a very positive force and should not be viewed as a personal attack. Opposition from others tests our commitment to change and strengthens our resolve to succeed. The resistance that we so often condemn can help us develop inner strength. Like weight training, we may find that when greater resistance is applied, we become stronger. Opposition produces determination and, therefore, is a necessary step toward achieving our goals.

When the Seven of Wands appears in a reading, it is important to identify exactly what is threatening us. Our intense ambition might threaten our personal relationships, a friend may threaten our marriage, or a recession may threaten our financial future. Identifying a threat is the first step in dealing with it. Then we must confront the threatening situation instead of avoiding it or hoping it will magically disappear. If we can find the psychological courage to face our fears, we can quickly conquer anything that threatens us.

This card also reflects the difficulty we have in setting boundaries. The man's defensive stance immediately conveys to his enemies that they must keep their distance and proceed no further. When we set boundaries, we tell others that certain behavior cannot be tolerated and that our privacy cannot be invaded. By setting clear boundaries with others, we can protect ourselves from intrusive behavior and protect our most important territory: peace of mind.

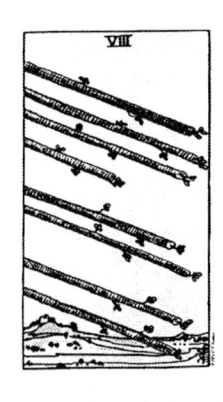

THE EIGHT OF WANDS: GOALS

Aim at the sun, and you may not reach it, but your arrow will fly far higher than if aimed at an object on a level with yourself.

—Joel Hawes

The Eight of Wands shows several wands flying over a pastoral landscape. An unknown archer seems to have shot his arrows toward a distant target. These swift-traveling wands resemble our intuition, which, like a revelation, comes all at once into our minds. Brilliant ideas or divinations, coming from an unknown source, suddenly appear from nowhere, hitting us with their power. Intuition, as well as the Tarot readings which depend upon it, can either hit or miss its target of reality. Readings can be totally on target by accurately revealing the future, or can be way off target. Even if our intuition should prove inaccurate from time to time, we still need to trust our intuition and stay open to any divine guidance that suddenly appears.

Depending on our point of view, the wands on this card are either headed in an upward trajectory or directed on a downward course. This is the essence of an either optimistic or pessimistic outlook in life. Like the eight wands set in motion, our belief in either the best or worst possible outcome will determine the direction our lives will take. Those who are optimistic see adversity as fleeting, just like the wands quickly passing through the air. This positive attitude gives them the constant reassurance that, even though they may be experiencing problems, they are headed in the right direction. On the other hand, pessimists view problems as permanent roadblocks to their goals, so they become trapped in feelings of helplessness and futility. Wands symbolize the way in which we use energy. Those who are optimistic use their energy to propel themselves into a better future, while pessimists waste their energy in self-pity.

The wands eternally traveling toward their target are reminiscent of all the goals we are constantly moving toward. Goals have the power to give a clear direction and meaning to our lives. In fact, goals are a form of prophecy, as they provide us with a clear picture of our future in advance. Setting goals provides us with a road map of our journey, but there are a few simple rules that may guide us along the way. It is best to begin by choosing a realistic goal. Achieving even an insignificant goal enhances our self-esteem and gives us the confidence to work toward bigger achievements. Once we've set our goal, we need to break it down into small, manageable steps that can be accomplished within a relatively short period of time. Success is to be found, not in the attainment of the final goal, but in the successful completion of each step along the way. Each step is a short-term goal in itself which, when completed, can be considered a great achievement.

Along with short-term goals, there are also medium- and long-range goals symbolized by the three groups of wands on the card. As the two lowest wands will come to earth first, they should be considered short-term goals we can attain almost immediately. For example, a mature woman who wishes to return to college orders a college catalog as her first goal. Medium-range goals require more effort but are, nonetheless, important stepping-stones toward fulfillment. In the case of the returning student, her medium-range goal would be to arrange financing for her education. Medium-range goals are symbolized by the middle group of wands, which come to rest later. Long-range goals, represented by the largest group of four wands, are usually measured in years. They are created by visualizing where we will be in the not too distant future, such as when the student visualizes her goal of graduating from college. When we have finally achieved our long-range goal, we can look back to review all the small details which contributed to making our dreams manifest.

While setting goals can be a useful mental exercise, we really need to put our goals into practice if we are going to succeed. It is very helpful to write out a list of short-, medium-, and long-term goals. This list can be reviewed daily, and goals that have been completed can be crossed off our ambitious list of things to do. Every time we accomplish a goal that we've set for ourselves, whether large or small, we need to immediately reward ourselves in some way. Whether this is an ice cream cone or a trip to Europe, rewards create positive reinforcement that keeps us moving forward. Positive self-talk can also sustain our momentum during the long journey toward achievement. Telling ourselves daily that we deserve happiness or that we are worthy of success builds self-confidence in our abilities. Affirming that we have all the time, energy, enthusiasm, and resources to accomplish our goal opens a doorway into a fabulous future.

While we are busy striving toward our self-directed goals, we are unable to see the ultimate goal: our life's purpose. All the seemingly disconnected events in our lives direct us toward our ultimate purpose here on earth. That task may be to give birth to a child, create a work of art, or save someone's life, but our destiny is not revealed to us. Nevertheless, we can be sure that, like the wands hurtling through the air toward their destination, we are always headed toward a divinely specified purpose in life. We are not pushed toward this ultimate goal by circumstance, but rather are inevitably drawn toward our destiny by unseen forces. Seen in this way, we are pulled toward our inexorable destiny very much like the eight wands are pulled to the earth by the force of gravity. Our purpose in life creates an invisible pathway that we must follow to meet our fate.

In a reading, the Eight of Wands signifies constant motion as the wands eternally fly through the air. Motion creates time, and we may find ourselves constantly in a hurry, trying to cope with increasing time pressures. There may be a great sense of urgency in meeting business deadlines or conceiving a child. As we approach the landmark years of thirty, forty, or fifty, these pressures to achieve can become all-consuming. The advice contained in this card is to act quickly before time runs out.

There is also a hidden warning in the wand's accelerating momentum. We must be very careful in choosing the particular journey we embark upon because we may not be able to accurately foresee our final destination. Drug addiction or a life of crime often starts out innocently as small deviations from the straight path but ends up in tragedy. We can easily get caught up in the momentum of corruption and suddenly find ourselves in a strange land far from home.

THE NINE OF WANDS: VIGILANCE

That which does not kill me makes me stronger.

—Johann Wolfgang von Goethe

In this scene, a warrior defensively clutches his wand while watching for the enemy's approach. There is a wariness in his gaze, as if he expects to be attacked at any moment. The reason for this aroused watchfulness is to be found in the bandage covering his recent head wound. When we have been hurt in the past, either physically or emotionally, we naturally develop an instinctive distrust of others. Self-preservation forces us to become suspicious of other people's motives, particularly when we wish to avoid being hurt again. The man pictured is obviously a survivor, and survival often depends upon a healthy distrust of other people. It is said that "nature favors the nervous," and we can hardly ignore the natural nervousness learned through hundreds of millennia of man's evolution. Vigilance is just as important to the survival of modern man as it was to our ancestors living in the Stone Age. Those who are vigilant are very cautious and reserved in all their interactions until they are certain that others are worthy of their trust. They are easily threatened, believing some possible harm will descend upon them in the near future. Therefore, they are constantly on guard against potential harm to themselves or their loved ones. By anticipating a future attack, they can adequately prepare for the assault or even prevent its occurrence.

Of course, distrust can quickly turn into a paranoid state of mind in which everyone is seen as a potential enemy and every encounter is a potential battle. People who are paranoid view themselves as part of a very hostile world where bad things happen despite all the precautions taken. Expecting to be exploited or harmed by others, they constantly question the trustworthiness of friends and family. They typically overreact to the smallest slight and believe other people are constantly talking about them behind their backs. All these defensive behaviors prevent them from developing intimate relationships. Because they fear another person will exploit their weaknesses, they never let down their guard to reveal their true selves to others. Trust, if developed at all, is usually predicated upon the other party passing some sort of test to prove their loyalty. Although we may have difficulty understanding the paranoid person, we have all, at one time or another, felt overly suspicious about a particular person or project. Sometimes our suspicions are confirmed, while at other times we may feel foolish for suspecting an innocent person. Whether our fears are realistic or exaggerated, we need to respect them, for as Sigmund Freud once said, "Even paranoids have enemies."

For most of us, the suspicion and distrust we sometimes feel stems from our essential woundedness. Like a flowering wand, woundedness has roots in the past that cause repercussions in the future. The warrior on the card has sustained a head wound, which has not entirely healed. Past traumas can be like unhealed wounds causing constant psychic pain. We may try to cover over the wound with a bandage of frantic activity, denial or addiction, but it remains an open sore nonetheless. Only by exposing this terrible wound to the light of consciousness and re-experiencing the pain of the original trauma can healing finally take place.

The warrior's bandage also serves to hide his wound from others. Our wounds of rejection or betrayal are not visible to those around us because we have carefully hidden them beneath a façade of status, wealth, or professionalism. Most people invest a great deal of their energy in concealing their pain for fear of exposing their vulnerability. Men often hide behind their anger, women behind their tears. The real tragedy is our failure to recognize that we are all wounded soldiers trying to valiantly carry on in an uncaring world.

We may also summon up all our defenses to protect ourselves from a hidden, painful memory. Repressed memories (symbolized by the warrior's head wound) usually generate so much anxiety that they are permanently banished from consciousness. To prevent these painful memories from surfacing into conscious awareness, our egos must be constantly vigilant. However, the memory of a past trauma can slip past the defenses of the ego in the symbolic form of dreams, or surface as psychological disorders. Physical pain can also mirror the psychological pain that has been repressed. For example, in some cases migraine headaches can substitute for a painful childhood memory that literally hurts.

No one goes through life unscathed, but we can strive to change the way we perceive hurtful experiences from our past. Instead of seeing the past as a time in which we were victimized by our parents or boss, we can view life as a series of situations in which we developed strength through adversity. Like the heavily muscled warrior, we have built up certain strengths or skills in order to survive in our family or workplace. The often trying circumstances of childhood molded our personalities so that many of the positive qualities we embody today can be directly attributed to earlier trauma. The inner strength and resilience we take for granted today probably developed in response to adversity in our parental home. If some members of our family behaved irresponsibly, we reacted by becoming the responsible person in the home who took care of the others. When conflict followed us into the workplace, we learned to become more assertive. In order to fully understand where we stand as adults, we need to recognize the true value of traumatic experience in the development of our character and fate.

In divination, this card symbolizes preservation. Just as the warrior stands guard protecting his wands from the enemy, we must protect what is ours. Sometimes the task in life is not to acquire more things, but to hold onto what we already possess. Consequently, any financial investment that involves risk should be avoided as well as anything that could endanger an important relationship.

THE TEN OF WANDS: PERSEVERANCE

God is with those who persevere.

—The Koran

On this card, a man clutching ten wands staggers toward his home in the distance. The man's back is bent from carrying his heavy burden, reflecting our underlying belief that life is a monumental struggle. We struggle daily with our finances, relationships, illnesses, desires, the irrevocableness of the past, and the uncertainly of the future. The individual must carry his burden alone, with all the courage he can command, through an indifferent world that cares little for his personal struggle. Modern man adds to his burden considerably by believing in a godless, mechanistic universe in which humankind's struggles seem meaningless. Still, we must continue on our journey, for it is ours alone. Armed only with acceptance and determination, we must find a way to make sense of our struggle through life.

In order to find meaning in life, our personal struggle must be understood within the context of a larger framework. If we believe in a divine plan for our lives, then our fate becomes our way to serve God's will. Likewise, our burdens become lighter when we understand our struggle to be a sacred duty to a higher power. Even those of us who lack faith in God can become aware of the valuable lessons provided by struggle that strengthens our character. Whether we see our burdens as serving God or self-serving, the vital meaning we find in our struggle can sustain us through the most challenging times.

This is also a card dealing with the burden of responsibility. The responsibilities of doing our job, taking care of others, and trying to take care of ourselves can be overwhelming at times. Like the man carrying his heavy wands, most people have very heavy demands placed upon them by others that they cannot easily put down. When these responsibilities become too stressful, we earnestly wish for some relief from the crying baby or the interminable car payments. However, the wise person within us would say that we should not pray for a lighter load, but rather we should pray for a stronger back. The responsibilities we carry with us daily are a necessary part of our development. Instead of seeking rest from our labors, we should develop the inner strength to labor more wholeheartedly. If we can totally accept our God-given responsibilities, then every burden will be light and every duty will be a profound joy.

There are also the unnecessary burdens we place on ourselves by demanding too much of ourselves. We feel we "should" or "have to" accomplish a never-ending series of tasks simply because of our exacting standards. These self-imposed demands put constant pressure on us to meet internal deadlines (we have to produce a child by age twenty-five), or meet particular requirements (we should lose ten more pounds). These are not ordinary goals for self-improvement, but rather are unrealistic demands that create constant tension and worry. In effect, we put a tremendous burden on ourselves and then suffer under the pressure of it. We may need to unload the burden of expectations we've placed on ourselves and consider less stressful options.

Some of us carry too many self-imposed demands because of our perfectionism. We incorrectly believe that unless we do everything perfectly, we will be labeled as a failure. This heavy burden of perfectionism has a negative impact on ourselves as well as those around us. Trying to maintain the perfect relationship, a perfect appearance, or find the perfect solution to a problem can be exhausting. Perfectionists also demand that their family and fellow workers maintain the same impossibly high standards that they have adopted. Their children should be model students, and their spouses must always create a good impression. Unfortunately, like the overburdened man struggling toward home, we will never reach our destination if our goal is perfection. Eventually, when we finally become too tired to carry the burden of perfectionism, we will let go of some of our responsibilities so we can continue on our journey disencumbered.

Sometimes, the responsibilities we assume are a necessary part of life. In this case, the Ten of Wands reflects the perseverance necessary to reach a realistic goal. Although he is weighed down by an enormous load, the man pictured continues on his arduous journey. Continuing to put one foot in front of the other, he is the personification of perseverance. Likewise, we may have to persevere through tough times when every laborious step we take seems destined to put us farther behind. It is in times like these that we need to remind ourselves that nothing worthwhile in life is ever easy. It is only through the relentless perseverance of the human spirit that we are able to bear the unbearable. Perseverance is more important than either education or experience, for without determination to succeed we cannot use these attributes. Sometimes, we must even persevere when our destination is unknown. The heavy burden of wands that the man carries obscures his vision so he can't see where he is going. Spiritual progress is a very similar situation, because we may not be able to see the results of our meditations or prayers in the usual sense. We can only persevere in our spiritual practices, confident that our faith will guide us safely to our destination.

Finally, the Ten of Wands can also illustrate the burden of guilt that we all carry. The injuries we have inflicted on others in the past stay with us long after our transgressions. Nevertheless, by making amends or apologizing for our errant behavior, we may be able to unburden ourselves of guilty feelings. Like the flowering wands, guilt is associated with our growth because it is often an impetus for positive change.

In a reading, we can consider this card a warning that we are shouldering too many responsibilities. The workload at home or on the job may be too heavy for our limited resources. When we feel there are not enough hours in the day to complete all our tasks, it is time to let go of some of our responsibilities. Pursuing part-time work or equalizing the division of labor in a household can relieve some of the weight of our obligations.

THE PAGE OF WANDS: INTUITION

Intuition is more important than knowledge.

—Albert Einstein

A young man stands alone in the desert contemplating a flowering wand. It seems miraculous that anything could grow in this barren desert landscape, yet the wand continues to blossom. There are many times in our lives when life seems devoid of the vital elements that previously sustained us. Periods of grief, unemployment, or illness can transform our lives into a bleak, barren landscape. However, we may be surprised to find that these empty times are our greatest opportunity for growth. They give us a golden opportunity to look beyond our usual preoccupation with the externals of life in order to fully explore what is hidden within our hearts and minds.

The three pyramids in the card's background symbolize the three different aspects of ourselves which can be examined to hasten our inner growth: the rational, the emotive, and the intuitive mind. When faced with isolation or illness, our rational mind must immediately re-evaluate our priorities in life. What was once thought to be significant may be seen as unimportant in the light of catastrophe. Lofty goals that were at one time consuming passions are suddenly abandoned in favor of higher priorities. As the mind makes these new adjustments, we begin to see ourselves in a new way. When our self-concept changes, we realize we are not who we thought we were. Like the flowering wand in the desert, a new person has emerged from an empty sea of sand.

When we examine our emotions, we naturally find discouragement and depression in periods of emptiness. Nevertheless, if we embrace these dark emotions, we can grow. A dark night of the soul often yields a deeper understanding of ourselves than the bright light of happiness. Like the shifting sands of the desert, we may also feel insecure and uncertain at this trying time. Actually, uncertainty provides us with another opportunity for growth because it discloses options that we may not have previously considered. In bleak times, the distressing emotions we experience can change us for the better.

The intuitive mind concerns itself with the future, but in difficult times the future may resemble a wasteland of unfulfilled desires. Tomorrow may seem like a vast desert in which nothing appears on the endless horizon. Perhaps the days and years ahead seem barren without the person or abilities we have lost. With nothing to look forward to, it is very easy to succumb to despair. However, this inner empty landscape may be the perfect place to make a new start in life. Like a young page who has his whole life in front of him, we can use youthful optimism to envision the possibilities contained in our future.

The Page of Wands is a young student who is learning to use his intuition. He focuses all of his energy on the wand he holds because his first lesson is to pay strict attention to his intuition. Intuitive insights are very fleeting, as a word or image may suddenly come into conscious awareness and then disappear just as quickly. If we are paying attention to these transitory clues provided by the universe, we will be able to capitalize on them. It may be helpful to record our previous insights so that they are not lost in the daily stream of consciousness. We can recognize these insights because they differ from normal, everyday perceptions. Intuitions appear from out of nowhere such as, for example, when a popular song pops into our head and we can't stop singing it all day. Similarly, a particular woman's name constantly appears in newspaper articles, television programs, or books we are reading. These are not random events, but are messages sent to us from a place beyond our ordinary awareness.

Once we have realized that there is a hidden message contained in certain words or images, we need to discern their meaning. Because there is no dictionary of intuition we can consult to find the meaning of these events, we must look to our own experience to find an answer. If the recurrent word or image is a familiar one (for example, if we repeatedly come across the name Emily and we have a sister by the same name), then we should try to make contact with that person or image. If the image is unfamiliar to us, we can use word association or fantasy to amplify the meaning of the strange experience.

Dreams and Tarot readings are fertile ground for intuitive messages, which is why they have been used through the generations to provide insights into life's problems. As students of intuition, we can also use everyday experiences as opportunities to learn more about our intuitive gifts. The world is a magic mirror filled with images of our future. The peculiar behavior of animals, particularly birds, is often a vital connection to future events. There is also symbolic meaning hidden in the problems we routinely encounter. Mechanical problems with our car sometimes mirror physical illness. A faulty fuel pump could reflect a heart problem, for example. A flat tire could symbolize how we are stuck in our present job. Similarly, a clogged drain may be a clue to our inability to express our feelings. Other exercises include paying particular attention to synchronicities and overheard conversations. These interesting coincidences not only reflect our difficulties, but also usually provide needed answers to our most pressing problems.

One problem that affects us all is losing an important possession such as our car keys. As an exercise in using our intuition, we can draw a single Tarot card and try to discern where the lost object is by contemplating the symbolism of the card. The Empress, for example, may send us to our mother's house to look for our lost keys. Traditionally, pages have symbolized messengers in Tarot readings, and the Page of Wand's message is that abundant messages are all around us. We are in a constant dialogue with a universe that reaches out daily to communicate with us through the universal language of symbolism.

In divination, this card shows the need for optimism. If the wand pictured can blossom in the desert, then we can certainly blossom where we are planted. We must make the best of our situation by always viewing ourselves in positive circumstances. If we use our intuition to envision a positive outcome, there is every possibility that our vision will be confirmed.

THE KNIGHT OF WANDS: RESTRAINT

Reason lies between the spur and the bridle.

—George Herbert

In this card, a dashing knight on horseback travels over the Egyptian desert. While his horse seems very eager to gallop over the endless expanse of desert sand, the knight has reined in his horse, impeding his swift progress. In our lives, we must also rein in the destructive parts of our nature. There is a need to restrain our actions or feelings before they get out of control. The two reins we use to control our wild impulses are willpower and reason. When we possess enough strength of mind to stop our destructive actions, we will gain control over the untamed animal within us. By steering ourselves gently, but firmly on the predetermined course we have set for ourselves, we can successfully direct our energies toward worthwhile goals.

Like a wild horse, unbridled emotions can quickly lead us into tragedy. This is particularly true when the uncontrolled emotion is anger. The knight's fiery plumage and red horse reflect the smoldering anger that we all valiantly try to control. This anger is most commonly caused by frustration when we don't get what we most desire in life. Like a knight on a failed quest, we can become extremely angry when we fail to obtain our personal objectives. Any attack upon our ego or integrity can also fuel our anger, creating a fury that threatens to run off with us. Our anger, once unleashed in either malevolent words or deeds, can carry us far away from those we love. Because there are very serious consequences to fully expressing our anger, we must make a concerted effort to rein in our fury before it is too late. One helpful technique is to simply count to ten before taking any action. If we can stop for a moment before venting our angry feelings, we may calm down long enough to consider the consequences of our actions. By practicing self-restraint, even if it is for a few minutes, we can learn to develop the self-control necessary to become masters of our emotions.

This card also represents a turning point in our lives. While we spur ourselves onward, trying to gain the momentum to succeed, there is always a part of us that hesitates. Like the knight who reins in his horse just as he is leaping forward, we may lack the self-confidence to see a project to its conclusion. When we constantly procrastinate, life becomes a long series of undeveloped ideas and uncompleted projects. Hesitation leads to failure, and our hope for a better future becomes a barren desert of unfulfilled dreams. When we realize this past pattern, we can make positive strides toward changing our previous behavior. Completing even a small task on time can give us the confidence to finish larger projects in the future. If, like the horse, we continue to balk at the idea of completion, we will simply have to take a leap of faith and persevere regardless of our hesitancy.

When the Knight of Wands spurs his horse to go forward and then uses the reins to pull him back, he is expressing two conflicting wishes. On the one hand, he wishes the horse to proceed, but on the other, he wants him to stop. Human beings also give themselves contradictory commands. We wish to leave a relationship, but force ourselves to stay, for example. A simplistic view of human nature theorizes that there are only two forces operating in our lives: reward and punishment. We impulsively desire something forbidden, but the fear of punishment automatically reins in our actions. Torn between the desire for freedom and constraint, impulse and inhibition, we find ourselves in the no-man's-land of ambivalence. It is in this place of uncertainty that we must decide how we will proceed. When conflicting desires threaten to overwhelm us, we need to make decisions based upon reason rather than emotion. First, consider if the potential loss is worth what we may gain. Second, we can make a list of advantages and disadvantages for the satisfaction of each desire and then select the one that offers us the greatest rewards with the fewest risks. By reviewing all our options, we can choose the appropriate action rather than have the action choose us.

Like the other knights, the Knight of Wands seeks to transcend his own mortality through his momentous deeds. The Egyptian pyramids in the background are very potent symbols of immortality, and the knight aligns himself with these ancient monuments that have withstood the test of time. While architects and builders are certainly aware of their ability to create a building that will stand long after they are gone, many other artisans also leave behind immortal works. Books, paintings, and successful businesses are all lasting monuments to their creators. The things we have created in life live after us as our representatives on earth.

In divination, the pyramids in the background are also a reminder that we must learn from the past if we wish to move forward into the future. Like a questing knight, we may want to explore our personal past as well as our family heritage to find our own Holy Grail. Our survival depends upon our ability to learn from the past and a willingness to take that knowledge into the future.

THE QUEEN OF WANDS: SEPARATION

You can never have a greater or a lesser dominion than that over yourself.

—Leonardo da Vinci

The Queen of Wands serenely surveys her desert kingdom while a beautiful black cat sits at her feet. Black cats are the traditional companions of witches and sorceresses, those women believed to possess extraordinary gifts of prophecy. The witch is a seer who can skillfully use the Tarot, as well as other tools of divination, to predict future events. When she gazes into the distance, the Queen of Wands can see through the material world into the spiritual realm where past, present, and future meet.

The Queen of Wands, as the archetypal witch, rejects the usual feminine ideals of wife and mother, replacing them with selfishness and a desire for power. Traditionally, the evil witch in fairy tales represents the negative side of femininity. Instead of giving birth to children, she devours them. Instead of nurturing innocent girls and boys, she typically takes advantage of children's helplessness. Wishing only to feed herself, she refuses to help anyone. The witch is also a very powerful figure, having secret knowledge and the desire to use her magical knowledge against anyone she perceives as weak. She typically has the power to turn men into animals (perhaps this is where the cat originates!), and she casts spells of enchantment on rivals.

Although the witch's actions are undoubtedly despicable, we would all secretly like to be her for at least one day. This is because her only responsibility is to satisfy her own desires, as she is an independent, self-centered woman with the freedom to do as she pleases. This is in sharp contrast to the self-sacrificing image we usually have of ourselves. However, sometimes we need to get in touch with this darker side of our personality, if only to acknowledge its existence. The Queen of Wands reminds us that underneath our nurturing selves lives a greedy, selfish witch whose needs must be satisfied. This devouring aspect of the witch is a reminder that we need to feed ourselves with emotions and ideas in order to survive. Furthermore, her need for power is our own need to reclaim our personal power from those who have taken it. When we contact the hidden witch within us, we automatically strike an important balance between giving and taking.

The witch's companion is her black cat. Cats have always represented feminine power, which is one reason why many men fear or dislike the feline species. Women's power is contained in their intuition, and the cat's ability to see in the dark naturally symbolizes women's psychic abilities. Being able to sense something rather than seeing it is our extraordinary gift. Like the instincts of a cat, a woman's intuition can warn of danger or sense love at first sight. Our psychic abilities may also be like an untamed cat that refuses to come at our bidding and refuses to be controlled. Psychic insights often burst into consciousness uninvited whether we want them or not. Nevertheless, we must trust our intuition to guide us through the delusions of life.

The Queen of Wands holds a sunflower in her left hand. This beautiful flower has been cut off from its roots and will soon fade. People, as well as flowers, do not hold up well when they are severed from their roots. Likewise, we may feel cut off from the family roots which sustain us. A rift between family members can quickly lead to estrangement, or a bitter divorce may separate us from our spouse's family. Also, simply moving from place to place puts considerable distance between family members who may find it difficult to connect with one another. Because of all these factors, many of us lack the continuity and stability that an extended family can provide. The cut off sunflower also represents our disconnection from our family history. Our family roots extend back in time many generations, yet few of us are familiar with our family history beyond that of our grandparents. Even if we have problems with certain family members, we need to talk with them about their life experience. Through this oral family history, we may come to know that we are not isolated individuals, but rather are an important link in the great chain of being.

THE MINOR ARCANA

Our sense of rootlessness may also originate from a feeling of detachment from ourselves. Women in particular need to stay in one place in order to put down roots in their home and community. The transience of modern life, with its constant relocation to satisfy business concerns, conflicts with a woman's primal nature and causes her to lose touch with herself. It is also easy to lose touch with those around us when there is little time to establish friendships before we have to be uprooted again.

On a deeper level, feelings of rootlessness can stem from the modern woman's new role as a professional in the workplace. Our quest for professional status and prosperity may have cut us off from our instinctual female base. We no longer have the vital connection to the earth that sustained many generations of women before us. This results in many modern women having wings, but no roots. Permanently estranged from the guidance of Mother Earth, they develop male personas in order to compete with men in their world. This often results in worldly success accompanied by feelings of emptiness. There is a sense that something vital is missing from women's lives that cannot be replaced by status or money. The Queen of Wands wears a crown intertwined with leaves to remind us to become reacquainted with the natural world that sustains our spirits.

In divination, the Queen of Wands is a reigning monarch of the lifeless desert and, therefore, may represent barrenness. Surrounded by figures of lions, the queen also symbolizes the many inner strengths of women. Leonine characteristics such as courage and boldness may be needed to solve the current problem. Lions are also associated with verbal aggression that may be necessary in this situation.

THE KING OF WANDS: ADAPTING

He was capable of adapting himself to place, time, and person, and of playing his part appropriately under whatever circumstances.

—Diogenes Laetius

A king dressed in resplendent robes surveys his vast desert kingdom. Alone in the desert, his only companion seems to be the tiny salamander at his feet. Salamanders are capable of changing their color in order to blend in with their surroundings, thus eluding capture. We may also have to make certain adaptations to ensure our psychological and physical survival. Life is a series of constantly changing circumstances, and the ability to change ourselves to meet new requirements in a necessary survival skill. Some of these vital adaptations are to internal states, while others are adaptations to a changing environment. Both require us to alter our behavior or attitudes in response to change.

Internal adaptations usually arise from changes in our body or mind. Through the course of our lives, we have had to adapt to different life stages. The first of these adjustments was to the natural changes of maturation. While we were growing up, we were thought to be "well adjusted" if we used age-appropriate behavior and met the developmental tasks for each stage of development. However, adjustment doesn't end when we mature into adults. Childhood, adolescence, adulthood, middle age, and old age all require us to adapt to new bodies and new mindsets. Each stage of life produces bodily changes that we must gradually adapt to and accept. Our beliefs about growing up and growing older need adjustment as well. Most children eagerly look forward to the independence conferred by adulthood, but few of us enthusiastically anticipate old age. Because our minds are directly connected to our bodies, readjusting our beliefs about getting older can be just as important as adapting to bodily changes.

External adaptations are necessary when we must alter our behavior to fit a changing environment. Our first environment was our family home, and through the years we had to cleverly adapt ourselves to all the usual upheavals of family life. We had to become accustomed to a new baby brother or sister, had to make new friends after relocating to a new town, or had to cope with the death of a grandparent. Most of these early adjustments were to accommodate others' needs, but as we got older, we had to adapt to our own needs. Finding a job, a mate, and a place to live all required us to make psychological adjustments. One of the most important modifications we have had to make is to our self-concept. Each external change brings a subtle shift in our perception of who we are: student, store manager, husband, or mother. Naturally, we adjust to the roles we must play. We become more authoritarian when we are given authority, more trusting if we are given others' trust.

This is particularly true if we find ourselves in a harsh environment. Like the unforgiving sands of the desert, many professions present difficult working environments that we adapt to only at great personal cost. Doctors and policemen, for example, are exposed to so much human misery that they can only adjust to it by becoming cynical or uncaring. Bored office workers adapt to the tediousness of their jobs by generating exciting office gossip. Whatever our chosen profession, we need to become more aware of the impact of our jobs on our mental health.

Other environmental factors we must adjust to are new locations and new technologies. Some people find it easy to adapt to the impersonal environment of a big city, while others fare better in the friendly atmosphere of a small town. Adapting to different climates can also present problems. If the climate is extreme (tropical, arid, or frigid), it can take considerable time to adjust to the challenges of trying to stay comfortable. While the interiors of our houses are climate controlled, we seem to have little control over the gadgetry we currently bring into our homes. New technology, which quickly becomes outdated, forces us to adapt to it or risk being left behind on the technological superhighway. As the world progresses at a faster rate, we find we must adapt quickly to new technologies. We should remember, however, that when we connect to the latest technology, it also connects to us. As we adapt to the faster pace of our machines, we may find ourselves emulating them with frenetic behavior. Occasionally unplugging ourselves from technology can give us back our sanity and humanity.

Some of us adapt very easily to new circumstances, while others find adjustment to be difficult, if not impossible. An underlying reason for this may be our temperaments. Introverts typically do not like changes in their environment, while extraverts welcome change with open arms. Whether we like it or not, life is constantly changing, and we must change with it. Adaptation requires flexibility in both our thinking and our behavior. Like the king's rigid wand, we can be too inflexible to the changes that surround us, and this can produce unfortunate results. When adaptation is required, it is far better to bend than to break.

The King of Wands, when present in a reading, represents a very unreliable person. The salamander symbolizes an elusive person who likes to hide in the shadows. Salamanders are also mythological creatures that can live in fire. Fire can warm, but like the hot desert sands, it can also burn. Care should be taken that a relationship that promises to warm our hearts does not reduce us to ashes.

CHAPTER FOUR
READING THE TAROT

I must complain the cards are ill shuffled till I have a good hand.
—Jonathan Swift

Reading the Tarot is very much like reading a foreign language, only in this case it is the pictures on the cards that are translated into words. When we do a reading for ourselves or others, we find relevant meanings for the cards and then verbalize our thoughts. Like learning a foreign language, Tarot reading takes practice before we can develop the requisite skills needed to interpret the cards.

Tarot readings are performed by laying out a few chosen cards in particular patterns known as Tarot spreads. Each position in the spread puts the card placed on it in a particular context in which to view the card's meaning. For example, there are separate positions for the past, the environment, and the future. Because there are a multitude of meanings for each card, it is probably best to start out by doing single-card readings and then proceed to more complicated spreads after becoming better acquainted with the deck.

To become more familiar with the cards, we simply pick a single card at random every morning. In the evening, we try to relate the card we've chosen to the day's events. Did we have a problem with our car when we picked the Chariot? Did our mother call the day we chose the Empress card? In this way, we can become familiar with the card's meanings while we test the Tarot's predictive ability. This is similar to the faith we develop in a Tarot reader. If the reader can tell us, through her psychic abilities, intimate facts about our lives that she could not have known otherwise, then we will begin to trust her ability to accurately foretell our future. In a similar fashion, when the single card we pick each day accurately mirrors our experiences, we begin to trust the Tarot as a powerful oracle. Picking a card a day also encourages us to accept the transience of experience, for tomorrow we will choose a new card, releasing today's card along with its good or bad fortune.

When we have gained enough confidence to attempt more complex spreads, we may wish to use traditional Tarot rituals in the performance of our readings. Rituals help to focus the mind, banishing distractions arising from the everyday world so we can contact our source of higher wisdom. First, the cards need to be carefully shuffled by the questioner (also known as the querent) while the questioner concentrates on the question she wants answered. It is possible to ask the Tarot any question; however, the question should be open-ended rather than one requiring a simple yes or no answer. So, the question, "Will I get the job?" is unsatisfactory, while, "How can I improve my chance of getting the job?" is much better. After shuffling, the cards should be cut twice by the questioner, and the three piles then picked up in reverse order by the reader to form a single pack of cards. Dealing from the top of this deck, the reader then places a single card face down in each of the chosen positions forming the spread. The remaining cards are then put aside. These unused cards are called the Da'ath pack (named for the hidden sephira on the Kabbalistic Tree of Life) and contain information that cannot be revealed at this time. The reader then carefully turns over the cards from left to right, being careful not to reverse any of the cards. After these rituals are completed, reading the cards can begin.

It is helpful to first look at the spread in its entirety before discussing the meanings of individual cards. Counting the number of Major and Minor Arcana cards is a helpful place to start this analysis. If a majority of the cards are Majors, then we could say that the questioner has little control over his situation because the powerful archetypes of the Major Arcana are strongly influencing the outcome. Next, the number of cards from each suit of the Minor Arcana should be counted to see if there is a predominant suit. A majority of pentacles indicates that the Tarot wishes to address work or money issues, many cups denotes relationships, a preponderance of swords indicates conflicts with others, and a majority of wands indicates issues involving time or energy. Next, we notice the numbers on the cards, particularly those numbered ace through ten. When two or three of the same numbered cards appear in a reading, we can look for the hidden meaning contained in that particular number. Many aces denote beginnings, twos are opportunities, threes are growth, fours are manifestation, fives are conflict, sixes are balance, sevens are completion, eights are organization, nines are integrity, and tens are fulfillment.

When looking at all the cards as a whole, many other interesting patterns may emerge. If the central card is surrounded by many men or women, this may indicate the possibility of multiple relationships. We may also want to look carefully at the court cards to see if they are facing toward or away from each other, as this can reflect the level of intimacy or antagonism between two people. If most of the people are looking downward, this reflects a pessimistic outlook. Are many of the people moving or are they stationary? The Tarot may be trying to tell us that it is time to move on, either emotionally or geographically. When the majority of the figures are either working or playing, we should consider either making a more strenuous effort or taking it easy for a while. Younger people indicate getting in touch with our younger, playful selves, while many older figures suggest the need for wisdom. Our emotional outlook can also be reflected in the weather, as many cards with stormy skies symbolize sorrow or anger looming on the horizon. The story we lay out in the cards is dependent upon the interaction between all the characters pictured as well as between the characters and their environment. By looking at the reading as if it were one large scene, we can readily see these important interactions and make the appropriate recommendations.

After making these vital connections between all the cards in the spread, we can address the meanings of individual cards as they apply to each position in the layout. There are many different meanings for each card ranging from simple definitions to highly esoteric descriptions. It is probably best to consult more than one book when looking for card meanings, for each book will have its own point of view. After awhile, we may find ourselves drawn to particular authors who present either a mythological, psychological, or philosophical context in which we can understand the cards. Alternately, we may adopt an eclectic approach by consulting many different Tarot books, as we try to develop a more well-rounded approach. However, when pursuing these myriad definitions, our intuition will usually lead us to the correct meaning. It is very common to feel surprise and delight when we find just the right meaning. This triumphant feeling occurs when the right definition seems to leap off the page into our hearts.

Finally, each of the card's meanings has to be interpreted according to their position in the spread. The most common spread is the Celtic cross layout (see Figure 1). It consists of ten cards, six of which form a cross, with the remaining four cards forming a vertical staff to the right of the cross. Each position, numbered one through ten, has its own meaning. The first four cards represent a timeline of the past, present, and future. Position one is the questioner as she appears in the present. Crossing this card is card number two, which is an obstacle to the questioner's progress. Position three is the near future, while position four is the past. Position five is what we really need to solve our problems, while position six is what we want instead. Position seven is ourselves, as we see ourselves. Position eight is our environment. Position nine is our hopes and fears for the future, while position ten is the final outcome.

These ten positions can be divided into five opposing pairs, symbolizing the need for balance in our lives. The central cross made by positions one and two represents our personal will (position one), opposed by the circumstances in which we find ourselves (position two). This is the eternal conflict between inner desire and outer reality. These two cards may also mirror an internal conflict when we desire two opposing things. We want to stay, yet want to leave; we want to work, but want to play. The Appendix in the back of this book lists these conflicts or opposing pairs for all seventy-eight cards. Any mutually antagonistic feelings or desires can produce a conflict in our lives. Conflicts can generate guilt, anxiety, anger, or neurotic symptoms in response to the two contradictory tendencies in our mind. Like the central cross, understanding of these conflicts may be central to our understanding the real problems underlying the querent's question.

Positions three and four are opposite each other on the timeline, representing the future and the past respectively. In some cases, position two (the crossing card) can be seen as a connecting bridge between these two periods in time, so that we do not repeat past mistakes in the future. The future position may tell us more about what we believe will happen in the future than what will actually occur. The past position mirrors our personal history including childhood experiences, previous marriages, or previous employment.

Positions five and six represent the constant, internal battle between what we want (position six) and what we really need (position five). The conflict usually arises when we realize that what we want may not be good for us, while what we need may not necessarily be pleasurable. We need to keep in mind that the want position may show us alternate ways of achieving what we want, while the need position alerts us to unconscious needs we may not be able to verbalize. The need position is also where the Tarot dispenses most of its sage advice, so the card occupying this space should always be carefully considered.

The staff to the right of the cross also has opposing pairs. Positions seven and eight signify the nature versus nurture controversy, as they represent our self (position seven) and our environment (position eight). Another way of looking at this conflict is to view it as the questioner's inner resources pitted against her outer circumstances. When looking at the card occupying position seven, it is helpful to expand the term "self" to include self-esteem and professional persona in order to get a clearer picture of the questioner. A card placed here can also represent someone with whom the questioner closely identifies such as her mother, father, or religious figure. Position eight reminds us that we are largely a product of our environment. Our fundamental beliefs about the world and how it operates are also revealed in this position. Because this card represents the environment, it is imperative that the reader carefully look at the background of the card appearing in this position. A rocky or dangerous landscape warns of an inhospitable environment either at home or at work.

The next to last position is our hopes and fears, which often conflicts with the final card. This is because our hopes or fears for the future will not necessarily be reflected in the final outcome. The hopes and fears position itself seems to be one of contradiction until we understand that there is fear in every hope and hope in every fear. Many of us dread what we most desire: love, change, commitment, or success. As we vacillate between attraction and repulsion, we only become more ambivalent about the future. However, the hopes and fears position does offer us one piece of sage advice: "Hope for the best, prepare for the worst."

The final outcome position is the culmination of all the cards that have been read. This is where our present path leads, whether we like our destination or not. Even if the final card offers us a poor prognosis for the future, predictions are not carved in stone. We can use the insights gained from the reading to change our beliefs and, therefore, change our future.

If we have experienced some difficulty in discerning the meanings of the cards within the context of the different positions in the spread, it is helpful to ask more than one question during the reading. Each position contains its own question that the card's meaning will answer. The following questions can be asked during the course of the reading:

Position one and two: "What conflict would I like to resolve in this situation?"

Position three: "What do I believe will happen in this situation?"

Position four: "How have I tried to resolve this situation in the past?"

Position five: "What do I need to change in this situation?"

Position six: "What do I want to change in this situation?"

Position seven: "How did I contribute to this situation?"

Position eight: "How did others contribute to this situation?"

Position nine: "What are my hopes and fears for this situation?"

Position ten: "How will I be affected by the resolution of this situation?"

If after all this effort, the reading is still an enigma, we may be tempted to reshuffle the cards and try another reading. However, as anyone who has tried this will attest, the result of the second reading will be almost identical to the first. Many of the same cards will reappear, although in different positions. Obviously, the Tarot is trying to tell us something important even if our current knowledge doesn't allow us to understand the message. While it is easy to repeat a reading several times in the hope of getting a positive outcome, it is ill-advised. Proverbial wisdom dictates that "he who questions cannot avoid the answers."

Tarot Insights

Figure 1

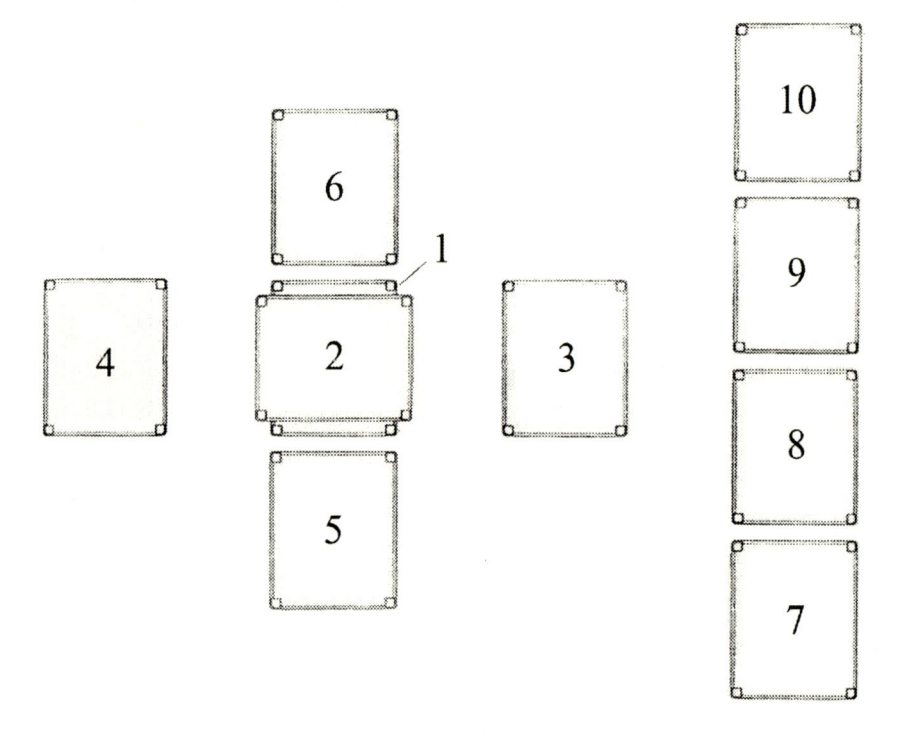

<u>Celtic Cross</u>

APPENDIX
CONFLICTING PAIRS

The Fool	Eight of Pentacles	nonconformity vs. conformity
The Magician	The Tower	intentional vs. unintentional
The High Priestess	The Star	hidden vs. revealed
The Empress	The Tower	creation vs. destruction
The Emperor	Seven of Cups	reality vs. fantasy
The Hierophant	Five of Pentacles	insider vs. outsider
The Lovers	The Devil	choice vs. no choice
The Chariot	Eight of Swords	movement vs. restriction
Strength	The Emperor	gentleness vs. harshness
The Hermit	Three of Cups	isolation vs. connection
The Wheel of Fortune	Four of Swords	change vs. changeless
Justice	Five of Pentacles	justice vs. injustice
The Hanged Man	The Emperor	powerlessness vs. power
Death	The Empress	death vs. birth
Temperance	Nine of Cups	temperance vs. overindulgence
The Devil	Six of Wands	punishment vs. reward
The Tower	Three of Pentacles	destruction vs. construction
The Star	Five of Pentacles	abundance vs. scarcity
The Moon	The Chariot	fear vs. courage
The Sun	The Moon	conscious vs. unconscious
Judgment	The Empress	criticism vs. acceptance
The World	The Hanged Man	resolved vs. unresolved
Ace of Pentacles	Death	beginning vs. ending
Two of Pentacles	The Emperor	adaptability vs. rigidity
Three of Pentacles	Eight of Cups	commitment vs. abandonment
Four of Pentacles	Six of Pentacles	greed vs. generosity
Five of Pentacles	Seven of Cups	needs vs. wants
Six of Pentacles	Two of Cups	inequality vs. equality
Seven of Pentacles	Ten of Cups	worried vs. untroubled
Eight of Pentacles	Nine of Pentacles	work vs. leisure
Nine of Pentacles	Six of Pentacles	independence vs. dependence
Ten of Pentacles	Six of Wands	ordinariness vs. specialness
Page of Pentacles	The Fool	focus vs. distraction
Knight of Pentacles	The Emperor	potential vs. reality
Queen of Pentacles	The Emperor	nature vs. nurture
King of Pentacles	Five of Pentacles	harvest vs. famine

Ace of Cups	The Emperor	effusive vs. reserved
Two of Cups	Ten of Swords	loyalty vs. betrayal
Three of Cups	Four of Cups	gratitude vs. ingratitude
Four of Cups	The Hanged Man	rejection vs. acceptance
Five of Cups	Six of Cups	loss vs. gain
Six of Cups	Nine of Wands	trust vs. mistrust
Seven of Cups	Nine of Cups	desire vs. fulfillment
Eight of Cups	Eight of Wands	departure vs. arrival
Nine of Cups	Four of Cups	satisfaction vs. dissatisfaction
Ten of Cups	The Emperor	idealism vs. pragmatism
Page of Cups	Five of Cups	found vs. lost
Knight of Cups	The Chariot	hesitation vs. action
Queen of Cups	Ace of Cups	repression vs. expression
King of Cups	Six of Swords	drifting vs. steering
Ace of Swords	Seven of Swords	honesty vs. dishonesty
Two of Swords	The Lovers	indecisiveness vs. decisiveness
Three of Swords	Four of Swords	wounded vs. recovered
Four of Swords	The Wheel of Fortune	resisting vs. accepting change
Five of Swords	Six of Wands	defeat vs. victory
Six of Swords	Two of Cups	separation vs. reunion
Seven of Swords	The Hierophant	rebellion vs. obedience
Eight of Swords	The Chariot	helplessness vs. control
Nine of Swords	Ten of Cups	sorrow vs. happiness
Ten of Swords	Ten of Cups	pessimism vs. optimism
Page of Swords	The Fool	influenced vs. independent
Knight of Swords	The Hanged Man	impatience vs. patience
Queen of Swords	The Hanged Man	transformation vs. stasis
King of Swords	The Fool	rational vs. irrational
Ace of Wands	Eight of Swords	opportunity vs. impossibility
Two of Wands	Queen of Cups	objectivity vs. subjectivity
Three of Wands	Two of Swords	vision vs. blindness
Four of Wands	The Fool	safety vs. risk
Five of Wands	Three of Pentacles	competition vs. cooperation
Six of Wands	Two of Pentacles	self-confidence vs. self-doubt
Seven of Wands	Six of Cups	enemy vs. friend
Eight of Wands	Four of Pentacles	expenditure vs. conservation of energy

Nine of Wands	Six of Cups	danger vs. safety
Ten of Wands	Eight of Wands	struggle vs. ease
Page of Wands	The Hierophant	student vs. teacher
Knight of Wands	Judgment	restraint vs. liberation
Queen of Wands	Two of Cups	separating vs. reuniting
King of Wands	The Fool	demanding vs. undemanding

BIBLIOGRAPHY

Abadie, M. J. *Tarot for Teens*. Bindu, 2002.

Abraham, Sylvia. *How to Use Tarot Spreads*. Llewellyn, 1997.

Almond, Jocelyn, and Keith Seddon. *Tarot for Relationships*. Aquarian, 1990.

Amaral, Geraldine, and Nancy Brady Cunningham. *Tarot Celebrations*. Samuel Weiser, 1997.

Anderson, Vikki. *Totally Tarot: How to Be a Tarot Detective*. Rose International, 2000.

Anderton, Bill. *Tarot*. Paragon, 1996.

Anonymous. *Jewels of the Wise*. Epiphany Press, 1979.

Anonymous. *Keystone of Tarot Symbols*. Holy Order of Mans, 1971.

Anonymous. *Meditations on the Tarot*. Amity House, 1985.

Arrien, Angeles. *The Tarot Handbook: Practical Applications of Ancient Visual Symbols*. Arcus, 1987.

Aviza, Edward A. *Thinking Tarot*. Simon and Schuster, 1997.

Banzhaf, Hajo, and Elisa Hemmerlein. *Tarot as Your Companion*. U.S. Games Systems, 1999.

Baxter, Aza. *Sense Dominance Tarot Workbook*. Intuitive Psychology Press, 1995.

Benares, Camden. *Common Sense Tarot*. Newcastle, 1992.

Berti, Giordano, and Tiberio Gonard. *Visconti Tarots*. Lo Scarabeo, 2002.

Betts, Timothy. *Tarot and the Millennium*. New Perspective Media, 1998.

Blakeley, John. *The Mystical Tower of the Tarot*. Watkins, 1974.

Blank, William. *Torah, Tarot, and Tantra*. Coventure, 1991.

Braden, Nina Lee. *Tarot for Self Discovery*. Llewellyn, 2002.

Buess, Lynn. *The Tarot and Transformation*. DeVorss, 1977.

Bunning, Joan. *Learning the Tarot: A Tarot Book for Beginners*. Samuel Weiser, 1998.

Burger, Evelin, and Johannes Fiebig. *Tarot Basics*. Sterling, 1994.

Butler, Bill. *Dictionary of the Tarot*. Schocken Books, 1977.

Calvino, Italo. *The Castle of Crossed Destinies*. Harcourt Brace Jovanovich, 1976.

Campbell, Joseph, and Richard Roberts. *Tarot Revelations*. Vernal Equinox, 1982.

Case, Paul Foster. *The Tarot: A Key to the Wisdom of the Ages*. Builders of the Adytum, 1974.

Cavendish, Richard. *The Tarot*. Crescent Books, 1986.

Clarson, Laura E. *Tarot Unveiled: The Method to its Magic*. U.S. Games Systems, Inc., 1988.

Colin, Didier. *Tarot: Reading the Future*. Hachette, 2001.

Compton, L. C. *Archetypes on the Tree of Life: The Tarot as Pathwork*. Llewellyn, 1991.

Connolly, Eileen. *Tarot: A New Handbook for the Apprentice*. Newcastle, 1979.

———. *Tarot: A New Handbook for the Journeyman*. Newcastle, 1987.

———. *Tarot: The First Handbook for the Master*. Newcastle, 1994.

Cowie, Norma. *Exploring the Patterns of the Tarot*. NC Publishing, 1987.

———. *Tarot for Successful Living*. NC Publishing, 1979.

Crowley, Aleister. *The Book of Thoth*. U.S. Games Systems, 1977.

———. *Tarot Divination*. Samuel Weiser, 1985.

Crystal. *The Inner Truth and Wisdom of the Tarot*. Mermaid Press, 1988.

Curtiss, Harriette, and F. Homer Curtiss. *The Key to Destiny*. Newcastle, 1983.

———. *The Key to the Universe*. Newcastle, 1983.

D'Agostino, Joseph. *The Tarot: The Royal Path to Wisdom*. Samuel Weiser, 1976.

Dante. *Share: Tarot Meditations*. Peyto Books, 1993.

De Saint Phalle, Niki. *Tarot Cards in Sculpture*. Ponsio, 1985.

———. *The Tarot Garden*. Charta, 1998.

Decker, Ronald, Thierry Depaulis, and Michael Dummett. *A Wicked Pack of Cards: The Origin of the Occult Tarot*. St. Martin's Press, 1986.

Decker, Ronald, and Michael Dummett. *A History of the Occult Tarot*: 1870–1970. Duckworth, 2002.

Denning, Melita, and Osborne Phillips. *The Llewellyn Practical Guide to the Magick of the Tarot*. Llewellyn Publications, 1983.

Dhingra, Guneeta. *All You Wanted to Know About the Tarot*. New Dawn, 2000.

Doane, Doris Chase. *Secret Symbolism of the Tarot*. American Federation of Astrologers, 1993.

Doane, Doris Chase, and King Keyes. *How to Read Tarot Cards*. Harper & Row, 1979.

Donaldson, Terry. *Step-by-Step Tarot*. Thorsons, 1995.

———. *The Tarot Spellcaster*. Barrons, 2001.

———. *Thorsons Principles of Tarot*. Thorsons, 1996.

Douglas, Alfred. *The Tarot: The Origins, Meaning and Uses of the Cards*. Penguin Books, 1972.

Drane, John, Ross Clifford, and Philip Johnson. *Beyond Prediction: The Tarot and Your Spirituality*. Lion, 2001.

Drury, Nevill. *Inner Visions: Explorations in Magical Consciousness*. Routledge & Kegan Paul, 1979.

———. *Music for Inner Space: Techniques for Meditation & Visualization*. Prism Press, 1985.

Dummett, Michael. *The Game of Tarot*. Duckworth, 1980.

———. *The Visconti-Sforza Tarot Cards*. George Braziller, Inc., 1986.

Eason, Cassandra. *Tarot Talks to the Woman Within*. Quantum, 2000.

Echols, S. E., R. Mueller, and S. A. Thomson. *Spiritual Tarot: Seventy-Eight Paths of Personal Development*. Avon Books, 1996.

Fairfield, Gail. *Choice Centered Tarot*. Newcastle, 1985.

Fairfield, Gail, and Patti Provo. *Inspiration Tarot: A Workbook for Understanding and Creating Your Own Tarot Deck*. Samuel Weiser, 1991.

Fenton, Sasha. *Fortune-Telling by Tarot Cards: A Beginner's Guide to Understanding the Future Using Tarot Cards*. The Aquarian Press, 1985.

———. *Tarot in Action*. The Aquarian Press, 1985.

Fimlaid, Louise. *The Spiritual Study of the Tarot*. Galaxy, 1997.

Fiorini, Jeanne. *Invitation to Wonder: Real Life Insights Through the Tarot*. Suite One, 2002.

Franklin, Stephen E. *Origins of the Tarot Deck: A Study of the Astronomical Substructure of Game and Divining Boards*. McFarland & Company, 1988.

Freer, Jean. *The New Feminist Tarot*. The Aquarian Press, 1987.

Gad, Irene. *Tarot and Individuation: Correspondences with Cabala and Alchemy*. Nicolas-Hays, 1994.

Garcia, Carole. *Tarot Poetry*. Avon Books, 1997.

Gardner, Richard. *Evolution Through the Tarot*. Samuel Weiser, 1970.

———. *The Tarot Speaks*. Rigel, 1971.

Garen, Nancy. *Creating Your Own Tarot Cards*. Fireside, 1991.

———. *The Tarot According to You: A Workbook*. Fireside, 2001.

Gearhart, Sally, and Susan Rennie. *A Feminist Tarot: A Guide to Intrapersonal Communication*. Persephone Press, 1977.

Gettings, Fred. *The Book of Tarot*. Triune Books, 1973.

Giles, Cynthia. *The Tarot: History, Mystery and Lore*. Simon and Schuster, 1992.

———. *The Tarot: Methods, Mastery and More*. Simon and Schuster, 1996.

Golowin, Sergius. *The World of the Tarot: The Secret Teachings of the 78 Cards of the Gypsies*. Samuel Weiser, 1988.

Gordon, Richard, and Dixie Taylor. *The Intuitive Tarot*. Blue Dolphin, 1994.

Gregory, James. *How to Perform a Psychic Reading*. Zymore, 1999.

Graves, F. D. *The Windows of Tarot*. Morgan and Morgan, 1973.

Gray, Eden. *Complete Guide to the Tarot*. Bantam, 1971.

———. *Mastering the Tarot*. New American Library, 1988.

Greer, Mary K. *The Complete Book of Tarot Reversals*. Llewellyn, 2002.

———. *Tarot Constellations: Patterns of Personal Destiny*. Newcastle, 1988.

———. *Tarot for Your Self: A Workbook for Personal Transformation*. Newcastle, 1984.

———. *Tarot Mirrors: Reflections in Personal Meaning*. Newcastle, 1988.

———. *Women of the Golden Dawn*. Park Street Press, 1995.

Gwain, Rose. *Discovering Your Self Through the Tarot*. Destiny Books, 1994.

Haich, Elizabeth. *Wisdom of the Tarot*. Aurora Press, 1983.

Hall, Manly P. *The Tarot: An Essay*. Philosophical Research Society, 1978.

Hanmaker-Zondag, Karen. *Tarot as a Way of Life: A Jungian Approach to the Tarot*. Samuel Weiser, 1994.

Hasbrouck, Muriel. *Tarot and Astrology*. Inner Traditions, 1987.

Hederman, Mark Patrick. *Tarot: Talisman or Taboo? Reading the World as Symbol*. Currach, 2003.

Heline, Corinne. *The Bible & the Tarot*. DeVorss, 1981.

Herbin, Evelyn, and Terry Donaldson. *Way of Tarot*. Thorsons, 2001.

Hoeller, Stephan A. *The Royal Road: A Manual of Kabalistic Meditations on the Tarot*. The Theosophical Publishing House, 1975.

Hoffmann, Detlef, and Margot Dietrich. *Tarot Art*. Leinfelden-Echterdingen, 1989.

Hounsome, Steve. *Tarot Therapy*. Capall Bann, 1999.

Hoy, David. *The Meaning of Tarot*. Aurora, 1971.

Huson, Paul. *The Devil's Picturebook*. G.P Putnam's Sons, 1971.

Irwin, Lee. *Gnostic Tarot*. Samuel Weiser, 1998.

Isabella. *Mystic Sciences: Tarot and Numerology*. Santa Monica Press, 1994.

Jacobs, Michael. *Ten and Twenty-Two: A Journey Through the Paths of Wisdom*. Jason Aronson, 1997.

Japikse, Carl. *Exploring the Tarot*. Ariel Press, 1989.

Jayanti, Amber. *Living the Tarot*. Borgo Press, 1988.

———. *Tarot for Dummies*. Hungry Minds, 2001.

Jedrziewski, Anna. *Tarot as a Tool for Personal Growth: The Getting There from Here Spreads*. Inanna Works, 1996.

———. *Tarot as a Tool for Personal Growth: The Numerology Spreads*. Inanna Works, 1996.

———. *Tarot as a Tool for Personal Growth: The Sacred Geometry Spreads*. Inanna Works, 1997.

Jette, Christine. *Tarot for All Seasons*. Llewellyn Publications, 2001.

———. *Tarot Shadow Work*. Llewellyn Publications, 2000.

Johnson, Cait. *Tarot for Every Day*. Shawangunk Press, 1994.

Johnson, Cait, and Maura D. Shaw. *Tarot Games*. Harper San Francisco, 1994.

Jorgensen, Danny L. *The Esoteric Scene, Cultic Milieu, and Occult Tarot*. Garland, 1992.

Jung, Carl Gustav. *Synchronicity: An Acausal Connecting Principle*. Princeton, 1973.

Junjulas, Craig. *Psychic Tarot*. Morgan and Morgan, 1985.

Kalinkova, Ivarna. *The Wisdom Well*. Barrons, 2003.

Kaplan, Stuart R. *The Encyclopedia of Tarot*. Vol. I. U.S. Games Systems, Inc., 1978.

———. *The Encyclopedia of Tarot*. Vol. II. U.S. Games Systems, Inc., 1986.

———. *The Encyclopedia of Tarot*. Vol. III. U.S. Games Systems, Inc., 1990.

———. *Tarot Classic*. U.S. Games Systems, 1972.

Kaser, R. T. *Tarot in Ten Minutes*. Avon, 1992.

Kelly, Dorothy. *Tarot Card Combinations*. Samuel Weiser, 1995.

Ketch, Tina. *Get a Life: Archetypal Personalities as Seen Through Tarot.* Boaz, 1991.

Kettlewell, Sarah. *Guide to Tarot.* Caxton, 2000.

Knight, Gareth. *The Magickal World of Tarot.* The Aquarian Press, 1991.

———. *The Treasure House of Images.* Destiny Books, 1986.

Konraad, Sandor. *Classic Tarot Spreads.* Schiffer, 1985.

———. *Numerology: Key to Tarot.* Schiffer, 1983.

Krafchow, Dovid. *Listening to the Soul: A Cabalistic Guide to the Tarot.* Shadiam, 2002.

Lammey, W. C. *Karmic Tarot: A New System for Finding Your Lifetime's Purpose.* Borgo Press, 1988.

Laurence, Theodor. *The Sexual Key to the Tarot.* New American Library, 1973.

Leary, Timothy. *The Game of Life.* Peace Press, 1979.

LeGette, Bernard Spencer. *The Rational Tarot.* Arthur Barker, 1976.

LeMieux, David. *The Ancient Tarot and Its Symbolism.* Cornwall Books, 1985.

———. *Forbidden Images: The Secrets of the Tarot.* Barnes & Noble Books, 1985.

Lewis, Keren. *The Joy of Tarot.* Astrolog, 2002.

Lionnet, Annie. *Secrets of Tarot*. Dorling Kindersley, 2000.

———. *The Tarot Directory*. Chartwell, 2002.

Lotterhand, Jason C. *Thursday Night Tarot*. Newcastle, 1989.

Lucia, Linda. *Releasing Through the Tarot*. Lucia, 1988.

McCarrdl, Amber. *A Kaleidoscope of Day Dreams: A Spiritual Journey Through the Tarot*. J.J. Publishing, 1998.

MacCormack, Kathleen. *Beginner's Tarot*. Barrons, 2001.

MacGregor, Trish, and Phyllis Vega. *Power Tarot*. Fireside, 1998.

Martello, Leo Louis. *Reading the Tarot*. Avery Publishing Group, 1990.

Masino, Marcia. *Easy Tarot Guide*. ACS Publications, 1983.

Mathers, S. L. *Tarot*. Gordon, 1973.

Maxwell, Joseph. *The Tarot*. Neville Spearman Ltd., 1975.

Michelsen, Teresa. *Designing Your Own Tarot Spreads*. Llewellyn, 2003.

Moakley, Gertrude. *The Tarot Cards Painted by Bonifacio Bembo*. New York Public Library, 1966.

Montalban, Madeline. *The Prediction Book of Tarot*. Blandford, 1983.

Moore, Daphna. *The Rabbi's Tarot: An Illumination from the Kundalini to the Pineal to the Pituitary*. Hughes Henshaw Publications, 1987.

Morag, Hali. *All About Tarot*. Astrolog, 1999.

———. *Tarot: The Ultimate Full-Color Guide*. Astrolog, 2002.

Morgan, Diane. *Magical Tarot, Mystical Tao*. St. Martin's Griffin, 2003.

Morgan, Frederick. *The Tarot of Cornelius Agrippa*. Sagarin Press, 1978.

Moura, Ann. *Tarot for the Green Witch*. Llewellyn, 2003.

Muchery, Georges. *The Astrological Tarot*. Crescent Books, 1989.

Newman, Kenneth D. *The Tarot: A Myth of Male Initiation*. C.G. Jung Foundation for Analytical Psychology, 1983.

Nichols, Sallie. *Jung and Tarot: An Archetypal Journey*. Samuel Weiser, 1980.

Noble, Vicki. *Motherpeace: A Way to the Goddess through Myth, Art, and Tarot*. Harper & Row, 1983.

Nordic, Rolla. *Let's Talk About the Tarot: A Tarot Story for Children and the Young at Heart*. Vantage, 1992.

———. *The Tarot Shows the Path*. Regency Press, 1960.

Olmstead, Kathleen. *The Girl's Guide to Tarot*. Sterling, 2002.

Olsen, Christina. *The Art of Tarot*. Abbeville Press, 1995.

O'Neill, Robert V. *Tarot Symbolism*. Fairways Press, 1986.

Osho. *Tarot in the Spirit of Zen*. St. Martin's Griffin, 2003.

Ouspensky, P. D. *The Symbolism of the Tarot*. Dover, 1976.

Ozaniec, Naomi. *The Element Tarot Handbook*. Element, 1994.

———. *The Illustrated Guide to Tarot*. Godsfield, 1999.

Papus. *Tarot of the Bohemians*. Chapman and Hall, 1892.

Payne-Towler, Christine. *The Underground Stream: Esoteric Tarot Revealed*. Noreah Press, 1999.

Peters, Roberta. *Elementary Tarot*. Caxton, 2000.

Pielmeier, Heidemarie, and Marcus Schirner. *Illustrated Tarot Spreads*. Sterling, 1999.

Pollack, Rachel. *The Complete Illustrated Guide to the Tarot*. Element, 1999.

———. *The Forest of Souls: A Walk Through the Tarot*. Llewellyn, 2002.

———. *The Open Labyrinth*. Borgo Press, 1988.

———. *The New Tarot: Modern Variations of Ancient Images*. Overlook Press, 1990.

———. *Salvador Dali's Tarot*. Salem House, 1985.

———. *Seventy-Eight Degrees of Wisdom*. Volumes 1 and 2. Borgo Press, 1986.

Porter, Tracy. *Tarot Companion*. Llewellyn, 2000.

Prosapio, Richard. *Intuitive Tarot*. Morgan & Morgan, 1990.

Pushong, Carlyle. *The Tarot of the Magi*. Regency, 1969.

Quntanna, Beatrex. *Tarot: A Universal Language*. Art Ala Carte, 1989.

Raine, Kathleen. *Yeats, The Tarot, and the Golden Dawn*. Dolman Press, 1972.

Rakoczi, Basil. *The Painted Caravan*. Boucher, 1954.

Reiher, Jim. *The Message in the Tarot*. N.p., 1998.

Renee, Janina. *Tarot Spells*. Llewellyn, 1990.

Ricklef, James. *Knighthawk's Tarot Readings*. Writer's Club Press, 2001.

Riley, Jana. *The Tarot Book*. Samuel Weiser, 1992.

———. *Tarot Dictionary and Compendium*. Samuel Weiser, 1995.

Roberts, Richard. *The Original Tarot and You*. Vernal Equinox, 1987.

Rose, Carol Jean. *Tarot Comparisons: 78 Packs of 78 Cards*. Rosehips Productions, 1999.

Rosengarten, Arthur. *Tarot and Psychology: Spectrums of Possibility*. Paragon House, 2000.

Roszak, Theodore. *Fool's Cycle—Full Cycle: Reflections on the Great Trumps of the Tarot*. Robert Briggs Associates, 1988.

Sadhu, Mouni. *The Tarot*. Wilshire, 1962.

Sandbach, John. *Astrology, Alchemy, and the Tarot*. Seek-It Publications, 1981.

———. *The Golden Cycle: A Text on the Tarot.* Aries, 1976.

Sargent, Carl. *Personality, Divination and the Tarot.* Destiny Books, 1988.

Sariol, Elsa. *Tarot of an Old Gypsy.* Writers Club Press, 2000.

Sharman-Burke, Juliet. *The Complete Book of Tarot.* St. Martin's Press, 1987.

———. *Mastering the Tarot: An Advanced Personal Teaching Guide.* St. Martin's Griffin, 2000.

Shavick, Nancy. *The Tarot.* Prima Materia, 1985.

Shephard, John. *The Tarot Trumps: Cosmos in Miniature.* Aquarian, 1985.

Sisson, Pat. *The Royal Path: A Layman's Look at the Tarot.* Earthtide, 1989.

Skafte, D. *Listening to the Oracle.* Harper SanFrancisco, 1997.

Starbird, Margaret. *The Tarot Trumps and the Holy Grail.* Wovenword, 2000.

Sterling, Stephen Walter. *Tarot Awareness.* Llewellyn, 2000.

Steward, Alan. *Down to Earth Tarot.* ABACO, 1992.

———. *The World's Easiest Tarot Book.* ABACO, 1995.

Stewart, Rowenna. *Collins Gem Tarot.* Harper Collins, 1998.

Sturzaker, James. *Tarot Symbolism Revealed.* Kingfisher, 1987.

Summers, Catherine, and Julian Vayne. *The Inner Space Work Book: Developing Counseling Skills Through the Tarot*. Capall Bann, 1994.

———. *Personal Development with the Tarot*. Quantum, 2002.

Thierens, A. E. *The General Book of the Tarot*. David McKay, 1928.

Tobin-Gray, Alarnah. *Time Tarot*. Simon and Schuster, 2002.

Tognetti, Arlene, and Lisa Lenard. *The Intuitive Arts on Love: Use Astrology, Tarot and Psychic Intuition to See Your Future*. Alpha, 2003.

———. *The Intuitive Arts on Work: Use Astrology, Tarot, and Psychic Intuition to See Your Future*. Alpha, 2003

Uecker, Ellen Z. *Tarot Looking Glass: Alternative New Age Guide to the Psychology of Tarot*. Mass Media Publications, 1994.

Waite, Arthur Edward. *The Pictorial Key to the Tarot*. Rider, 1910.

Walker, Ann. *Living Tarot*. Capall Bann, 1994.

Walsh, Allyson. *The Sacred Tarot Unveiled*. Allyson Universal Ministry, 1994.

Wang, Robert. *The Qabalistic Tarot*. Samuel Weiser, 1983.

———. *Tarot Psychology: Handbook for the Jungian Tarot*. Urania Verlags Ag, 1990.

Wanless, James. *The New Age Tarot: Guide to the Thoth Deck*. Merrill-West, 1986.

———. *Strategic Intuition for the Twenty-First Century: Tarot for Business*. Merrill-West, 1996.

Warwick-Smith, Kate. *The Tarot Court Cards*. Destiny Books, 2003.

Webster, Roger St. John. *The Teach Yourself Tarot Course and the Cabbalistic Wheel*. Arthur Stockwell, 2002.

Weinstein, Marion. *Marion Weinstein's Handy Guide to Tarot Cards*. Earth Magic Publications, 2000.

Weor, Samael Aun. *Tarot and Kabbalah*. Gnostic Editions, 1996.

Willis, Tony. *Magick and the Tarot*. The Aquarian Press, 1988.

Wilson, Marie Claire. *The Spiritual Tarot: The Keys to the Divine Temple*. The Spiritual Tarot, 1995.

Wirth, Oswald. *The Tarot of the Magicians*. Samuel Weiser, 1990.

Woudhuysen, Jan. *Tarot Therapy: A Guide to the Subconscious*. J.P. Tarcher, 1979.

Younger, J. Kelley, ed. *New Thoughts on Tarot*. Newcastle Publishers, 1989.

Zain, C. C. *The Sacred Tarot*. Church of Light, 1994.

Ziegler, Gerd. *Tarot: Mirror of the Soul*. Samuel Weiser, 1988.

Index

A

Acceptance 120
Ace of Cups 125, 126, 127, 268
Ace of Pentacles 78, 80, 267
Ace of Swords 170, 171, 172, 268
Ace of Wands 213, 214, 215, 268
Active waiting 106
Adam and Eve 28, 56, 57
Adaptation 258
Anger 13, 31, 150, 196, 233
Approval 230
Archetypes 272
Aristotle 32
Art 277, 281, 283
Assertiveness 168
Asthma 115
Attraction 128, 129, 130
Avoidance 173
Awakening 195, 197
Awareness 284

B

Becoming 9, 205, 208, 233
Belief 25
Betrayal 198
Blame 57
Blood 140
Buddhists 71, 145
Business 286

C

Castle 271
Catastrophe 60
Celtic cross 262
Change 66, 104, 235
Chariot 31, 32, 33, 34, 259, 267, 268
Charity 95
Childhood 28, 70, 92, 142, 256
Children 91, 118, 281
Choice 28, 274
Circumstance 185

Color 281
Commitment 85, 86
Communication 275
Compensation 95
Conflict 226
Conscience 188
Conscious 29
Consequences 44
Contentment 120
Control 31
Cooperation 34
Coping 82
Correspondences 275
Courage 50
Criticism 235
Cups 7, 8, 78, 127, 128, 130, 132, 133, 135, 137, 138, 142, 144, 145, 146, 149, 150, 152, 155, 156, 162, 164, 267, 268, 269
Cycle 283, 284

D

Death 50, 51, 52, 73, 162, 267
Death card 50, 52, 162
Demands 23
Demeter 19, 21
Deprivation 91, 93
Desire 145
Devil 30, 56, 57, 58, 267, 277
Diana complex 35
Disappointment 153
Discrimination 153
Disease 198
Distortion 56
Distrust 162
Divorce 222
Dreams 65, 111, 158, 249, 280
Drifting 167, 168

E

Eden 28, 29, 57, 276
Emanation 120, 125

Emperor 22, 23, 24, 267, 268
Empress 7, 19, 20, 21, 30, 249, 259, 267
Energy 69, 140
Envy 147
Experience 115

F

Failure 100
Faith 30, 50
Farming 99
Fate 40, 85
Fatherlessness 94
Fear 13, 60, 186
Fool iv, 7, 9, 10, 11, 37, 77, 267, 268, 269, 283
Forgiveness 198
Fortitude 30, 146
Fortuna 40, 41
Fortune 40, 41, 43, 268, 274
Fulfillment 75, 153
Future 271, 274, 285

G

Garden 28, 29, 57, 272
Giving 55, 88, 96, 142
Goals 237
God 14, 25, 28, 29, 42, 47, 48, 57, 70, 76, 93, 102, 120, 121, 132, 136, 140, 144, 155, 177, 181, 186, 233, 244, 245
Gothic arch 87
Gothic period 7
Gratification 152
Gratitude 132, 133
Greed 145, 147
Growth 277, 278
Guidance 63

H

Hanged Man 30, 47, 48, 49, 51, 267, 268
Harvest 123
Helplessness 42

Hermetic Order of the Golden Dawn 6
Hermit 37, 38, 39, 111, 267
Hesitation 161, 251
Hestia 132
Hierophant 7, 25, 26, 27, 28, 30, 199, 267, 268, 269
High Priestess 16, 18, 267
Holy Grail 161, 252, 284
Hope 30, 64, 155, 264
Humility 146

I

Independence 187
Infidelity 57
Influence 201
Insight 106, 158
Inspiration 274
Integration 53, 55
Intention 12
Introverts 258
Intuition 237, 247, 285, 286
Isis 63

J

Jealousy 58, 178
Judgment 72, 73, 74, 267, 269
Jung, Carl 278
Justice 30, 44, 45, 46, 95, 267

K

Kabbalists 120
King of Cups 167, 268
King of Pentacles 123, 124, 267
King of Swords 210, 211, 212, 268
King of Wands 256, 258, 269
Knight of Cups 118, 161, 162, 163, 268
Knight of Pentacles 117, 118, 267
Knight of Swords 118, 204, 205, 206, 268
Knight of Wands 118, 250, 251, 269
Krishnamurti 191

L

Last Judgment 72
Law of Polarity 210, 211
Leaving 78, 149
Limitation 191
Lion 273
Loss 94, 133, 138, 139, 140, 150
Lovers 28, 29, 30, 56, 57, 267, 268
Lucan 51
Lust 146

M

Magician 12, 13, 14, 18, 199, 267
Magick 14, 273, 286
Major Arcana 3, 30, 31, 33, 49, 74, 75, 77, 78, 162, 260
Marcus Aurelius 40, 75
Maya 76
Meditation 181, 274
Memory 16
Middle Ages 1, 29, 86, 87, 99, 152
Minor Arcana 3, 4, 6, 12, 78, 95, 121, 260
Miserliness 88
Moon 5, 30, 66, 68, 70, 267
Mother 19, 120, 140, 255
Mother Nature 19, 120, 140
Mourning 139

N

Nature 19, 120
Negativity 23
Neglect 92, 178
Night 280
Nurturing 19

O

Objectivity 216
Optimism 50
Other 23, 58, 85, 97, 128, 173, 221, 249, 257
Overintellectualization 171
Overreaction 204

P

Page of Cups 6, 158, 159, 268
Page of Pentacles 113, 114, 267
Page of Swords 201, 203, 268
Page of Wands 247, 248, 269
Pain 13, 170, 176
Parents 58, 165
Past 73, 242
Path 272, 281, 284
Patience 235
Pentacles 7, 78, 79, 82, 85, 87, 88, 91, 95, 99, 102, 103, 105, 109, 110, 118, 120, 121, 132, 267, 268
Permanence 179
Perseverance 244, 246
Pluto 21
Possession 88
Potential 117
Power 22, 280
Problem-solving 83
Psychic 254, 275, 278, 285
Purpose 279

Q

Queens 122
Queen of Cups 121, 164, 165, 268
Queen of Pentacles 120, 121, 122, 165, 267
Queen of Swords 121, 207, 208, 268
Queen of Wands 121, 253, 254, 255, 269

R

Rationalization 210
Reason 170, 250
Redemption 72
Rejection 135, 137
Relationships 270
Reoccurring cards 202
Repression 164
Resistance 233, 234
Restraint 250
Retirement 138

Revelation 109, 111
Reward 50
Rider-Waite Tarot iv, 6

S

Sacrifice 47
Searching 149
Seasons 278
Secrets 71, 279, 280
Security 222
Seeker 151
Self-denial 135
Self-development 20
Self-help groups 100
Self-improvement 99, 232
Self-respect 135
Self-revelation 65
Seneca 58
Separation 253
Shadow 278
Skills 285
Sloth 146
Spirituality 273
Spreads 270, 277, 278, 279, 280, 282
St. Paul 47
Star 30, 63, 64, 267
Strength 30, 34, 35, 36, 267
Styx 162
Success 144, 238
Sun 5, 30, 69, 70, 71, 267
Swords 78, 170, 172, 173, 174, 176, 178, 179, 182, 184, 185, 188, 191, 192, 195, 197, 198, 199, 200, 202, 203, 205, 212, 267, 268
Symbol 276
Symbolism 3, 273, 279, 281, 284
Synchronicity 159, 278

T

Tarot readings 2, 158, 167, 216, 237, 249, 259
Temperance 30, 53, 54, 55, 148, 267
Time 85, 285

Timing 106
Tower 30, 60, 61, 62, 267, 271
Transformation 207, 271, 276
Transition 78
Tree of Life 16, 109, 260, 272
Trust 242

V

Victimization 194
Victory 182
Vigilance 241
Vision 219

W

Waite, Arthur Edward 285
Waiting 105
Wands 8, 78, 213, 216, 219, 220, 222, 224, 226, 230, 231, 232, 233, 235, 237, 239, 241, 244, 246, 253, 267, 268, 269
Water 164
Wheel of Fortune 30, 40, 41, 42, 43, 267
Will 260
Wisdom 37, 271, 272, 276, 277, 278, 282
Witch 281
Work 33, 278, 285
World 30, 75, 76, 77, 78, 267, 275, 276, 279, 284

Z

Zen 71, 281

About The Author

Laurie Watts-Amato, Ph.D., holds advanced degrees in clinical nutrition and library science. She has over thirty years of experience reading, researching, and designing Tarot cards. She can be contacted through her website <*www.tarotinsights.com*>.

Printed in the United Kingdom
by Lightning Source UK Ltd.
127922UK00001B/65/A

PARIS

Restaurant Guide

HIGHLY RECOMMENDED RESTAURANTS
FOR YOUR DINING EXPERIENCE IN PARIS

DEREK M. VISAGE

2023'S PARIS RESTAURANT GUIDE
Highly Recommended Restaurants for Your
Dining Experience in Paris.

© Derek M. Visage
© E.G.P. Editorial

ISBN-13: 9798391223566

Copyright © All rights reserved.

PARIS
TOP 50 RESTAURANTS

Welcome to the vibrant city of Paris, the gastronomic capital of the world! I am delighted to present to you this book, which will guide you through the 50 most popular restaurants in this charming metropolis. In the following pages, we will explore the culinary gems of five iconic neighborhoods: Montmartre, Le Marais, Saint-Germain-des-Prés, Quartier Latin, and Île de la Cité. Get ready to delight your taste buds with exquisite dishes and immerse yourself in the authentic Parisian flavor!

Montmartre, known for its cobblestone streets and iconic Sacré-Coeur, is the perfect place to get lost and discover romantic bistros and cafes. In this picturesque corner of Paris, I will recommend 10 exceptional restaurants that will allow you to taste the best of French cuisine and experience the bohemian spirit of the area.

Le Marais, with its narrow medieval streets and lively nightlife, is a true gastronomic treasure. Here, I will show you 10 splendid restaurants where you can enjoy a diversity of flavors, from sophisticated French dishes to the most delicious falafels and dishes of Jewish tradition.

Saint-Germain-des-Prés, the cradle of Parisian intellectuals, is home to some of the most iconic restaurants and cafes in the city. Immerse yourself in the rich literary and artistic history of the neighborhood as I take you to 10 restaurants that blend culinary excellence with the unmistakable Parisian elegance.

The Quartier Latin, with its lively squares and student atmosphere, will offer you a unique and unforgettable culinary experience. Let me be your guide as I introduce you to 10 exceptional establishments that celebrate the diversity of international cuisine and the richness of French cuisine in this fascinating neighborhood.

Last but not least, Île de la Cité, the historical heart of Paris, is a paradise for food lovers. Amidst its stunning monuments and romantic alleys, I will reveal 10 restaurants that reflect the grandeur and sophistication of the French capital.

So, dear travelers, get comfortable and join me on this delicious journey through the exquisite culinary landscape of Paris! I am sure you will enjoy every bite, every sip, and every discovery this magnificent city has to offer. Bon appétit and long live France!

LIST OF RESTAURANTS

MONTMARTRE
LE BASILIC 9
LE REFUGE DES FONDUS 12
LA TABLE D'EUGÈNE 14
LE HIDE 16
CHEZ TOINETTE 17
L'ETE EN PENTE DOUCE 19
LE COQ RICO 20
CHEZ GINETTE 23
LE BISTROT POULBOT 25
AU PIED DE COCHON 27

LE MARAIS
L'AMBROISIE 29
CHEZ JANOU 31
LE COMPTOIR DU RELAIS 32
BREIZH CAFÉ 33
LES ENFANTS ROUGES 36
LE HANGAR 37
LES PHILOSOPHES 39
LE VOLTIGEUR 41
CAFÉ DES MUSÉES 44
MIZNON 46

SAINT-GERMAIN-DES-PRÉS
LES DEUX MAGOTS 48
CAFÉ DE FLORE 50
LE PROCOPE 51
L'ÉPICERIE 54

L'ATELIER DE JOËL ROBUCHON 56
LE COMPTOIR DU RELAIS 58
RALPH'S 60
LE SAINT-GERMAIN 61
LE PETIT ZINC 63
CHEZ FERNAND 65

QUARTIER LATIN
LA TOUR D'ARGENT 67
LE COUPE CHOU 69
LE COMPTOIR DU PANTHÉON 72
LE PETIT PONTOISE 74
AUX VERRES DE CONTACT 77
L'ÉTOILE MANQUANTE 80
POLIDOR 82
LA CRÊPERIE DU CLUNY 83
LA BOUTEILLE D'OR 85
L'ÎLOT 87

ÎLE DE LA CITÉ
LA BRASSERIE DE L'ISLE SAINT-LOUIS 89
LE SAINT RÉGIS 90
LE FLORE EN L'ÎLE 92
AUX ANYSETIERS DU ROY 94
LA RÉSERVE DE QUASIMODO 97
LE CAVEAU DU PALAIS 98
AU BOUGNAT 100
LA ROSE DE FRANCE 102
L'ORANGERIE 103
SORZA 106

MONTMARTRE RESTAURANTS

LE BASILIC

Le Basilic is a delightful French restaurant that offers a truly unique culinary experience. With its classic Parisian décor and mouth-watering menu, Le Basilic has become a go-to destination for both locals and tourists alike.

The restaurant is located in a beautifully restored building that dates back to the 19th century, giving it an old-world charm that is hard to resist. The interior is adorned with vintage chandeliers, original stonework, and elegant French artwork, which transports diners to a bygone era of Parisian elegance and sophistication.

Le Basilic is renowned for its French cuisine, which showcases the very best of classic French cooking techniques and locally sourced ingredients. From the succulent escargots de Bourgogne to the velvety foie gras, each dish is prepared with the utmost care and attention to detail, ensuring that every bite is an explosion of flavor.

One of the standout dishes at Le Basilic is the iconic duck confit, which is cooked to perfection and served with a side of crispy, golden pommes frites. Another must-try dish is the boeuf bourguignon, a hearty beef stew that is slow-cooked for hours to create a depth of flavor that is simply unforgettable.

In addition to its exquisite menu, Le Basilic also boasts an impressive wine list that features some of the finest vintages from France and beyond. Whether you prefer a full-bodied red or a crisp white, the knowledgeable sommelier will help you select the perfect wine to complement your meal.

Aside from its culinary offerings, Le Basilic is also a fascinating destination for history buffs. The restaurant is located just a stone's throw away from the iconic Sacré-Cœur Basilica, which offers panoramic views of Paris and is a must-see attraction for any visitor to the city.

Interestingly, Le Basilic gets its name from the basilica, which is said to have inspired the restaurant's owner to open the establishment. Legend has it that he was so taken with the beauty and grandeur of the basilica that he decided to name his restaurant after it.

Overall, Le Basilic is a fantastic destination for anyone looking to experience the best of French cuisine in a historic and elegant setting. With its delicious food, impeccable service, and stunning surroundings, this restaurant is sure to leave a lasting impression on all who visit.

One of the most unique aspects of Le Basilic is its location in the heart of Montmartre, which is known for its artistic and bohemian vibe. After a delicious meal at the restaurant, visitors can take a leisurely stroll through the charming cobbled streets of Montmartre, which are lined with galleries, boutiques, and street performers.

Montmartre is also famous for its connections to many famous artists, including Pablo Picasso, Vincent van Gogh, and Henri de Toulouse-Lautrec. Visitors can follow in their footsteps by visiting landmarks such as the Moulin Rouge cabaret and the famous Place du Tertre, which is home to many artists and their works.

Le Basilic is open for lunch and dinner, and reservations are highly recommended as the restaurant can get quite busy, especially during peak tourist seasons. The dress code is smart casual, and visitors are advised to dress appropriately for the occasion.

Aside from its regular menu, Le Basilic also offers a set menu for special occasions such as Valentine's Day and New Year's Eve. These menus often feature exclusive dishes and are paired with the finest wines, making them the perfect way to celebrate a special occasion in style.

In addition to its indoor dining areas, Le Basilic also has a beautiful outdoor terrace that offers stunning views of the surrounding area. This terrace is particularly popular during the summer months when visitors can enjoy their meal al fresco while soaking up the warm Parisian sunshine.

Overall, Le Basilic is a fantastic choice for anyone looking to experience the very best of French cuisine in a historic and elegant setting. With its delicious food, impressive wine list, and exceptional service, this restaurant is a must-visit destination for anyone traveling to Paris.

LE REFUGE DES FONDUS

Le Refuge des Fondus is a unique restaurant located in the picturesque neighborhood of Montmartre in Paris. This cozy eatery is a must-visit for anyone seeking an authentic French dining experience with a twist. Le Refuge des Fondus is famous for its quirky atmosphere and its unconventional approach to serving wine.

Upon entering the restaurant, guests are greeted with a cozy, rustic ambiance. The walls are adorned with vintage skis, bicycles, and other eclectic items, adding to the cozy and welcoming atmosphere. The seating arrangement is equally unique - diners are seated on long wooden benches, encouraging a convivial atmosphere where strangers quickly become friends.

One of the most distinctive features of Le Refuge des Fondus is its wine service. Rather than serving wine in traditional glasses, patrons are given baby bottles filled with wine. This unconventional method of serving wine has become a beloved tradition at the restaurant and adds to the playful and jovial ambiance.

The menu at Le Refuge des Fondus features classic French dishes such as cheese fondue and charcuterie boards, all of which are prepared with fresh, high-quality ingredients. Diners can also choose from a selection of French wines to pair with their meals. One popular dish is the "Chaudron du Refuges," a hearty stew made with beef, bacon, and vegetables, perfect for a chilly evening in Montmartre.

Located in the heart of Montmartre, Le Refuge des Fondus is surrounded by some of the most iconic landmarks in Paris. Just a short walk away is the Sacré-Cœur Basilica, a stunning landmark known for its breathtaking views of the city. Visitors can also explore the winding streets of Montmartre, which are filled with charming cafés, art galleries, and boutiques.

For those looking to experience a unique and memorable dining experience in Paris, Le Refuge des Fondus is the perfect choice. Its cozy ambiance, delicious cuisine, and playful approach to wine service make it a must-visit for travelers seeking an authentic taste of French culture.

In addition to its unique dining experience, Le Refuge des Fondus has a fascinating history that dates back over a century. The building that now houses the restaurant was originally a bakery in the early 1900s. In the 1920s, it was converted into a wine shop and then later transformed into a restaurant.

Over the years, Le Refuge des Fondus has attracted a diverse clientele, from locals to tourists from around the world. It has also been featured in numerous travel guides and food publications, cementing its status as one of the most unique dining destinations in Paris.

Despite its popularity, Le Refuge des Fondus maintains a warm and welcoming atmosphere, with friendly staff and a convivial vibe. It's the perfect place to unwind with friends after a day of exploring Montmartre, or to enjoy a romantic evening with a loved one.

For those looking to experience something truly out of the ordinary, Le Refuge des Fondus is a must-visit in Paris. Whether you're sipping wine from a baby bottle or enjoying a traditional cheese fondue, you're sure to have a memorable and enjoyable evening at this beloved restaurant in Montmartre.

LA TABLE D'EUGÈNE

Located in the charming neighborhood of Montmartre, Paris, La Table d'Eugène is a hidden gem that offers a unique dining experience to its guests. This restaurant is nestled on a quiet street, away from the bustling tourist crowds, and offers a cozy and intimate ambiance to those who seek it.

The restaurant is named after its founder and head chef, Eugène, who has been running the place for more than a decade. The restaurant's decor is simple yet elegant, with wooden furniture and soft lighting, creating a warm and inviting atmosphere that complements the food perfectly.

La Table d'Eugène's menu is a celebration of French cuisine, with a modern twist. The restaurant prides itself on using only the freshest, locally sourced ingredients, and the menu changes regularly to reflect the season and availability of ingredients. The dishes are beautifully presented, and the flavors are rich and complex, making every bite a gastronomic delight.

Some of the signature dishes at La Table d'Eugène include the pan-fried foie gras with fig compote and brioche toast, the roasted duck breast with orange and ginger sauce, and the caramelized apple tart with vanilla ice cream. The restaurant also offers an excellent selection of French wines, carefully curated by the knowledgeable staff, to complement each dish.

One of the unique features of La Table d'Eugène is the chef's table, where guests can enjoy a front-row seat to the kitchen action. This intimate dining experience allows guests to watch as the chefs prepare their meals, and they can even chat with the chefs and ask questions about the dishes.

In addition to the delicious food and intimate ambiance, La Table d'Eugène also has a fascinating history. The building that houses the restaurant dates back to the 19th century and was once a bakery. The restaurant has preserved some of the original features of the building, such as the brick walls and the original fireplace, adding to its charm and character.

Another interesting fact about La Table d'Eugène is that it has earned a prestigious Michelin star for its exceptional cuisine. This accolade is a testament to the restaurant's commitment to quality and excellence and makes it a must-visit destination for food lovers visiting Paris.

If you're planning a trip to Montmartre, La Table d'Eugène is definitely worth a visit. The restaurant's location on a quiet street in a charming neighborhood adds to its allure, and the food and ambiance make it a memorable dining experience. Whether you're looking for a romantic dinner for two or a special night out with friends, La Table d'Eugène is the perfect destination.

LE HIDE

Located on Rue du Pot de Fer, Le Hide is a cozy and intimate restaurant that exudes a sense of warmth and comfort. The ambiance is elegant yet relaxed, with soft lighting, exposed brick walls, and wooden accents that create a cozy and welcoming atmosphere.

The menu at Le Hide is a blend of French and international cuisine, with a focus on fresh and seasonal ingredients. From the classic French onion soup to the succulent steak tartare, every dish is prepared with precision and care, using only the finest ingredients.

One of the standout dishes at Le Hide is the slow-cooked pork belly, which is cooked to perfection and served with a flavorful sauce that perfectly complements the tender and juicy meat. Another must-try dish is the seafood risotto, which is creamy and indulgent, with a generous serving of plump and juicy shrimp.

In addition to the delicious food, Le Hide also boasts an impressive selection of wines, with an emphasis on French and European varietals. Whether you are a wine connoisseur or a casual drinker, there is sure to be a wine that suits your taste and budget.

Le Hide is not just a restaurant, it is an experience. The attentive and friendly staff go above and beyond to ensure that every guest feels welcome and comfortable, and the attention to detail in every aspect of the dining experience is truly impressive.

For those interested in history, Le Hide has a fascinating backstory. The building was originally used as a hideout for resistance fighters during World War II, hence the name "Le Hide". The restaurant pays homage to this history with a collection of vintage photographs and memorabilia from the era, creating a unique and memorable dining experience.

Located in the heart of Montmartre, Le Hide is a perfect spot for a romantic dinner or a special occasion. The restaurant is just a short walk from the iconic Sacré-Cœur Basilica, making it an ideal destination for tourists looking to explore the neighborhood and enjoy a memorable meal.

CHEZ TOINETTE

Chez Toinette's menu features a range of classic French dishes, with a focus on locally-sourced and seasonal ingredients. From the rich and creamy escargots de Bourgogne to the hearty boeuf bourguignon, every dish is made with care and attention to detail. And of course, no visit to Chez Toinette would be complete without trying their signature dish, the Coq au Vin - a succulent chicken stew cooked in red wine and served with a side of crispy French bread.

One of the most fascinating things about Chez Toinette is its history. The building itself dates back to the 18th century and has been a popular meeting place for artists and intellectuals throughout the years. In fact, it is rumored that the famous writer Ernest Hemingway was a regular patron of the restaurant during his time in Paris.

Today, Chez Toinette remains a popular spot for artists and writers, with its cozy atmosphere and friendly staff inspiring creativity and conversation.

Another unique aspect of Chez Toinette is its location. Situated in the heart of Montmartre, the restaurant is just a short walk away from some of the most iconic landmarks in Paris, including the Sacré-Cœur Basilica and the Moulin Rouge. After a day of exploring the city, Chez Toinette provides the perfect refuge for weary travelers, with its comforting cuisine and relaxed atmosphere.

But perhaps the most charming thing about Chez Toinette is the warm welcome that guests receive from its owner, Madame Toinette herself. With her bright smile and infectious personality, Madame Toinette greets every guest like an old friend, making sure that everyone feels at home in her restaurant. Her love for food and for people is evident in every aspect of the restaurant, from the carefully crafted menu to the cozy decor.

The interior of Chez Toinette is cozy and inviting, with warm lighting, rustic wooden furniture, and vintage decor. The walls are adorned with old photographs and paintings, giving the restaurant a sense of history and character. The intimate atmosphere makes it a perfect spot for a romantic date or a quiet evening with friends. One interesting fact about Chez Toinette is that the restaurant has been featured in several films and TV shows over the years, including Woody Allen's "Midnight in Paris" and the popular French crime drama "Engrenages". These appearances have only added to the restaurant's charm and allure, attracting even more visitors from around the world.

L'ETE EN PENTE DOUCE

L'Ete en Pente Douce, located in the charming Montmartre neighborhood of Paris, is a hidden gem that offers a unique and unforgettable dining experience for travelers seeking an authentic taste of French cuisine.

As you step into the restaurant, you'll be immediately struck by its warm and inviting atmosphere, with soft lighting and cozy seating that creates an intimate and romantic ambiance. The décor is inspired by the French countryside, with rustic wooden furniture, lush green plants, and subtle floral accents that add a touch of charm and elegance.

The menu at L'Ete en Pente Douce is a true masterpiece, featuring classic French dishes that are expertly crafted with the freshest and highest-quality ingredients. Start your meal with a tantalizing appetizer, such as escargots de Bourgogne, a traditional French dish of baked snails in garlic butter, or the delicate foie gras with fig compote.

For your main course, indulge in the restaurant's signature dish, the succulent coq au vin, a hearty stew made with chicken, bacon, mushrooms, and red wine. Other mouthwatering options include the tender beef bourguignon, the classic ratatouille, or the perfectly grilled steak frites.

No French meal would be complete without a decadent

dessert, and L'Ete en Pente Douce does not disappoint. Satisfy your sweet tooth with the creamy crème brûlée, the rich chocolate mousse, or the delicate tarte tatin, a classic French pastry made with caramelized apples and buttery pastry.

Aside from the delicious food, one of the unique features of L'Ete en Pente Douce is its location. The restaurant is situated on a charming cobblestone street in Montmartre, a historic and picturesque neighborhood that was once home to famous artists such as Picasso, Van Gogh, and Toulouse-Lautrec. The area is filled with quaint shops, art galleries, and stunning views of the city, making it the perfect place to explore before or after your meal.

Finally, a fun fact about L'Ete en Pente Douce: its name translates to "Summer on a Gentle Slope," which perfectly captures the restaurant's warm and welcoming ambiance. Whether you're traveling solo, with a partner, or with a group of friends, L'Ete en Pente Douce is the perfect place to savor the flavors of French cuisine and immerse yourself in the rich culture and history of Montmartre.

LE COQ RICO

Le Coq Rico is a must-visit restaurant for foodies and travelers alike. Located in the heart of Montmartre in Paris, this rustic and charming restaurant serves up some of the best poultry dishes in the city. From farm-to-table ingredients to expertly prepared dishes, Le Coq Rico is a true culinary gem.

The restaurant's menu is centered around one main

ingredient: poultry. Whether it's chicken, duck, or pigeon, the dishes at Le Coq Rico are cooked to perfection. The restaurant prides itself on using only the highest quality ingredients, with all poultry coming from small-scale farms in France. This commitment to using locally sourced ingredients results in dishes that are not only delicious but also sustainable.

One of the standout dishes at Le Coq Rico is the roasted chicken. Cooked in a rotisserie, the chicken is juicy and flavorful, with a crispy skin that is hard to resist. The restaurant also offers a range of other poultry dishes, such as duck confit and pigeon with foie gras, that are equally as delicious.

In addition to the poultry dishes, Le Coq Rico also serves up a range of tasty sides and desserts. The potato puree is a popular side dish that is creamy and flavorful, while the chocolate tart is the perfect way to end the meal on a sweet note.

The restaurant's interior is just as impressive as the food. The decor is rustic and charming, with wooden tables and chairs, exposed brick walls, and vintage lighting. The cozy atmosphere makes it the perfect place to enjoy a meal with friends or family.

For those looking to learn more about the culinary traditions of France, Le Coq Rico also offers cooking classes. Led by the restaurant's head chef, these classes provide a hands-on experience in preparing and cooking poultry dishes.

One interesting fact about Le Coq Rico is that the restaurant's name translates to "The Rich Rooster". This nod to the restaurant's focus on poultry is reflected in the decor, with rooster motifs and paintings adorning the walls.

Le Coq Rico is located in Montmartre, one of the most picturesque and vibrant neighborhoods in Paris. The restaurant is just a short walk from the famous Sacré-Cœur Basilica and offers stunning views of the city.

Overall, Le Coq Rico is a must-visit restaurant for anyone looking to experience the best of French cuisine. With its commitment to locally sourced ingredients, expertly prepared dishes, and charming atmosphere, it's no wonder that this restaurant has become a favorite among locals and travelers alike.

In addition to its delicious food and charming atmosphere, Le Coq Rico has also been recognized for its culinary excellence. The restaurant has been awarded a Michelin star, a prestigious accolade in the culinary world that is only given to the very best restaurants.

One of the unique features of Le Coq Rico is its focus on nose-to-tail cooking. This means that every part of the bird is used in the cooking process, from the breast to the liver to the feet. This approach not only reduces waste but also ensures that every part of the bird is used to create delicious and flavorful dishes.

For those looking to pair their meal with the perfect wine, Le Coq Rico offers an extensive wine list that features a range of French and international wines. The restaurant also has a sommelier on staff who can help guests select the perfect wine to complement their meal.

Another interesting feature of Le Coq Rico is its commitment to sustainability. The restaurant sources all of its poultry from small-scale farms in France, which not only supports local farmers but also ensures that the animals are treated humanely and raised in a sustainable manner. Additionally, the restaurant uses eco-friendly materials for its packaging and takeout containers.

Le Coq Rico has become a favorite among locals and tourists alike and is often recommended as a top dining destination in Paris. Reservations are highly recommended, as the restaurant can get quite busy, particularly during peak tourist season.

CHEZ GINETTE

Located in the heart of Montmartre, Chez Ginette is a charming restaurant that offers a warm and friendly atmosphere that is sure to make diners feel right at home. With a reputation for serving up some of the best French cuisine in the area, this restaurant is a must-visit for foodies and travelers looking to experience the flavors of Paris.

As soon as you step inside, you'll be greeted by the cozy ambiance of the restaurant, which is decorated in a traditional Parisian style with exposed brick walls, vintage posters, and wooden furniture. The staff is also incredibly friendly, welcoming you with a smile and offering recommendations on the menu.

Speaking of the menu, Chez Ginette offers a range of classic French dishes that are sure to satisfy any craving. From escargot to boeuf bourguignon, there's something for everyone here. One of the standout dishes is the Coq au Vin, a hearty chicken dish that is slow-cooked in red wine and served with creamy mashed potatoes. For dessert, don't miss the Crème Brûlée, a rich and decadent custard with a crunchy caramelized sugar topping.

But it's not just the food that makes Chez Ginette special. The restaurant is steeped in history and has been a fixture of the Montmartre neighborhood since it first opened its doors in 1933. Over the years, it has welcomed famous patrons such as Edith Piaf, Maurice Chevalier, and Pablo Picasso, who were drawn to its authentic Parisian atmosphere and delicious cuisine.

In fact, Chez Ginette has become something of a cultural landmark in Montmartre, with locals and tourists alike flocking to the restaurant to soak up its old-world charm. From the vintage decor to the live accordion music that fills the air, every aspect of Chez Ginette is designed to transport diners back in time to the golden age of Parisian dining.

Despite its popularity, Chez Ginette manages to maintain a sense of intimacy and warmth that is rare in larger, more touristy restaurants. The staff take the time to chat with customers and make them feel at home, and the cozy atmosphere encourages diners to linger over their meals and savor every bite.

So if you're looking for a truly authentic Parisian dining

experience, Chez Ginette is the place to be. With its delicious food, rich history, and cozy atmosphere, it's no wonder that this restaurant has become a beloved institution in the heart of Montmartre.

LE BISTROT POULBOT

Le Bistrot Poulbot with its warm and cozy ambiance makes it a popular spot for locals and tourists alike, seeking to indulge in the rich flavors of French cuisine. The restaurant takes its name from the famous French artist Francisque Poulbot, who was known for his depictions of the Parisian working class, and whose artwork adorns the walls of the restaurant, creating a nostalgic atmosphere.

Le Bistrot Poulbot offers a unique and authentic dining experience, serving classic French dishes with a modern twist. The menu features a wide range of delicious options, from escargots to beef bourguignon, and of course, a variety of fresh baguettes and cheeses. The dishes are made with the freshest ingredients, sourced locally whenever possible, ensuring that each bite is bursting with flavor.

One of the restaurant's most popular dishes is the "Cassoulet," a hearty stew of white beans, sausage, and duck confit, cooked to perfection and served with a crispy baguette. The dish is a staple of French cuisine, and Le Bistrot Poulbot's version is one of the best in the city. Other favorites include the "Coq au Vin," a classic chicken stew, and the "Poulet Roti," a roasted chicken with garlic and thyme.

The restaurant's location in Montmartre is also a draw for travelers, as the area is steeped in history and culture. Montmartre was once the center of the bohemian movement in Paris, and today it is still home to many artists and musicians. Visitors can wander the winding streets and explore the vibrant cafés, shops, and galleries that line the neighborhood's cobblestone streets.

Le Bistrot Poulbot's interior is a cozy and welcoming space, with exposed brick walls, wooden beams, and vintage décor. The restaurant's warm lighting and intimate seating make it the perfect spot for a romantic dinner or a meal with friends. The outdoor terrace, overlooking the charming streets of Montmartre, is also a popular spot for al fresco dining during the warmer months.

Interesting fact: Le Bistrot Poulbot was once a haunt of famous artists and writers, including Pablo Picasso and Ernest Hemingway. The restaurant's rich history and artistic heritage make it a must-visit destination for anyone interested in the cultural history of Paris.

In addition to its delicious food and historic location, Le Bistrot Poulbot also offers a unique cultural experience for travelers. On select evenings, the restaurant hosts live music performances, featuring local musicians and singers. Visitors can enjoy a meal while listening to the sounds of traditional French music, adding an extra layer of authenticity to their dining experience.

Overall, Le Bistrot Poulbot is a delightful restaurant that captures the essence of traditional French cuisine and culture. Its delicious food, warm ambiance, and historic location make it a must-visit destination for anyone traveling to Paris. Whether you're seeking a romantic dinner for two or a meal with friends, Le Bistrot Poulbot is sure to leave a lasting impression.

AU PIED DE COCHON

Au Pied de Cochon is a legendary restaurant located in the heart of Montmartre, Paris. It is a place that has been drawing in diners for over 100 years, and is famous for its traditional French cuisine, particularly its namesake dish of pig's feet.

The restaurant has a warm and welcoming atmosphere, with its classic Parisian brasserie decor, white tablecloths, and dark wood furniture. The space is filled with the buzz of conversation and the clinking of glasses, creating a lively and convivial ambiance.

One of the most popular dishes at Au Pied de Cochon is, of course, the eponymous pig's feet, or pied de cochon in French. The dish is a classic of French cuisine, and at this restaurant it is served with creamy mashed potatoes and a rich sauce. But there are plenty of other delicious options on the menu as well, including hearty soups, fresh seafood, and perfectly cooked steaks.

Beyond the food, there are plenty of interesting facts and curiosities about Au Pied de Cochon. For example, the restaurant is open 24 hours a day, 7 days a week, which makes it a popular destination for late-night revelers and early-morning diners alike. It has also played host to a number of famous patrons over the years, including Ernest Hemingway and Pablo Picasso.

In addition to its great food and atmosphere, Au Pied de Cochon is also located in a fantastic spot in Montmartre. The restaurant is just a stone's throw from the iconic Sacré-Cœur Basilica, and is surrounded by charming cobblestone streets and historic buildings. It is a great place to stop for a meal after exploring the many sights and sounds of this vibrant neighborhood.

For travelers looking to experience the best of traditional French cuisine in a lively and welcoming atmosphere, Au Pied de Cochon is an excellent choice. With its classic decor, delicious food, and fascinating history, it is a true gem of the Parisian dining scene.

LE MARAIS RESTAURANTS

L'AMBROISIE

L'Ambroisie is a legendary restaurant located in the heart of Le Marais district in Paris. It is known for its classic French cuisine, elegant atmosphere, and exceptional service, making it a must-visit destination for food lovers and connoisseurs from around the world.

The restaurant is situated in a beautifully restored 16th-century building, boasting a warm and inviting ambiance that sets the perfect tone for a memorable dining experience. The interior is tastefully decorated with intricate woodwork, crystal chandeliers, and plush seating, exuding a refined and sophisticated vibe that complements the exquisite cuisine.

L'Ambroisie's menu features a range of classic French dishes that have been expertly crafted to perfection. The restaurant sources only the freshest, highest-quality ingredients, and each dish is beautifully presented with artistic flair. The menu changes seasonally, ensuring that guests can savor the best of each ingredient when it's at its peak.

One of the most popular dishes at L'Ambroisie is the iconic Bresse chicken, which is roasted to perfection and served with a decadent foie gras sauce. The restaurant's desserts are equally impressive, with classics such as crème brûlée, tarte Tatin, and chocolate soufflé leaving guests wanting more.

Aside from its exceptional cuisine, L'Ambroisie is also known for its extensive wine list, which features an impressive selection of French and international wines. The restaurant's sommelier is highly knowledgeable and can recommend the perfect wine pairing to complement each dish, ensuring a complete gastronomic experience.

In addition to its culinary offerings, L'Ambroisie's location in Le Marais makes it an ideal spot for exploring the area's charming streets and historic landmarks. Le Marais is one of Paris's most vibrant and eclectic neighborhoods, home to numerous art galleries, boutiques, and cultural attractions.

Travelers visiting L'Ambroisie should also take note of the restaurant's interesting history. It was founded in 1986 by Bernard Pacaud, a celebrated French chef who had previously worked at the Michelin-starred restaurant Lasserre. Over the years, L'Ambroisie has earned numerous accolades and awards, including three Michelin stars, making it one of the most renowned restaurants in Paris.

Despite its prestigious reputation, L'Ambroisie maintains a warm and welcoming atmosphere, ensuring that guests feel comfortable and at ease. The restaurant's staff is friendly and attentive, going above and beyond to ensure that every detail is taken care of and that guests leave with unforgettable memories.

CHEZ JANOU

This beloved restaurant has been a fixture in the area for over 80 years, and its rustic interior and traditional French cuisine continue to delight locals and tourists alike.

Located on the Rue Roger Verlomme, Chez Janou boasts a warm and inviting atmosphere that immediately transports diners to a bygone era. The walls are adorned with vintage posters and old-fashioned knick-knacks, while the wooden tables and chairs provide a cozy and intimate setting for a meal with friends or loved ones.

The menu at Chez Janou is a celebration of classic French dishes, with a focus on the freshest seasonal ingredients. Start your meal with a plate of escargots de Bourgogne, or snails cooked in garlic butter and parsley, a true French delicacy. For the main course, try the restaurant's signature dish, the bouillabaisse, a hearty fish soup with an array of seafood that will leave you feeling satisfied and content. Or, if you're in the mood for something lighter, go for the salade niçoise, a refreshing mix of lettuce, tuna, anchovies, and olives.
Chez Janou also has an extensive wine list featuring some of the best wines from France's various regions. Don't hesitate to ask the friendly and knowledgeable staff for their recommendations.

What sets Chez Janou apart from other restaurants in Le Marais is its charming and whimsical ambiance. The restaurant is famous for its bright blue shutters and colorful façade, which have become a staple of the neighborhood's landscape. It's not uncommon to see tourists stopping outside the restaurant to take pictures of the vibrant exterior.

If you're lucky enough to visit Chez Janou during the summer months, make sure to reserve a table on the restaurant's terrace. Situated on a quiet pedestrian street, the terrace is the perfect spot to soak up the sun and enjoy a glass of rosé while watching the world go by.

One of the most interesting facts about Chez Janou is that it was once a popular hangout spot for the famous artist Pablo Picasso. Legend has it that Picasso would often come to the restaurant with his friends and fellow artists to enjoy a meal and discuss their latest creations.

Chez Janou is also known for its friendly and attentive staff, who go above and beyond to make sure that every guest feels welcome and taken care of. The restaurant's owner, Madame Janou, can often be seen chatting with diners and ensuring that everything is running smoothly.

LE COMPTOIR DU RELAIS

Located on the bustling Carrefour de l'Odéon, this classic bistro has become a beloved fixture of the neighborhood's dining scene.

The restaurant's warm and inviting atmosphere is immediately apparent upon entering. The decor is classic and elegant, with vintage photographs and paintings adorning the walls, giving diners a sense of the rich history of the area. The intimate dining room features wooden floors, dark wooden chairs, and tables adorned with white tablecloths, all of which contribute to the restaurant's refined ambiance.

Le Comptoir du Relais is renowned for its traditional French cuisine, with a menu that changes regularly to reflect the freshest seasonal ingredients. Diners can start their meal with the restaurant's signature escargots de Bourgogne, a classic dish of snails cooked in garlic butter, or the refreshing gazpacho soup, perfect for a hot summer day. The main course options are equally delicious, with classic dishes such as coq au vin and steak frites being staples of the menu. For dessert, diners can indulge in the rich and creamy crème brûlée, a perfect end to a fantastic meal.

One of the most interesting facts about Le Comptoir du Relais is its association with renowned French chef Yves Camdeborde. Camdeborde started his career as a sous chef at the iconic Hôtel de Crillon, before going on to become the head chef at the prestigious Le Bristol hotel. In 1998, he and his wife opened Le Comptoir du Relais, which quickly became a favorite among locals and visitors alike. Camdeborde's unique blend of classic French cuisine and modern culinary techniques has won him numerous accolades and awards, and he remains a fixture of the French culinary scene to this day.

Beyond the food, Le Comptoir du Relais also offers a prime location for travelers. Situated in the heart of Le Marais, the restaurant is surrounded by a plethora of attractions, including the iconic Sainte-Chapelle and the Musée Picasso. It is also within walking distance of many of Paris's famous landmarks, such as Notre-Dame Cathedral and the Louvre Museum.

For curious travelers looking for something special, Le Comptoir du Relais also has a secret upstairs dining room, known as the Cave du Comptoir. This intimate space is perfect for private events, with a menu tailored to the specific needs of each group. Diners can enjoy an exclusive meal in this cozy room, complete with a fireplace and a view over the bustling street below.

BREIZH CAFÉ

Breizh Café is a charming little restaurant located in the heart of Le Marais, Paris. This cozy eatery specializes in traditional French crepes, which are made using only the finest ingredients and prepared with an authentic Breton recipe.

The restaurant is housed in a beautifully restored 16th-century building that perfectly captures the rustic charm of the Breton countryside. The interior is warm and inviting, with exposed brick walls, wooden beams, and cozy seating that make it the perfect place to unwind after a long day of exploring the city.

One of the most interesting things about Breizh Café is its commitment to using only the best ingredients. All of the flour used in their crepes is organic and sourced from the best producers in France, while the fillings are made with locally-sourced and seasonal ingredients.

Their menu offers a wide variety of savory and sweet crepes, as well as a selection of artisanal ciders from small producers in Brittany. The menu also includes other Breton specialties, such as galettes (a savory buckwheat crepe) and kouign-amann (a buttery Breton pastry).

One of the must-try items on the menu is the "Complète" crepe, which is made with ham, emmental cheese, and a farm-fresh egg. It's a classic French dish that's been given a Breton twist, and it's sure to satisfy even the most discerning palate.

Another interesting fact about Breizh Café is that it's owned and operated by a Breton couple, Bertrand and Fanny Larcher, who are passionate about sharing the cuisine and culture of their homeland with the rest of the world. They've even opened additional locations in Tokyo, Cancale, and Saint-Malo, which speaks to the popularity of their delicious and authentic cuisine.

The restaurant is located in the heart of Le Marais, one of Paris's most vibrant and fashionable neighborhoods. This area is known for its beautiful architecture, trendy boutiques, and lively nightlife, making it the perfect destination for travelers looking to immerse themselves in the culture of the city.

Overall, Breizh Café is a charming and authentic restaurant that offers a delicious taste of Breton cuisine in the heart of Paris. Whether you're in the mood for a savory crepe or a sweet treat, you're sure to find something to satisfy your appetite here. So if you're looking for a unique dining experience in Paris, be sure to add Breizh Café to your list of must-visit destinations.

LES ENFANTS ROUGES

First opened in 2008, Les Enfants Rouges takes its name from the red uniforms worn by the children of a nearby orphanage in the 16th century. The restaurant is located in a historic building that dates back to the 17th century, with exposed stone walls, high ceilings, and elegant decor that transport diners to another era.

Les Enfants Rouges is helmed by Japanese chef Daï Shinozuka, who has earned a Michelin star for his innovative and inspired cuisine. The menu features a mix of French and Japanese influences, with creative dishes that use the freshest ingredients from local markets. Signature dishes include the black cod with miso glaze, seared foie gras with spiced apple compote, and the mouth-watering beef filet with wasabi butter.

But Les Enfants Rouges is more than just a restaurant - it's a true Parisian experience. The intimate setting, attentive service, and carefully crafted atmosphere make it the perfect spot for a romantic evening or special occasion. The wine list features a curated selection of French and international wines, with knowledgeable staff on hand to help you choose the perfect bottle to complement your meal.

One of the most unique aspects of Les Enfants Rouges is its location in Le Marais, one of the most dynamic and eclectic neighborhoods in Paris. The area is known for its trendy boutiques, art galleries, and historic landmarks, including the Place des Vosges and the Musée Picasso. Le Marais is also home to a thriving Jewish community, and Les Enfants Rouges offers a menu of kosher dishes for observant diners.

For travelers looking for an authentic taste of Parisian culture, Les Enfants Rouges is a must-visit destination. The restaurant's commitment to locally sourced ingredients, inventive cuisine, and warm hospitality make it a beloved fixture of the Parisian dining scene.

Whether you're in the mood for a romantic evening, a special celebration, or simply a delicious meal, Les Enfants Rouges is the perfect place to indulge your senses and savor the flavors of Paris. With its rich history, cozy ambiance, and exceptional cuisine, this restaurant is sure to be a highlight of any trip to the City of Light.

LE HANGAR

The restaurant's decor is sleek and contemporary, with exposed brick walls, wooden accents, and industrial-style lighting fixtures that create a warm and inviting atmosphere. Le Hangar's cozy seating arrangement makes it the perfect place for a romantic dinner or a catch-up with friends.

The menu at Le Hangar is a culinary journey through France, featuring classic dishes from different regions. Starters include escargots, foie gras, and a delicious French onion soup. Main dishes range from grilled meats to fish and seafood, with options like steak frites, bouillabaisse, and pan-seared duck breast.

One of the restaurant's signature dishes is the coq au vin, a hearty French stew made with chicken, mushrooms, and red wine. Another popular choice is the bœuf bourguignon, a tender beef stew slow-cooked with red wine and vegetables.

Le Hangar also boasts an impressive wine list, with a carefully curated selection of French and international wines to complement your meal. The knowledgeable staff can help you choose the perfect wine pairing for your dish.
Located in the heart of Le Marais, Le Hangar is just a short walk away from some of Paris's most iconic landmarks, including the Notre-Dame Cathedral and the Place des Vosges. The neighborhood itself is known for its vibrant nightlife, trendy boutiques, and picturesque cobblestone streets.

If you're looking for something unique to do after your meal, check out the many art galleries and museums in the area. The Picasso Museum, for example, is just a few blocks away and showcases an impressive collection of the artist's work.

But there's more to Le Hangar than just its location and delicious food. The restaurant has a rich history, having once served as a warehouse for goods transported along the nearby Canal Saint-Martin. The building's original features have been preserved, giving the space a rustic and authentic feel.

In addition to its storied past, Le Hangar is also known for its commitment to sustainability. The restaurant sources its ingredients from local, organic farms and supports eco-friendly practices in all aspects of its operation.

Overall, Le Hangar is a must-visit destination for foodies and travelers looking to experience the best of French cuisine in a unique and inviting setting. Whether you're in the mood for a romantic dinner or a night out with friends, Le Hangar is the perfect place to indulge in delicious food and fine wine while immersing yourself in the rich history and culture of Le Marais.

LES PHILOSOPHES

Les Philosophes is a charming and cozy restaurant located in the heart of Le Marais, one of the most historic and fashionable neighborhoods in Paris. With its quaint ambiance and delicious cuisine, this eatery is a favorite among locals and visitors alike.

Upon entering Les Philosophes, guests are greeted by a warm and inviting atmosphere. The restaurant's walls are adorned with vintage posters and artwork, and the cozy seating arrangements make for an intimate dining experience. The restaurant's outdoor seating is equally charming, with cozy bistro chairs and tables nestled in the heart of the Marais.

The menu at Les Philosophes features classic French dishes with a modern twist, all prepared with fresh and locally sourced ingredients. Guests can enjoy savory dishes like coq au vin and steak tartare, as well as lighter fare like salads and soups. The restaurant's wine list is equally impressive, with a wide variety of French and international wines to choose from.

One interesting fact about Les Philosophes is that the restaurant has been a staple in the Marais for over 30 years, having opened its doors in 1980. The restaurant has remained popular throughout the years, attracting both locals and tourists with its delicious food and charming ambiance.

Another interesting feature of Les Philosophes is its proximity to some of the most historic and culturally significant sites in Paris. Just a short walk from the restaurant, guests can visit landmarks like the Place des Vosges and the Musée Picasso, as well as the many boutiques and galleries that line the charming streets of the Marais.

For those looking to experience the true essence of Parisian cuisine and culture, a visit to Les Philosophes is a must. With its cozy atmosphere, delicious cuisine, and historic location, this restaurant offers a truly unique dining experience in the heart of one of the city's most iconic neighborhoods.

In addition to its savory cuisine, Les Philosophes also offers a delectable selection of desserts. Guests can indulge in classic French treats like crème brûlée and tarte tatin, as well as more modern creations like chocolate mousse and fruit sorbets.

For those seeking a lively atmosphere, Les Philosophes also offers a vibrant bar scene. The bar is located in the front of the restaurant and offers an extensive list of cocktails, beers, and wines. With its cozy seating and friendly staff, the bar is the perfect spot for a pre-dinner drink or a night out with friends.

One of the unique features of Les Philosophes is its commitment to sustainable and eco-friendly practices. The restaurant uses locally sourced ingredients whenever possible and works to reduce its carbon footprint through energy-efficient lighting and recycling programs.

When visiting Les Philosophes, be sure to take a moment to admire the restaurant's charming decor. The walls are adorned with vintage posters and artwork, creating a cozy and intimate atmosphere that is both welcoming and stylish.

LE VOLTIGEUR

The restaurant's décor is a perfect blend of modern and traditional French design, featuring plush banquettes, wooden beams, and elegant lighting fixtures. The space is cozy yet spacious enough to accommodate both intimate dinners and larger groups.

The menu at Le Voltigeur showcases the best of French gastronomy, with a focus on seasonal, locally-sourced ingredients. Guests can start with an array of mouth-watering appetizers, such as foie gras terrine, escargots, and oysters. For the main course, the restaurant offers an extensive selection of classic French dishes, including steak frites, roasted duck, and seafood platters. Vegetarian options are also available, such as the creamy risotto with seasonal vegetables or the truffle linguine.

To accompany the meal, Le Voltigeur has an impressive wine list that features a range of French and international wines. The knowledgeable staff is happy to make recommendations based on guests' preferences and the dishes they've ordered. For those who prefer a cocktail, the bar offers a creative selection of signature drinks, including the refreshing Voltigeur Spritz and the spicy Bloody Mary.

Apart from its delicious food and drinks, Le Voltigeur also has a rich history. The restaurant is housed in a building that dates back to the 17th century and has served as a military barracks and a stable for the French cavalry. The name "Le Voltigeur" pays homage to the soldiers who were part of the French Imperial Guard, known as "les voltigeurs," who were known for their agility and precision on the battlefield.

Le Marais is one of Paris' most fascinating districts, known for its charming cobblestone streets, beautiful architecture, and trendy shops and cafes. The neighborhood has a rich history, dating back to the Middle Ages when it was the center of Jewish life in Paris. Today, Le Marais is a popular destination for travelers looking to experience Parisian culture and cuisine.

In addition to its many attractions, Le Marais is also known for its thriving LGBTQ+ community. The neighborhood is home to many gay bars and clubs, as well as the Centre Pompidou, one of the world's leading modern art museums.

For travelers looking to experience the best of Parisian cuisine and culture, Le Voltigeur is a must-visit. The restaurant's delicious food, welcoming atmosphere, and rich history make it a perfect destination for a romantic dinner, a night out with friends, or a special occasion. With its prime location in Le Marais, guests can also explore the neighborhood's many attractions and experience the vibrant energy of Paris.

Le Voltigeur is a popular spot among locals and tourists alike, so reservations are highly recommended. The restaurant is open for lunch and dinner, and the menu changes seasonally to showcase the freshest ingredients. For a truly unforgettable dining experience, guests can opt for the chef's tasting menu, which offers a selection of the restaurant's most popular dishes.

One of the standout dishes at Le Voltigeur is the classic French onion soup, which is made with rich beef broth, caramelized onions, and topped with a crispy layer of gruyere cheese. The restaurant's version is a must-try for anyone visiting Paris, and it's the perfect comfort food on a chilly evening.

Another dish that's highly recommended is the roasted duck breast with honey and thyme glaze. The dish is cooked to perfection and served with a side of creamy mashed potatoes and sautéed vegetables. The duck breast is tender and flavorful, and the honey and thyme glaze adds a touch of sweetness that complements the rich flavor of the meat.

Le Voltigeur also offers a selection of decadent desserts, including the classic crème brûlée, which is made with creamy vanilla custard and topped with a layer of caramelized sugar. The restaurant's version is rich and indulgent, and it's the perfect way to end a delicious meal.

CAFÉ DES MUSÉES

This restaurant has become a favorite among locals and tourists alike, thanks to its warm atmosphere, excellent cuisine, and historic setting.

One of the things that sets Café des Musées apart from other restaurants in the area is its rich history. The building that houses the restaurant dates back to the 17th century and has served many purposes over the years. It was once a stable, a blacksmith's workshop, and a tavern before it was transformed into the cozy bistro that it is today. Despite the modernization, the restaurant has managed to maintain much of its historic charm, with its stone walls, wooden beams, and cozy decor.

One of the highlights of Café des Musées is the food. The menu is full of classic French dishes, such as escargots, foie gras, and coq au vin, as well as daily specials that showcase the freshest seasonal ingredients. The portions are generous, and the prices are reasonable, making it a popular spot for both lunch and dinner. The wine list is also impressive, with a great selection of French wines from different regions.

Aside from the food, the atmosphere is another draw for Café des Musées. The restaurant has a warm and welcoming ambiance that is perfect for a relaxed meal with friends or family. The walls are adorned with paintings and vintage posters, and the lighting is dimmed, creating a cozy and romantic atmosphere.

One of the best times to visit Café des Musées is during the lunch hour. The restaurant offers a three-course prix fixe menu that is an excellent value for the quality of food. The lunch menu changes every day, depending on what's fresh and in season, and includes a starter, main course, and dessert.

If you're a fan of museums, you'll appreciate the name of the restaurant, which translates to "Café of Museums." The name is a nod to the fact that the restaurant is located just a stone's throw away from the Musée Picasso and the Musée Carnavalet, both of which are worth a visit.

In addition to its proximity to museums, Café des Musées is also located in one of the most vibrant neighborhoods in Paris. Le Marais is known for its beautiful architecture, trendy boutiques, and lively nightlife. After a meal at Café des Musées, be sure to take a stroll through the charming streets of Le Marais and discover all that this neighborhood has to offer.

Overall, Café des Musées is a must-visit for anyone looking for an authentic Parisian experience. With its historic setting, delicious food, and charming ambiance, it's no wonder that this restaurant has become a favorite among locals and tourists alike. Whether you're in Paris for a weekend or an extended stay, be sure to add Café des Musées to your list of places to visit.

MIZNON

Miznon is a vibrant and bustling restaurant located in the heart of Le Marais. Founded by the acclaimed Israeli chef Eyal Shani, Miznon has quickly become a favorite among locals and visitors alike for its delicious and innovative cuisine, lively atmosphere, and friendly service.

As you step inside Miznon, you will be greeted by a colorful and eclectic décor that reflects the restaurant's bold and playful spirit. The walls are adorned with graffiti and street art, and the open kitchen in the center of the space buzzes with energy and activity. The menu, which is written on a chalkboard above the counter, features a mouth-watering selection of Middle Eastern-inspired dishes, including pita sandwiches, vegetable salads, roasted meats, and savory pastries.

One of the most popular items on the menu is the famous "Miznon's Ratatouille," a deconstructed version of the classic French dish that is made with grilled eggplant, zucchini, and bell peppers, served with a poached egg and a slice of crusty bread. Another must-try is the "Whole Roasted Cauliflower," a show-stopping dish that is cooked in the oven for hours until it is tender and caramelized, then served with tahini, herbs, and spices.

But Miznon's real specialty is its pita sandwiches, which

are made with freshly-baked pita bread that is soft, chewy, and bursting with flavor. The sandwiches are filled with a variety of ingredients, from roasted lamb and beef to grilled vegetables and falafel, and are accompanied by a range of homemade sauces and dips, such as harissa, tzatziki, and tahini.

In addition to its delicious food, Miznon is also known for its lively and convivial atmosphere, which makes it the perfect spot for a casual meal with friends or family. The staff is friendly and welcoming, and the communal tables and bar seating encourage interaction and conversation among diners.

For those who are interested in the history of the restaurant, Miznon was first opened in Tel Aviv in 2011, and quickly became a sensation for its fresh and inventive take on Israeli street food. Since then, Miznon has expanded to other cities around the world, including Paris, where it opened its doors in 2019.

If you're looking for a unique and exciting dining experience in Le Marais, Miznon is definitely worth a visit. Whether you're a foodie looking to explore new flavors and ingredients, or simply seeking a fun and relaxed atmosphere to enjoy a meal, Miznon has something for everyone. So come on in, grab a pita sandwich, and get ready to be transported to the vibrant streets of Tel Aviv.

SAINT-GERMAIN-DES-PRÉS RESTAURANTS

LES DEUX MAGOTS

Nestled in the heart of Saint-Germain-des-Prés, one of Paris' most charming and historic neighborhoods, Les Deux Magots is a must-visit destination for any traveler looking to immerse themselves in the city's rich cultural heritage. This legendary restaurant and café has been a fixture on the Parisian scene since it first opened its doors in 1885, and has played host to some of the greatest artists, writers, and thinkers of the 20th century.

One of the most remarkable things about Les Deux Magots is its location. Situated on the bustling Boulevard Saint-Germain, the café boasts a prime position in the heart of one of the city's most vibrant districts. From here, visitors can soak up the atmosphere of the surrounding area, which is packed with quaint boutiques, charming cafés, and cultural landmarks.

But it's not just the location that makes Les Deux Magots so special. This historic establishment is steeped in history, and has played a key role in the cultural life of Paris for over a century. In the early 20th century, Les Deux Magots was a popular hangout for the city's intellectual elite, including writers such as Jean-Paul Sartre, Simone de Beauvoir, and Ernest Hemingway. Today, the café remains a popular spot for writers and artists, as well as tourists looking to experience a taste of old-world Paris.

The interior of Les Deux Magots is equally impressive. With its ornate Art Deco furnishings and rich mahogany paneling, the café exudes a sense of elegance and sophistication that is sure to transport visitors back in time. The walls are lined with photographs and memorabilia, offering a fascinating glimpse into the café's rich history and the famous figures who have passed through its doors.

Of course, no visit to Les Deux Magots would be complete without sampling some of the delicious food and drink on offer. The café is renowned for its coffee, which is served in traditional French style with a small glass of water on the side. There are also plenty of tasty treats to choose from, including croissants, macarons, and other French pastries.

For those looking for something heartier, Les Deux Magots also serves a range of classic French dishes, including onion soup, steak frites, and escargots. And if you're in the mood for a tipple, the café's extensive wine list is sure to satisfy even the most discerning palate.

If you're planning a trip to Paris, a visit to Les Deux Magots is an absolute must. With its prime location, rich history, and delicious food and drink, this iconic café is the perfect place to soak up the city's unique atmosphere and experience a taste of old-world Paris.

CAFÉ DE FLORE

Café de Flore, located in the heart of Saint-Germain-des-Prés in Paris, is a legendary café that has been serving locals and visitors since 1887. This charming café has been a hub of intellectual and artistic activity for over a century, attracting some of the world's most famous writers and artists.

One of the most interesting facts about Café de Flore is that it was one of the first cafés in Paris to install electric lighting, which made it a popular spot for people to gather in the evenings. This historic café has also been the subject of many books and films, and it has played an important role in the cultural history of Paris.

Located on the Boulevard Saint-Germain, Café de Flore is easily accessible by public transportation and is just a short walk from several major tourist attractions, including the Luxembourg Gardens and the Musée d'Orsay. The café's location in the heart of Saint-Germain-des-Prés also makes it an ideal spot for people watching and soaking up the atmosphere of this trendy and sophisticated neighborhood.

One of the unique features of Café de Flore is its décor, which has remained largely unchanged over the years. The café's art deco style interior features elegant red velvet banquettes, marble tables, and a stunning stained glass ceiling. The café also has an outdoor terrace, which is perfect for enjoying a coffee or a glass of wine while watching the world go by.

Café de Flore is famous for its traditional French cuisine, which includes classic dishes like croque-monsieur, omelettes, and escargots. The café also serves a wide selection of pastries and desserts, including their famous hot chocolate, which is made with pure melted chocolate and is one of the best in Paris.

For travelers interested in the literary history of Paris, a visit to Café de Flore is a must. The café has been frequented by some of the world's most famous writers, including Ernest Hemingway, Jean-Paul Sartre, and Simone de Beauvoir. In fact, the café still maintains a reading room upstairs, where visitors can browse through books and magazines while sipping their coffee.

Café de Flore has also been featured in several films and TV shows, including Woody Allen's "Midnight in Paris" and the Netflix series "Emily in Paris". This has helped to cement the café's status as a cultural icon and a must-visit destination for anyone visiting Paris.

LE PROCOPE

It is one of the oldest restaurants in the city and has a fascinating history that dates back to the 18th century. This iconic eatery has played host to many famous personalities over the years, including Voltaire, Napoleon Bonaparte, Benjamin Franklin, and Victor Hugo.

Located in the heart of Saint-Germain-des-Prés, Le Procope is easily accessible from all parts of the city. The restaurant is situated on Rue de l'Ancienne Comédie, just a short walk from the Saint-Michel metro station. The area is known for its bustling streets, charming cafes, and elegant boutiques, making it the perfect place for a leisurely stroll before or after your meal at Le Procope.

The restaurant's interior is a beautiful blend of traditional and modern styles. The walls are adorned with historic paintings and antique mirrors, giving the space a timeless feel. The dining room is spacious and elegant, with comfortable seating and soft lighting that creates a warm and welcoming ambiance.

Le Procope's menu is a celebration of classic French cuisine, with a range of dishes that are expertly prepared using the finest ingredients. The restaurant's signature dish is the 'coq au vin,' a hearty stew made with tender chicken, mushrooms, and red wine. Other standout dishes include the escargots de Bourgogne, a delicious snail dish served with garlic butter, and the bouillabaisse, a traditional fish soup that is packed with flavor.

One of the most interesting facts about Le Procope is that it was the birthplace of the French Revolution. The restaurant was a popular gathering spot for intellectuals and revolutionaries in the late 18th century, including Maximilien Robespierre and Georges Danton. It was here that they would meet to discuss politics and plan their strategies, leading to the eventual overthrow of the French monarchy.

Another fascinating feature of Le Procope is its collection of historical artifacts. The restaurant has an impressive collection of antique furniture, paintings, and documents that offer a glimpse into the past. Some of the highlights include a letter written by Napoleon Bonaparte and a chair that once belonged to Voltaire.

For travelers looking for a unique dining experience in Paris, Le Procope is an excellent choice. Its historic significance, elegant ambiance, and delicious cuisine make it a must-visit destination for anyone visiting the city. Whether you're looking to indulge in some classic French dishes or simply soak up the atmosphere of this iconic establishment, Le Procope is sure to leave a lasting impression.

Le Procope has a long and storied history that is intricately linked to the cultural and political life of France. The restaurant first opened its doors in 1686, making it one of the oldest continuously operating restaurants in the world. Over the years, it has played host to a wide range of notable figures from French and international society, including writers, politicians, and artists.

The restaurant's literary connections are particularly strong, and many famous writers have frequented its halls. Voltaire, one of France's most celebrated philosophers, was a regular at Le Procope, and he even rented an apartment above the restaurant for a time. Other literary figures who have visited the restaurant include Jean-Jacques Rousseau, Victor Hugo, and Alexandre Dumas.

In addition to its cultural significance, Le Procope is also known for its excellent food and drink. The restaurant has an extensive wine list featuring some of the best

French wines, as well as a range of classic cocktails and spirits. The food menu is similarly impressive, with a variety of dishes that showcase the best of French cuisine. From hearty stews to delicate seafood dishes, there is something for everyone on the menu.

One of the most interesting features of Le Procope is its decor, which is a blend of traditional and modern styles. The restaurant has been renovated several times over the years, but it has managed to maintain its historic charm while still offering modern amenities. The walls are adorned with antique mirrors and paintings, and the furniture is a mix of classic and contemporary styles.

Another unique aspect of Le Procope is its location in the heart of Saint-Germain-des-Prés. The neighborhood is known for its vibrant cultural scene, and it is home to a variety of art galleries, theaters, and museums. Visitors to the area can spend hours exploring its charming streets and alleyways, taking in the sights and sounds of one of Paris's most vibrant neighborhoods.

L'ÉPICERIE

L'Épicerie, located in the heart of Saint-Germain-des-Prés in Paris. Tucked away in a small alleyway off the bustling Boulevard Saint-Germain, this restaurant provides a cozy and intimate atmosphere perfect for a romantic dinner or a casual catch-up with friends.

The restaurant's interior is designed to resemble an old-fashioned grocery store, complete with shelves lined with jars of spices, cans of preserves, and bottles of wine. The decor is rustic and charming, with wooden tables and chairs and vintage lamps hanging from the ceiling. The walls are adorned with black-and-white photographs and vintage advertisements, adding to the restaurant's nostalgic ambiance.

The menu at L'Épicerie features classic French dishes with a modern twist. The ingredients are sourced locally and seasonally, ensuring the freshest and most flavorful meals. For starters, the goat cheese and fig tartine is a must-try, with the creamy cheese and sweet figs perfectly complementing each other. The mains include classic French dishes like coq au vin and bouillabaisse, but also offer options like roasted lamb with harissa and mint yogurt, showcasing the restaurant's modern flair.

L'Épicerie is also known for its extensive wine list, with over 200 bottles available. The restaurant's sommelier is knowledgeable and passionate about wine, and is happy to help diners select the perfect pairing for their meal. In addition to wine, L'Épicerie also serves a variety of craft beers and cocktails, including the restaurant's signature drink, the "Épicerie Sour".

Despite its prime location in the heart of Saint-Germain-des-Prés, L'Épicerie manages to maintain a relaxed and welcoming atmosphere. The staff is friendly and attentive, and the restaurant's small size allows for a more personalized dining experience. The outdoor seating area is particularly charming, with tables surrounded by plants and flowers, providing a peaceful retreat from the hustle and bustle of the city.

Aside from its excellent food and drink offerings, L'Épicerie also has some interesting historical significance. The building that houses the restaurant dates back to the 17th century, and was once a convent. During World War II, the building was used as a hideout for members of the French Resistance. Today, the restaurant pays homage to this history with its decor, which includes old photographs and newspaper clippings from the war era.

L'ATELIER DE JOËL ROBUCHON

This Michelin-starred establishment is situated in the heart of the city, just a stone's throw away from the iconic Place Saint-Germain-des-Prés. With its sleek, modern design and buzzing atmosphere, L'Atelier de Joël Robuchon offers a truly unforgettable dining experience.

The restaurant is the brainchild of Joël Robuchon, a culinary legend who has been dubbed the "Chef of the Century" by the prestigious Gault Millau guide. Robuchon was renowned for his innovative approach to French cuisine, and L'Atelier de Joël Robuchon continues his legacy by serving up an exciting and contemporary take on classic French dishes.

The menu at L'Atelier de Joël Robuchon is a true feast for the senses. Guests can choose from a variety of dishes, ranging from the classic to the avant-garde. The restaurant's signature dishes include the potato puree, which is made with a staggering 50% butter, and the langoustine ravioli, which is served with a rich, creamy truffle sauce. Other popular dishes include the pigeon with foie gras and the black cod with miso.

One of the unique features of L'Atelier de Joël Robuchon is its open kitchen, which allows diners to watch the chefs at work as they prepare their meals. The kitchen is designed in the style of a Japanese sushi bar, with a long, sleek counter where guests can sit and watch the action. This creates a lively and interactive atmosphere, and adds an extra dimension to the dining experience.

The restaurant also boasts an impressive wine list, with over 1,200 bottles to choose from. The sommeliers at L'Atelier de Joël Robuchon are highly knowledgeable and passionate about wine, and are always on hand to offer recommendations and advice.

In addition to its delicious food and wine, L'Atelier de Joël Robuchon is also notable for its stylish decor. The restaurant's interior is sleek and modern, with a minimalist design that puts the focus firmly on the food. The walls are adorned with striking black and white photographs of the chef, and the tables and chairs are made from dark wood and leather, creating a chic and sophisticated ambiance.

Another interesting fact about L'Atelier de Joël Robuchon is that it has branches all over the world, from Tokyo to New York to London. This makes it a truly international brand, and a favorite among foodies from all corners of the globe.

LE COMPTOIR DU RELAIS

The restaurant has a long and storied history, having been in operation for over 100 years. Originally a popular meeting place for writers and artists, Le Comptoir du Relais has retained its bohemian charm and continues to attract a diverse crowd of locals and tourists alike.

The menu at Le Comptoir du Relais is a testament to the restaurant's commitment to using only the freshest, highest-quality ingredients. The kitchen specializes in classic French cuisine with a modern twist, and their signature dishes include steak tartare, foie gras, and roasted chicken. The restaurant also offers an extensive wine list, featuring a carefully curated selection of reds, whites, and sparkling wines from France's finest vineyards.

One of the highlights of dining at Le Comptoir du Relais is the bustling atmosphere. The restaurant is always packed with diners enjoying lively conversation and the sounds of clinking glasses and sizzling pans. The staff is attentive and friendly, and the service is impeccable.

The decor of the restaurant is simple yet elegant, with exposed brick walls, wooden tables, and vintage lighting fixtures. The overall effect is warm and inviting, making it the perfect spot for a romantic dinner or a night out with friends.

In addition to its exceptional food and lively atmosphere, Le Comptoir du Relais also has some interesting historical connections. The restaurant is located in the same building as the Hotel Relais Saint-Germain, which was once a popular haunt of French literary legends such as Jean-Paul Sartre and Simone de Beauvoir. In fact, the hotel's famous bar is said to have inspired the name of the restaurant.

Le Comptoir du Relais is also just a short walk away from some of Paris's most iconic landmarks, including the Louvre Museum and Notre-Dame Cathedral. The restaurant's location in the heart of the Saint-Germain-des-Prés neighborhood means that visitors can easily explore the area's charming cafes, shops, and galleries before or after their meal.

For travelers looking for an authentic Parisian dining experience, Le Comptoir du Relais is an absolute must-visit. From its exceptional cuisine and lively ambiance to its rich history and prime location, this charming bistro has everything that makes Paris so special.

Reservations are highly recommended at Le Comptoir du Relais, as the restaurant tends to fill up quickly. Visitors should also keep in mind that the menu is only available in French, so it may be helpful to brush up on some basic French phrases before dining here.

One of the unique aspects of Le Comptoir du Relais is the fact that the restaurant is open for breakfast, lunch, and dinner, making it a versatile destination for any time of day. Visitors can start their morning off with a freshly baked croissant and a steaming cup of café au lait, or stop in for a quick lunch of quiche and salad before exploring the city.

For those looking to experience the full Le Comptoir du Relais experience, dinner is the way to go. The restaurant's cozy atmosphere and exceptional cuisine make it the perfect spot for a romantic dinner or a night out with friends. Diners should be sure to save room for dessert, as the restaurant's homemade sweets are not to be missed.

RALPH'S

The restaurant is located in a historic building that was once a townhouse, with a façade that exudes old-world charm and sophistication.

Ralph's interior is equally stunning, featuring a warm and inviting ambiance that perfectly complements its upscale menu. The decor is a perfect blend of classic and contemporary elements, with plush leather chairs, marble tables, and soft lighting that creates a cozy and intimate atmosphere. The walls are adorned with beautiful artwork and photographs, adding to the overall elegance of the space.

As for the menu, Ralph's offers a delightful selection of American-inspired cuisine, with a focus on quality ingredients and impeccable presentation. The menu includes dishes such as the classic Ralph's Burger, made with juicy beef, cheddar cheese, and crispy bacon, as well as fresh salads, seafood, and pasta dishes.

One interesting fact about Ralph's is that it is owned by the fashion brand Ralph Lauren, hence its name. The restaurant is just one of several Ralph Lauren establishments around the world, each of which showcases the brand's signature style and attention to detail.

In addition to its stunning interior and delicious menu, Ralph's also boasts an incredible location. The restaurant is situated in the heart of Saint-Germain-des-Prés, an area known for its lively atmosphere, historic landmarks, and trendy boutiques. Visitors to Ralph's can easily explore the neighborhood's charming streets, visit local museums and galleries, and experience the bustling nightlife.

For those looking for something extra special, Ralph's also offers private dining rooms for intimate gatherings and special occasions. The rooms feature the same elegant decor as the main dining area and can accommodate up to 20 guests.

LE SAINT-GERMAIN

This elegant establishment boasts a warm and inviting ambiance, complete with cozy lighting, rich wooden furnishings, and soft music that creates the perfect atmosphere for a romantic dinner or a lively evening with friends.

Le Saint-Germain's menu is a tribute to classic French cuisine, with a focus on fresh, locally-sourced ingredients and traditional recipes that have been passed down through generations of chefs. The restaurant's signature dishes include escargots de Bourgogne, beef bourguignon, and crème brûlée, all of which are beautifully presented and expertly prepared.

One of the standout features of Le Saint-Germain is its extensive wine list, which offers a curated selection of the finest French wines from the country's most renowned vineyards. Guests can savor a glass of red, white, or rosé wine to complement their meal, with knowledgeable sommeliers on hand to provide recommendations and advice.

The location of Le Saint-Germain is also a major draw for travelers, as it is situated in the heart of one of Paris's most vibrant and historic neighborhoods. Saint-Germain-des-Prés is known for its picturesque streets, charming cafes, and bustling markets, making it the perfect place to explore after a satisfying meal.

For those seeking a unique dining experience, Le Saint-Germain offers private dining rooms that can be reserved for special occasions, such as birthdays, anniversaries, or intimate gatherings with loved ones. The restaurant's attentive staff are on hand to provide personalized service and ensure that each guest has a memorable and enjoyable experience.

Interesting facts about Le Saint-Germain include its long history as a gathering place for writers, artists, and intellectuals. The neighborhood was once home to famous figures such as Jean-Paul Sartre, Simone de Beauvoir, and Ernest Hemingway, all of whom frequented the area's cafes and restaurants. Le Saint-Germain continues this tradition of intellectual and artistic exchange, providing a space for guests to enjoy good food and good conversation.

LE PETIT ZINC

Founded in 1912, Le Petit Zinc has a long and storied history. Originally a popular meeting spot for artists, writers, and intellectuals, the bistro has retained its bohemian charm and is now a favorite haunt of locals and visitors alike. With its red banquettes, black-and-white checkered floor, and vintage posters adorning the walls, the restaurant exudes an old-world charm that is hard to resist.

The menu at Le Petit Zinc is a celebration of classic French cuisine, with a focus on fresh and seasonal ingredients. From traditional dishes like escargots and onion soup to more contemporary creations like roasted duck breast with honey-glazed turnips, the food here is always expertly prepared and beautifully presented.

One of the restaurant's signature dishes is the steak tartare, which is prepared tableside and served with crispy fries and a side salad. Another must-try is the bouillabaisse, a rich and flavorful seafood stew that is a specialty of the region. And for dessert, be sure to indulge in the heavenly profiteroles, which are filled with vanilla ice cream and topped with warm chocolate sauce.

In addition to its outstanding cuisine, Le Petit Zinc is also known for its impressive selection of wines and spirits. The restaurant has an extensive wine list featuring both French and international varietals, as well as a wide range of cocktails, aperitifs, and digestifs.

But what really sets Le Petit Zinc apart is its atmosphere. With its intimate setting and attentive service, dining here feels like being transported back in time to the Paris of the early 20th century. Whether you're looking for a romantic dinner for two or a relaxed evening with friends, this bistro is the perfect place to unwind and savor the best of French cuisine.

For those interested in history and culture, Saint-Germain-des-Prés is an excellent neighborhood to explore. Located on the Left Bank of the Seine River, this area has a long and rich history, dating back to the Middle Ages. Over the centuries, it has been home to many famous writers, artists, and intellectuals, including Jean-Paul Sartre, Simone de Beauvoir, and Ernest Hemingway.

Today, Saint-Germain-des-Prés is a vibrant and lively neighborhood, with a thriving arts scene, fashionable boutiques, and some of the city's best restaurants and cafes. Visitors can spend hours exploring the charming streets and hidden alleyways, admiring the architecture and soaking up the atmosphere.

For travelers looking for a true taste of Parisian culture and cuisine, Le Petit Zinc is an absolute must-visit. With its impeccable service, delicious food, and unforgettable ambiance, this restaurant is a true gem of Saint-Germain-des-Prés, and a testament to the enduring appeal of classic French bistro fare.

CHEZ FERNAND

The restaurant is located on the charming rue Christine, just a stone's throw away from the famous Abbey of Saint-Germain-des-Prés. The location is perfect for a leisurely stroll around the neighborhood before or after your meal. The restaurant's unassuming exterior belies the cozy and inviting atmosphere that awaits inside.

Once inside, you'll be greeted by the friendly and knowledgeable staff, who will guide you through the menu and help you choose from a variety of traditional French dishes. The menu at Chez Fernand features classic bistro fare such as escargots, foie gras, and beef tartare, as well as heartier dishes like steak frites and coq au vin. Vegetarian options are also available, making Chez Fernand a great choice for all diners.

One of the most popular dishes at Chez Fernand is the confit de canard, a rich and savory duck leg slow-cooked in its own fat. The dish is served with crispy potatoes and a side of vegetables, and is a true French classic that should not be missed.

The wine list at Chez Fernand is extensive and carefully curated, with a variety of wines from all regions of France. The staff is happy to make recommendations to pair with your meal, and the prices are reasonable for the quality of the wines.

In addition to the delicious food and wine, Chez Fernand is known for its cozy and intimate atmosphere. The restaurant is small and intimate, with dim lighting and wooden tables that give it a rustic and authentic feel. The walls are adorned with vintage posters and photos, adding to the charm of the space.

Interesting fact: Chez Fernand has a long history of attracting famous clientele. In the 1950s and 60s, the restaurant was a favorite of writers and intellectuals such as Jean-Paul Sartre and Simone de Beauvoir. Today, you might still spot a celebrity or two dining at Chez Fernand.

If you're looking for a true French bistro experience in the heart of Saint-Germain-des-Prés, Chez Fernand is the perfect choice. With its classic cuisine, extensive wine list, and cozy ambiance, it's no wonder that this restaurant has been a favorite of Parisians and travelers for over a century.

QUARTIER LATIN
RESTAURANTS

LA TOUR D'ARGENT

La Tour d'Argent, located in the heart of the Quartier Latin in Paris, is a culinary institution that has been serving up traditional French cuisine since 1582. With its rich history, stunning views of the Seine, and renowned cuisine, it is no wonder that this restaurant has become a must-visit destination for foodies and travelers alike.

The restaurant's name, which translates to "The Silver Tower," comes from the fact that it was originally housed in a tower on the Seine River that was used to store silverware for the royal family. Today, the restaurant is still located in the same building, which has been beautifully restored to maintain its historic charm.

La Tour d'Argent is most famous for its signature dish, Canard à la Presse, which translates to "pressed duck." This traditional French dish involves pressing the juices from a whole roasted duck tableside and serving the resulting sauce with the meat. This unique preparation has become a symbol of the restaurant and is a must-try for any visitor.

Aside from the iconic dish, La Tour d'Argent offers an extensive menu featuring classic French cuisine with a modern twist. From escargots to foie gras, every dish is crafted with the utmost care and precision by the restaurant's talented chefs.

The dining experience at La Tour d'Argent is truly one-of-a-kind. The restaurant boasts stunning views of the Seine River, the Notre-Dame Cathedral, and the Eiffel Tower. Guests can choose to dine in the elegant main dining room or in one of the restaurant's private salons, each with its own unique character and charm.

La Tour d'Argent is also known for its impressive wine cellar, which boasts over 400,000 bottles of wine from around the world. The restaurant's sommeliers are experts at pairing wines with each dish, ensuring that guests have an unforgettable dining experience.

In addition to its renowned cuisine and stunning views, La Tour d'Argent is steeped in history and tradition. The restaurant has played host to many famous figures throughout the centuries, including Louis XIV and Napoleon III. Today, it remains a favorite of celebrities and dignitaries from around the world.

One of the restaurant's most unique traditions is its numbering system for its pressed duck dishes. Each time a duck is prepared, it is given a number and recorded in the restaurant's "duck registry." To date, over a million ducks have been served at La Tour d'Argent, and each one has its own unique number.

For travelers seeking a truly unforgettable dining experience in Paris, La Tour d'Argent is a must-visit destination. With its rich history, stunning views, and renowned cuisine, it is sure to leave a lasting impression. Whether you're a foodie or simply looking to experience the best of French cuisine, a visit to La Tour d'Argent is an experience not to be missed.

LE COUPE CHOU

Le Coupe Chou is a charming and historical restaurant located in the heart of Quartier Latin, Paris. Established in 1962, the restaurant has been serving delicious French cuisine for over 60 years, making it a popular destination for locals and tourists alike.

The restaurant's name, "Le Coupe Chou", translates to "The Cabbage Cutter" in English. This quirky name has its roots in the history of the building that the restaurant occupies. In the 17th century, the building was home to a hairdresser who also worked as a cabbage cutter on the side. The name has been preserved to this day, adding to the restaurant's unique character.

Stepping inside Le Coupe Chou is like taking a trip back in time. The interior is filled with old-world charm, featuring exposed wooden beams, stone walls, and flickering candles. The ambiance is warm and inviting, making it the perfect spot for a romantic dinner or an intimate gathering with friends.

The menu at Le Coupe Chou showcases classic French cuisine, with a focus on traditional dishes made with fresh, locally-sourced ingredients. From escargots to coq au vin, the dishes are prepared with care and attention to detail, ensuring a truly authentic dining experience.

One of the standout dishes at Le Coupe Chou is the signature duck confit. Slow-cooked to perfection, the duck is tender and succulent, with a crispy skin that melts in your mouth. Another must-try dish is the classic French onion soup, served bubbling hot with a layer of melted gruyere cheese on top.

In addition to the delicious food, Le Coupe Chou also has an extensive wine list, featuring a carefully curated selection of French wines. Whether you're a wine connoisseur or just looking to enjoy a glass of something delicious, the knowledgeable staff are always happy to recommend the perfect pairing for your meal.

Aside from the food and wine, one of the unique features of Le Coupe Chou is its location. The restaurant is situated in the heart of Quartier Latin, a vibrant and historic neighborhood in Paris known for its intellectual and artistic community. Surrounded by bustling cafes, bookshops, and theaters, Le Coupe Chou is the perfect place to stop and take a break from the busy city streets.

Whether you're looking for a romantic dinner for two, a casual night out with friends, or just want to experience a piece of Parisian history, Le Coupe Chou is a must-visit destination. With its delicious food, extensive wine list, and charming ambiance, it's no wonder this restaurant has been a beloved fixture of the Parisian dining scene for over six decades.

For those interested in the history of the restaurant, Le Coupe Chou has a story to tell. The building dates back to the 16th century and was once a monastery before becoming a private residence. During the French Revolution, the building was confiscated and turned into a courthouse, which it remained for over a century. In the early 20th century, the building was converted into a tavern and then into a hair salon, where the original cabbage cutting took place. Today, the restaurant still retains many of the building's original features, including the stone walls and wooden beams, giving diners a sense of the rich history of the space.

One interesting fact about Le Coupe Chou is that it has played a role in French literature and cinema. The restaurant was featured in the novel "Les Enfants Terribles" by Jean Cocteau, and the film adaptation of the book was shot in part at the restaurant. In addition, Le Coupe Chou was used as a location for the French film "The Clockmaker," adding to its cultural significance.

For those looking to experience the restaurant's unique ambiance, Le Coupe Chou has a variety of seating options to choose from. The main dining room features cozy booths and tables, while the outdoor terrace is perfect for dining al fresco on warm summer nights. For a more intimate experience, the restaurant also has a private dining room, which can accommodate up to 12 people.

In terms of pricing, Le Coupe Chou is considered a mid-range restaurant, with entrees ranging from 18-35 euros. While it may not be the cheapest option in Paris, the quality of the food and the ambiance make it well worth the price.

LE COMPTOIR DU PANTHÉON

Situated just a stone's throw away from the magnificent Panthéon, this restaurant is a must-visit for food lovers and travelers looking for a taste of traditional French cuisine.

The restaurant's décor is warm and inviting, with a rustic charm that makes you feel right at home. The walls are adorned with vintage posters and antique mirrors, and the wooden furniture and dim lighting create a cozy atmosphere that is perfect for a romantic dinner or a relaxed evening with friends.

Le Comptoir du Panthéon is renowned for its mouthwatering menu of classic French dishes, which are prepared with the freshest ingredients and served with a modern twist. Some of the restaurant's must-try dishes include the succulent beef bourguignon, the classic escargots de Bourgogne, and the rich and indulgent crème brûlée.

One of the most interesting facts about Le Comptoir du Panthéon is that it was founded by the renowned French chef, Yves Camdeborde. Camdeborde is widely regarded as one of the pioneers of the bistronomy movement in France, which focuses on serving high-quality cuisine in a more casual and relaxed setting. The restaurant's menu reflects this philosophy, with a focus on simple yet delicious dishes that showcase the flavors and ingredients of traditional French cuisine.

Located in the heart of the Quartier Latin, Le Comptoir du

Panthéon is perfectly situated for travelers looking to explore the historic and cultural attractions of Paris. The Panthéon itself is just a few steps away, and other nearby attractions include the Jardin du Luxembourg, the Sorbonne, and the Musée de Cluny.

But the restaurant's location isn't the only thing that makes it a popular destination for travelers. Le Comptoir du Panthéon has also been praised for its friendly and welcoming atmosphere, with many visitors describing it as a hidden gem that is well worth seeking out. Whether you're a first-time visitor to Paris or a seasoned traveler looking for a new culinary experience, Le Comptoir du Panthéon is a must-visit destination that is sure to leave a lasting impression.

As for curiosities, Le Comptoir du Panthéon is also known for its extensive wine list, which features a carefully curated selection of French and international wines that pair perfectly with the restaurant's menu. And if you're looking for a unique and unforgettable dining experience, be sure to ask about the chef's table, which offers a front-row seat to the kitchen and the chance to interact with the talented chefs as they prepare your meal. With its delicious cuisine, friendly service, and charming atmosphere, Le Comptoir du Panthéon is a restaurant that is not to be missed.

In addition to its delicious food and welcoming atmosphere, Le Comptoir du Panthéon is also known for its commitment to sustainability and supporting local farmers and producers. The restaurant sources its ingredients from small-scale and organic farmers, ensuring that the food is not only delicious but also environmentally conscious.

For those looking for a unique experience, Le Comptoir du Panthéon also offers cooking classes and workshops for visitors. These classes are led by experienced chefs and provide a hands-on opportunity to learn the secrets of French cuisine, from preparing classic dishes like ratatouille to mastering the art of making delicate French pastries.

Another interesting aspect of Le Comptoir du Panthéon is its connection to the history of the Quartier Latin. The neighborhood was historically known as a center of intellectual and artistic activity, and it has been home to some of the most famous writers, artists, and philosophers in history. The restaurant's cozy atmosphere and rustic décor pay homage to this history, creating a unique and memorable dining experience that is steeped in Parisian culture and tradition.

LE PETIT PONTOISE

With its cozy ambiance and warm hospitality, it is no wonder that this quaint bistro has become a go-to spot for those seeking an authentic Parisian dining experience.

Located on the historic Rue Pontoise, Le Petit Pontoise is just a stone's throw away from some of the city's most iconic landmarks, including the Notre-Dame Cathedral and the Sainte-Chapelle. Its location in the vibrant Quartier Latin also makes it the perfect spot for a post-sightseeing meal or a casual dinner with friends.

But what truly sets Le Petit Pontoise apart is its menu, which showcases the very best of French cuisine. From classic dishes like escargots and steak frites to more innovative creations like the roasted veal sweetbread with girolle mushrooms, the restaurant's offerings are a true celebration of the rich culinary traditions of France.

One must-try dish is the house specialty, the "tête de veau," a slow-cooked veal head served with a tangy sauce gribiche. Despite its unusual appearance, this dish is a true delicacy and a favorite among regulars. Another standout dish is the roasted duck breast with honey and lavender, a perfect balance of sweet and savory flavors.

Le Petit Pontoise's wine list is equally impressive, featuring a carefully curated selection of French wines that perfectly complement the restaurant's cuisine. Whether you prefer a bold red or a crisp white, the knowledgeable staff is always on hand to help you find the perfect pairing for your meal.

The restaurant's décor is also worth noting, with its warm lighting and vintage posters creating a cozy and inviting atmosphere. The restaurant's small size only adds to its charm, as diners are made to feel like they are part of a special community of food lovers.

Le Petit Pontoise is also known for its excellent value, with prices that are very reasonable considering the quality of the food and the ambiance. This makes it a popular choice among students and budget-conscious travelers who want to experience authentic French cuisine without breaking the bank.

In addition to its delicious food and welcoming atmosphere, Le Petit Pontoise is steeped in history and tradition. The building itself dates back to the 17th century and was once a popular meeting spot for artists and intellectuals. The restaurant's founder, Alain Ducasse, is a legend in the French culinary world and is credited with helping to elevate French cuisine to the highest levels of international acclaim.

Today, Le Petit Pontoise continues to uphold the traditions of French cuisine and hospitality, while also embracing innovation and creativity. It is a true gem in the heart of Paris and a must-visit destination for any food lover. So if you find yourself in the Quartier Latin, be sure to make a reservation at Le Petit Pontoise and experience the magic for yourself.

As you step inside Le Petit Pontoise, you'll be greeted by the warm and friendly staff, who are passionate about providing a memorable dining experience for every guest. The restaurant's intimate setting, with only a few tables, creates a cozy and romantic atmosphere that is perfect for a special date or a celebratory meal.

Le Petit Pontoise also offers a daily changing menu that is based on the freshest and most seasonal ingredients available. This means that each visit to the restaurant is a unique culinary adventure, with new flavors and dishes to discover.

One of the restaurant's standout features is its attention to detail, with every dish carefully crafted and beautifully presented. The portions are generous, and the flavors are bold, yet balanced, making for a truly satisfying dining experience.

Le Petit Pontoise is also known for its exceptional desserts, which are made fresh daily by the talented pastry chef. From the classic French crème brûlée to the decadent chocolate mousse, the desserts are the perfect ending to a memorable meal.

If you're a wine enthusiast, Le Petit Pontoise offers a wide selection of French wines from all over the country, including some lesser-known but equally delicious options. The sommelier is happy to provide recommendations and help you find the perfect bottle to accompany your meal.

Another unique aspect of Le Petit Pontoise is its commitment to sustainability and local sourcing. The restaurant works closely with local farmers and suppliers to ensure that the ingredients used in their dishes are of the highest quality and sourced responsibly.

AUX VERRES DE CONTACT

The decor of Aux Verres de Contact is both elegant and welcoming. With warm lighting and comfortable seating, the restaurant exudes a cozy ambiance that invites guests to settle in and enjoy a leisurely meal. The walls are adorned with artful photographs and paintings, adding a touch of sophistication to the space.

One of the most fascinating things about Aux Verres de Contact is its commitment to sustainability. The restaurant sources its ingredients locally, using only the freshest, seasonal produce from nearby farms. The chefs take great care in creating delicious, inventive dishes that showcase the flavors of the region. From classic French favorites like escargot and steak tartare to more modern creations like roasted duck breast with figs and balsamic reduction, the menu is full of exciting options for diners to explore.

In addition to its commitment to sustainability, Aux Verres de Contact is also known for its extensive wine list. With over 300 bottles to choose from, guests are sure to find the perfect pairing for their meal. The restaurant's knowledgeable staff is always happy to make recommendations and offer guidance, ensuring that every guest leaves satisfied.

Located in the heart of the Quartier Latin, Aux Verres de Contact is surrounded by some of Paris's most iconic landmarks. Just a short walk away is the world-famous Notre Dame Cathedral, which offers stunning views of the city from its towers. Other nearby attractions include the Pantheon and the Luxembourg Gardens, both of which are perfect for a leisurely stroll after a meal.

For those looking for a unique dining experience, Aux Verres de Contact offers private tastings and wine classes. Guests can learn about the different regions and varietals of French wine while enjoying delicious food and expert guidance from the restaurant's staff.

With its commitment to sustainability, extensive wine list, and central location, Aux Verres de Contact is the perfect destination for anyone looking to explore the vibrant Quartier Latin. Whether you're a seasoned traveler or a first-time visitor to Paris, this charming restaurant is sure to leave a lasting impression. So why not book a table today and experience the magic of Aux Verres de Contact for yourself?

Aux Verres de Contact is also known for its warm and welcoming atmosphere. The staff is friendly and attentive, always going above and beyond to ensure that every guest feels comfortable and well taken care of.

One of the restaurant's most popular dishes is the sea bass ceviche, which is prepared with fresh herbs and citrus juice, giving it a bright and zesty flavor. Another standout dish is the roasted lamb shoulder, which is cooked to perfection and served with a savory jus and root vegetables.

For dessert, guests can indulge in classic French treats like crème brûlée or try something new like the chocolate and hazelnut mousse. No matter what you choose, every dish at Aux Verres de Contact is made with care and attention to detail, ensuring a truly exceptional dining experience.

Aux Verres de Contact also offers a private dining area for groups and special events. Whether you're planning a romantic dinner for two or a larger celebration with friends and family, the restaurant can accommodate your needs.

L'ÉTOILE MANQUANTE

This cozy and intimate restaurant is located on Rue Mouffetard, one of the oldest and most picturesque streets in Paris, lined with traditional French food shops and artisanal boutiques.

L'Étoile Manquante, which means "the missing star" in English, is a fitting name for this restaurant as it is one of the few places in Paris where you can find authentic and inventive cuisine without the pomp and circumstance of Michelin-starred restaurants. The menu at L'Étoile Manquante changes frequently, depending on the season and availability of fresh ingredients, but always features a mix of classic French dishes with a modern twist and fusion cuisine inspired by the chef's travels around the world.

The decor of L'Étoile Manquante is cozy and rustic, with exposed brick walls, wooden beams, and warm lighting that creates a romantic and inviting atmosphere. The restaurant has a small number of tables, making it an ideal spot for an intimate dinner or a special occasion. There is also a small bar area where you can enjoy a glass of wine or a cocktail before or after your meal.

One of the standout dishes at L'Étoile Manquante is the foie gras terrine, which is served with a homemade chutney and toasted brioche. The terrine is perfectly balanced and has a silky texture that melts in your mouth. Another must-try dish is the duck breast with a cherry sauce, which is a classic French combination that is executed to perfection at L'Étoile Manquante. For dessert, the chocolate fondant with a salted caramel sauce is a decadent and indulgent treat.

Aside from the delicious food, L'Étoile Manquante is also known for its excellent wine list, which features a selection of both French and international wines. The knowledgeable staff are happy to recommend a wine pairing for your meal, and can also suggest lesser-known wines that are not often found on other wine lists in Paris.

If you're looking for a unique and memorable dining experience in Paris, L'Étoile Manquante is definitely worth a visit. With its charming location, cozy ambiance, and inventive cuisine, this hidden gem is sure to leave a lasting impression on any food lover. Be sure to book ahead, as the restaurant's popularity means that tables are often in high demand.

Interestingly, L'Étoile Manquante has an impressive history that adds to its charm. The building that houses the restaurant dates back to the 17th century and was originally a wine cellar. The restaurant's owners have maintained much of the building's original character, including the stone walls and vaulted ceiling.

Another unique aspect of L'Étoile Manquante is the personal touch that the owners and staff bring to the dining experience. The chef and owner, Patrick Sébile, is often seen in the dining room, chatting with customers and ensuring that everyone is enjoying their meal. The staff are also friendly and attentive, making for a warm and welcoming atmosphere.

For those who are interested in cooking, L'Étoile Manquante also offers cooking classes where participants can learn how to make some of the restaurant's signature dishes. The classes are taught by the chef himself and offer a hands-on experience in a small group setting.

Located in the heart of Quartier Latin, L'Étoile Manquante is surrounded by many other attractions that are worth exploring. The famous Sorbonne University is just a few blocks away, as is the Panthéon and the Jardin des Plantes. The restaurant is also a short walk from the Saint-Médard market, which is a great place to pick up fresh produce and other food items.

POLIDOR

Polidor is a charming bistro nestled in the heart of the Quartier Latin in Paris. Founded in 1845, it is one of the oldest continuously running restaurants in the city, and its rich history and traditional French cuisine make it a must-visit for any foodie or history buff visiting the area.

The interior of Polidor is a cozy and intimate space, with dark wood paneling and vintage mirrors adorning the walls. The tables are set with crisp white tablecloths and classic bistro chairs, and the atmosphere is warm and inviting. The restaurant has a loyal local following, but also attracts a fair share of tourists eager to sample its famous dishes.

The menu at Polidor is simple but delicious, featuring classic French dishes such as escargots, steak frites, and coq au vin. One of the most popular items on the menu is the beef bourguignon, a slow-cooked stew made with tender beef, mushrooms, and red wine. It is rich and hearty, perfect for a chilly Paris evening. The wine list is extensive, with a great selection of French wines to complement the meal.

But it's not just the food that makes Polidor special. The restaurant has a rich history that is woven into the fabric of the Quartier Latin. It was a favorite haunt of many famous writers and artists in the early 20th century, including Ernest Hemingway and James Joyce. Hemingway even mentioned the restaurant in his book "A Moveable Feast," describing it as a place where "one could eat well and cheaply and drink the house wine."

Polidor's connection to the literary world is still evident today, with the walls adorned with photos and memorabilia from its famous patrons. The restaurant has also been used as a filming location for several movies, including Woody Allen's "Midnight in Paris."

Another interesting fact about Polidor is that it was one of the few restaurants in Paris to remain open during World War II. It served as a refuge for many locals and resistance fighters, who would often hold secret meetings there. The restaurant's resilience during the war is a testament to its importance to the community and its enduring legacy in the city.

LA CRÊPERIE DU CLUNY

The restaurant is located on a small street just steps away from the famous Musée de Cluny, making it the perfect spot for a quick bite before or after exploring the museum's rich collection of medieval art and artifacts.

As the name suggests, La Crêperie du Cluny is all about delicious, freshly made crepes. The menu offers a wide variety of sweet and savory crepes, all made with locally sourced ingredients and cooked to perfection. From classic ham and cheese to the more adventurous goat cheese and honey, there is something for everyone on the menu.

The atmosphere of La Crêperie du Cluny is cozy and welcoming, with warm lighting and rustic decor. The small dining room is adorned with old photographs and artwork, creating a charming and intimate ambiance that is perfect for a romantic dinner or a casual meal with friends.

One of the most interesting facts about La Crêperie du Cluny is its history. The building that houses the restaurant dates back to the 17th century and was once a stable for the horses of the nearby Cluny Abbey. The restaurant's owners have worked hard to preserve the building's historic character, and diners can still see the original wooden beams and stone walls that have been standing for centuries.

Another interesting tidbit about La Crêperie du Cluny is that it has become a popular spot for locals and tourists alike, thanks in part to its appearance in the popular travel guide Lonely Planet. The restaurant's cozy atmosphere and delicious crepes have earned it a spot in the hearts of foodies and travelers from all over the world.

For those looking for a truly unique dining experience, La Crêperie du Cluny also offers a selection of traditional Breton ciders and other regional drinks. Served in rustic pottery bowls, these drinks are the perfect accompaniment to a savory galette or a sweet crepe.

Whether you're in the mood for a hearty meal or a sweet treat, La Crêperie du Cluny is a must-visit destination for anyone exploring the Quartier Latin in Paris. With its delicious food, historic charm, and welcoming atmosphere, this little gem of a restaurant is sure to delight any traveler looking for an authentic taste of Parisian culture.

One of the standout dishes at La Crêperie du Cluny is their Galette Complète, a savory crepe filled with ham, cheese, and a perfectly cooked egg. This hearty dish is a favorite among locals and is the perfect choice for a satisfying lunch or dinner.

For those with a sweet tooth, La Crêperie du Cluny also offers a tempting selection of sweet crepes. From the classic Nutella and banana to the indulgent caramel and apple, these crepes are the perfect way to satisfy any dessert craving.

LA BOUTEILLE D'OR

Upon entering La Bouteille d'Or, guests are greeted by a warm and welcoming atmosphere. The cozy interior is decorated with traditional French décor, including vintage posters and rustic wooden furniture. The walls are adorned with bottles of wine, which give the restaurant its name, and create a cozy and intimate ambiance.

The menu at La Bouteille d'Or is a true reflection of the restaurant's commitment to using fresh, locally sourced ingredients. The cuisine is classic French, with dishes such as escargots de Bourgogne and coq au vin, as well as more contemporary offerings like seared scallops and foie gras. The restaurant also offers an extensive wine list, with bottles sourced from all over France and beyond, making it the perfect place to indulge in a glass of your favorite vintage.

One interesting fact about La Bouteille d'Or is that it has been serving up delicious French cuisine for over 60 years. The restaurant has a rich history and has been passed down through the generations, with each new owner adding their own unique flair to the menu and décor.

Located just a short walk from the famous Sorbonne University and the Panthéon, La Bouteille d'Or is in the heart of one of the most historic and culturally rich neighborhoods in Paris. The Quartier Latin is known for its charming streets, iconic landmarks, and lively atmosphere, making it the perfect place to explore before or after your meal.

In addition to its delicious food and historic setting, La Bouteille d'Or also offers a number of curiosities and unique features. For example, the restaurant has a private dining room that can be booked for special events and celebrations. This room is decorated with antique mirrors and vintage chandeliers, creating a truly special ambiance for any occasion.

Another interesting feature of La Bouteille d'Or is its proximity to some of the most famous literary landmarks in Paris. The restaurant is just a short walk from the famous Shakespeare and Company bookstore, as well as the historic Café de Flore, both of which have been frequented by famous writers and artists over the years.

L'ÎLOT

The location of L'Îlot is perfect for travelers looking to explore the vibrant and historic Quartier Latin neighborhood. This area is known for its lively atmosphere, intellectual culture, and stunning architecture. It is also home to some of the city's best restaurants and cafes, making it a popular destination for foodies and locals alike.

When it comes to the food at L'Îlot, visitors can expect an impressive array of classic French dishes, expertly prepared and served with a touch of modern flair. From escargots to foie gras, each dish is carefully crafted to showcase the unique flavors and ingredients of the region. The menu changes seasonally, ensuring that every visit to L'Îlot is a new and exciting culinary adventure.

One interesting fact about L'Îlot is that it is actually a converted wine cellar. The building dates back to the 17th century and was originally used as a storage space for wine merchants. Today, the cozy dining room is decorated with vintage wine bottles and other wine-related paraphernalia, creating a warm and inviting atmosphere for diners.

Another unique feature of L'Îlot is the open kitchen, which allows diners to watch as their food is prepared right before their eyes. This not only adds to the overall dining experience but also provides a glimpse into the culinary techniques and traditions of the French kitchen.

While the food at L'Îlot is certainly a highlight, the restaurant also boasts an impressive wine list. The cellar is stocked with an extensive collection of French wines, including many rare and hard-to-find bottles. Whether you are a wine connoisseur or simply enjoy a good glass of red or white, the knowledgeable staff at L'Îlot can help you find the perfect pairing for your meal.

In terms of ambiance, L'Îlot exudes charm and character. The dining room is small and intimate, with just a handful of tables and a bar seating area. The lighting is warm and inviting, creating a cozy and romantic atmosphere that is perfect for a special occasion or a romantic night out.

ÎLE DE LA CITÉ
RESTAURANTS

LA BRASSERIE DE L'ISLE SAINT-LOUIS

La Brasserie de l'Isle Saint-Louis is a quintessential French brasserie located in the heart of Île de la Cité, Paris. Known for its charming atmosphere, impeccable service, and delicious food, this brasserie is a must-visit destination for anyone visiting Paris.

Situated on the famous rue Saint-Louis en l'Île, the Brasserie de l'Isle Saint-Louis is perfectly located for tourists looking to explore the rich history and culture of Paris. This restaurant is just a stone's throw away from Notre-Dame Cathedral, the Sainte-Chapelle, and the Pont Saint-Louis. As you step inside, you will be transported to a bygone era with its traditional décor and warm ambiance.

One of the most interesting facts about La Brasserie de l'Isle Saint-Louis is that it has been a fixture of the neighborhood since 1900. It has served the local community and visitors alike for over a century, and its timeless charm has been preserved through the years. This restaurant has also been a favorite among many famous artists and writers, including Ernest Hemingway and James Joyce, who found inspiration here for their works.

The Brasserie de l'Isle Saint-Louis offers a wide variety of French classics, including escargots, steak tartare, and crème brûlée. The menu also features an impressive selection of wines, with many options from the local Île de la Cité region. The brasserie's seafood dishes are particularly noteworthy, and the fresh oysters are a must-try for any seafood lover.

One of the unique features of this restaurant is its outdoor seating area. Located on a quiet pedestrian street, the terrace offers a perfect spot to relax and enjoy a meal while soaking up the atmosphere of Île de la Cité. Whether you're looking to people-watch or simply enjoy a leisurely meal, the terrace is an excellent choice.

Another fascinating feature of La Brasserie de l'Isle Saint-Louis is its role in French culture. The brasserie is a place where locals and visitors come together to share a meal, converse, and enjoy the vibrant atmosphere of Paris. It's an excellent example of the conviviality and community that is so central to French culture.

Overall, La Brasserie de l'Isle Saint-Louis is a delightful destination for anyone looking to experience the best of French cuisine and culture. With its historic charm, impeccable service, and delicious food, it's a place that will leave a lasting impression on any traveler.

LE SAINT RÉGIS

Le Saint Régis is a quintessential French bistro that offers a unique culinary experience. This charming restaurant has been delighting locals and tourists alike since 1907 with its traditional French cuisine, warm atmosphere, and stunning views of the Seine River.

Located just a stone's throw away from the iconic Notre-Dame Cathedral, Le Saint Régis is an ideal spot to take a break from the hustle and bustle of Paris and indulge in some delicious French cuisine. The restaurant's interior is adorned with vintage posters, checkered tablecloths, and a beautiful wooden bar that exudes a classic Parisian charm.

Le Saint Régis is renowned for its exquisite French cuisine that is prepared using only the freshest and finest ingredients. The menu features an array of classic French dishes, including escargots, foie gras, and beef bourguignon, all served with a modern twist that is sure to tantalize your taste buds.

One of the must-try dishes at Le Saint Régis is the famous duck confit, which is slow-cooked to perfection and served with crispy potatoes and a deliciously tangy orange sauce. The restaurant also offers an excellent selection of wines, including some of the best French wines that perfectly complement the food.

Apart from its delectable cuisine, Le Saint Régis also boasts stunning views of the Seine River and the Notre-Dame Cathedral. The restaurant's outdoor seating area is the perfect spot to enjoy a romantic dinner or a leisurely lunch while taking in the breathtaking scenery.

Le Saint Régis has a rich history that dates back to the early 20th century. It was originally a wine bar and grocery store that catered to the locals living on Île de la Cité. Over the years, it has evolved into a charming bistro that is popular with both locals and tourists.

One of the interesting facts about Le Saint Régis is that it has been featured in several films and TV shows, including Woody Allen's Midnight in Paris and the French crime drama Spiral. The restaurant has also played host to many famous personalities over the years, including Ernest Hemingway, who was a regular at the bistro during his time in Paris.

Le Saint Régis is located in the heart of Île de la Cité, making it easily accessible from all parts of Paris. The nearest metro station is Cité, which is just a short walk away from the restaurant.

LE FLORE EN L'ÎLE

Located just steps away from the iconic Notre Dame Cathedral, Le Flore en L'Île is situated on a picturesque corner overlooking the tranquil square of Place Louis Lépine. The restaurant's exterior is adorned with vibrant floral arrangements, adding to the overall ambiance of the location.

Upon entering Le Flore en L'Île, guests are immediately greeted by a warm and welcoming atmosphere. The interior is beautifully decorated with traditional French accents, including ornate chandeliers, intricate woodwork, and elegant table settings. The intimate space exudes a cozy and romantic vibe, making it the perfect spot for a romantic dinner for two or a celebratory meal with friends and family.

The menu at Le Flore en L'Île boasts an impressive selection of classic French cuisine, with an emphasis on fresh and locally-sourced ingredients. From savory crepes and escargot to succulent beef bourguignon and coq au vin, the dishes are expertly prepared and full of flavor. The restaurant also offers an extensive wine list, featuring a range of varietals from across France.

In addition to its exceptional cuisine, Le Flore en L'Île has some interesting historical ties. The building itself dates back to the 17th century and was once home to a bakery that supplied bread to the neighboring prison of La Conciergerie. It was also a popular haunt for the literary crowd during the 19th century, with renowned authors such as Victor Hugo and Alexandre Dumas known to frequent the establishment.

Le Flore en L'Île is a must-visit for anyone seeking an authentic French dining experience. Its prime location on Île de la Cité makes it the perfect spot to relax and indulge in a delicious meal after a day of exploring Paris's many attractions. Whether you're a foodie, a history buff, or simply looking for a charming spot to enjoy a meal, Le Flore en L'Île is sure to delight.

In addition to its delicious cuisine and rich history, Le Flore en L'Île also offers a range of unique dining experiences. During the summer months, guests can enjoy their meal on the restaurant's outdoor terrace, which offers stunning views of the Seine and the surrounding architecture. The terrace is also the perfect spot to watch the sun set over the city while sipping a glass of wine or enjoying a dessert.

For those seeking a more intimate dining experience, Le Flore en L'Île offers a private dining room, which can accommodate up to 20 guests. This cozy space is perfect for a special occasion or a romantic dinner for two.

One of the standout dishes on the menu at Le Flore en L'Île is the tarte tatin. This classic French dessert is made with caramelized apples and a buttery pastry crust, and is served warm with a dollop of crème fraîche. It's the perfect way to end a meal at this charming restaurant.

Le Flore en L'Île is open for lunch and dinner seven days a week, and reservations are recommended, especially during peak tourist season. The restaurant's central location and warm, welcoming atmosphere make it a popular spot among both locals and visitors, so be sure to book ahead to secure a table.

AUX ANYSETIERS DU ROY

This charming restaurant is located just a stone's throw from the Notre-Dame Cathedral, making it the perfect spot to enjoy a delicious meal after exploring one of Paris's most iconic landmarks.

The atmosphere at Aux Anysetiers du Roy is warm and inviting, with exposed stone walls, wooden beams, and soft lighting creating a cozy and intimate setting. The menu offers a delightful selection of classic French dishes, with a focus on fresh, seasonal ingredients and traditional cooking techniques.

One of the standout dishes at Aux Anysetiers du Roy is the boeuf bourguignon, a hearty beef stew that is slow-cooked to perfection in red wine and served with a side of creamy mashed potatoes. The restaurant's signature dish is the escargots de Bourgogne, which are plump, juicy snails that are cooked in a rich garlic butter sauce and served with crusty bread.

In addition to its delicious food, Aux Anysetiers du Roy is also known for its extensive wine list, which features an impressive selection of French wines from some of the country's top producers. Whether you're a wine connoisseur or just looking for a great glass to pair with your meal, the knowledgeable staff at Aux Anysetiers du Roy will be happy to help you find the perfect bottle.

But it's not just the food and wine that make Aux Anysetiers du Roy worth a visit. The restaurant is steeped in history, with a story that dates back to the 18th century. Legend has it that the restaurant's name comes from the "anysetiers," or spice merchants, who once sold their wares on the Île de la Cité. The spice merchants were said to be favored by King Louis XIV, who would often stop by their shops to sample their latest offerings.

Today, Aux Anysetiers du Roy continues to pay homage to this rich history, with its rustic decor and traditional French cuisine. The restaurant is a popular destination for both locals and tourists alike, and reservations are highly recommended.

One of the most unique features of Aux Anysetiers du Roy is its "spice cellar," where guests can explore a wide range of herbs, spices, and condiments from around the world. From exotic blends like Ras el Hanout to classic French staples like Herbes de Provence, there is something for every taste and palate.

For travelers looking to immerse themselves in the rich culinary traditions of Paris, Aux Anysetiers du Roy is a must-visit destination. With its delicious food, extensive wine list, and charming atmosphere, this hidden gem on the Île de la Cité is sure to delight even the most discerning of diners.

In addition to the restaurant's main dining room, there is also a private room available for special events and gatherings. The room can accommodate up to 20 guests and features its own fireplace, creating a cozy and intimate setting for small groups.

Another interesting feature of Aux Anysetiers du Roy is the restaurant's use of traditional French cookware. Many of the dishes are cooked and served in classic French pots and pans, such as Le Creuset Dutch ovens and Staub cocottes, which not only add to the rustic charm of the restaurant but also enhance the flavor of the food.

If you're looking to experience the best of classic French cuisine in a cozy and intimate setting, then Aux Anysetiers du Roy is the place for you. With its rich history, delicious food, extensive wine list, and unique spice cellar, this hidden gem on the Île de la Cité is a must-visit destination for any food lover traveling to Paris.

When visiting Aux Anysetiers du Roy, be sure to make a reservation in advance, as the restaurant is quite popular and tends to fill up quickly, especially during peak tourist season. The staff is friendly and welcoming, and they will be happy to help you navigate the menu and select the perfect wine to accompany your meal.

After your meal, take a stroll around the Île de la Cité and explore some of the other historic landmarks in the area, such as the Sainte-Chapelle and the Conciergerie. Or, if you're looking for something a little more off the beaten path, head to the nearby Marché aux Fleurs, one of Paris's oldest flower markets, and browse the colorful stalls for a unique souvenir to take home.

LA RÉSERVE DE QUASIMODO

This charming restaurant is located just a stone's throw away from the world-famous Notre-Dame Cathedral, and its romantic atmosphere is the perfect place to savor traditional French cuisine in a cozy and intimate setting.

La Réserve de Quasimodo's menu is a carefully crafted tribute to French gastronomy, with a selection of classic dishes made from the freshest and finest ingredients. From escargots de Bourgogne to beef bourguignon, every dish is cooked to perfection and served with a touch of elegance and sophistication. Their wine list is equally impressive, featuring a vast array of French wines carefully chosen to complement the menu's flavors and textures.

Aside from the exquisite food and wine, La Réserve de

Quasimodo's ambiance is one of its most unique features. The restaurant's intimate setting and rustic decor, with exposed stone walls and wooden beams, make it feel like a hidden treasure in the heart of the city. The attentive and friendly staff only add to the charm, providing a warm welcome and attentive service throughout the meal.

While La Réserve de Quasimodo is undoubtedly a destination for foodies, its location on Île de la Cité makes it an ideal choice for travelers seeking to immerse themselves in the rich history and culture of Paris. This small island is home to some of the city's most iconic landmarks, including Notre-Dame Cathedral, Sainte-Chapelle, and the Conciergerie. Walking along the island's narrow streets, visitors can feel the city's history come alive and appreciate the intricate architecture and charming details of each building.

A visit to La Réserve de Quasimodo is also a chance to learn about the restaurant's namesake, Quasimodo. The character, famously portrayed in Victor Hugo's novel "The Hunchback of Notre-Dame," is said to have lived in the bell tower of Notre-Dame and watched over the city from above. The restaurant's name is a nod to this literary figure and the island's rich history.

LE CAVEAU DU PALAIS

Le Caveau du Palais is a charming restaurant nestled in the heart of Île de la Cité, a small island located in the Seine River in the center of Paris. This hidden gem boasts a rich history dating back to the Middle Ages and has become a popular spot among locals and tourists alike.

Located just a stone's throw away from the Notre-Dame Cathedral, Le Caveau du Palais is a must-visit for anyone looking for an authentic French dining experience. The restaurant is situated in a cave-like setting, which creates a cozy and intimate atmosphere that transports guests back in time.

As you enter the restaurant, you'll be greeted by a warm and friendly staff who will guide you to your table. The decor is traditional, with exposed stone walls and wooden beams, giving the restaurant a rustic and authentic feel. The candlelit tables and soft music add to the romantic ambiance of the restaurant, making it a perfect spot for a date night or special occasion.

The menu at Le Caveau du Palais features classic French dishes, such as escargot, foie gras, and coq au vin, all made with fresh, locally-sourced ingredients. The wine list is extensive and features a variety of local and international wines, with the staff happy to provide recommendations to perfectly pair with your meal.

One of the most interesting facts about Le Caveau du Palais is that it was once a popular meeting place for the French Revolutionaries. The restaurant was a hotspot for secret meetings and plotting, with its hidden location and discreet atmosphere providing the perfect setting for conspiracies.

Despite its historical significance, Le Caveau du Palais has remained a popular dining spot for over 100 years, with famous visitors including Ernest Hemingway and Jean-Paul Sartre. Today, the restaurant continues to attract visitors from all over the world who come to experience its unique atmosphere and delicious cuisine.

Another interesting feature of the restaurant is the wine cellar, which is located underground and features a vast collection of rare and vintage wines. Guests can request a tour of the cellar and even participate in wine tastings to experience some of the finest wines from the region.

If you're looking for a truly authentic French dining experience, Le Caveau du Palais is a must-visit. With its rich history, charming decor, and delicious cuisine, this hidden gem is sure to leave a lasting impression on any traveler who visits. Whether you're in the mood for a romantic dinner for two or a memorable evening with friends, Le Caveau du Palais is the perfect destination for an unforgettable dining experience in the heart of Paris.

AU BOUGNAT

The restaurant's location is one of its most unique features. Situated on the Île de la Cité, which is one of the two natural islands in the Seine River that flow through Paris, Au Bougnat offers a peaceful escape from the bustling city. The restaurant is easily accessible via public transportation, and its central location makes it a great starting point for exploring other attractions in the area.

Upon entering the restaurant, visitors are immediately transported to a quaint, rustic French setting. The walls are adorned with antique decorations, and the dim lighting creates a cozy atmosphere perfect for a romantic dinner or intimate gathering. Guests can choose to dine in the main dining room or the outdoor terrace, which offers stunning views of the Seine River and the Notre-Dame Cathedral.

One of the highlights of Au Bougnat is its extensive menu of traditional French cuisine. From classic dishes like escargots and beef bourguignon to more contemporary options like foie gras and lobster risotto, there is something to satisfy every palate. The restaurant also offers a selection of French wines to complement each dish, making for a truly authentic dining experience.

But what sets Au Bougnat apart from other restaurants in Paris is its commitment to preserving traditional French cooking techniques. Many of the dishes are prepared using old-fashioned methods, such as slow-cooking and braising, which allow the flavors to develop over time. This attention to detail and dedication to preserving French culinary traditions is what makes Au Bougnat a true gem in the Parisian dining scene.

In addition to its delicious food and charming atmosphere, Au Bougnat is also steeped in history. The restaurant has been a fixture on the Île de la Cité since the early 1900s and has hosted many famous guests over the years, including Coco Chanel and Pablo Picasso. The restaurant's name, "Au Bougnat," is a reference to the Auvergnats, a group of people from the Auvergne region of France who were known for their culinary skills.

Whether you're a foodie looking for an authentic French dining experience or a history buff interested in exploring one of Paris's oldest restaurants, Au Bougnat is not to be missed. With its delicious food, charming atmosphere, and rich history, this restaurant is sure to leave a lasting impression on any traveler lucky enough to dine there.

To start your meal at Au Bougnat, be sure to try their famous onion soup gratinée. This traditional French soup is made with caramelized onions, beef broth, and a hint of white wine, topped with a layer of Gruyere cheese and baked until golden brown. It's the perfect comfort food on a chilly Parisian evening.

For the main course, you can't go wrong with the beef bourguignon, a classic French dish made with tender beef stewed in red wine with vegetables and herbs. Or, if you're feeling adventurous, try the escargots, a French delicacy of snails cooked with garlic butter and herbs.

For dessert, be sure to save room for the crème brûlée, a creamy custard topped with a crispy layer of caramelized sugar. It's the perfect ending to a delicious meal at Au Bougnat.

LA ROSE DE FRANCE

One of the most notable aspects of La Rose de France is its rich history. The restaurant has been in operation for over a century, and its décor and ambiance have remained largely unchanged over the years. The walls are adorned with antique paintings, old-fashioned light fixtures, and intricate woodwork that transport diners back in time to the Paris of old. The restaurant's name is a nod to the country's national flower, which is prominently featured in its décor.

But it's not just the ambiance that makes La Rose de France a must-visit for travelers. The restaurant's menu is equally impressive, offering a wide variety of classic French dishes made with fresh and locally-sourced ingredients. Some of the must-try items on the menu include the escargots de Bourgogne, coq au vin, and crème brûlée. Each dish is expertly prepared by the restaurant's talented chefs and served by the friendly and attentive waitstaff.

For those looking for a unique dining experience, La Rose de France also offers a private dining room that is perfect for intimate gatherings and special occasions. The room is elegantly decorated and can accommodate up to 12 guests, making it the perfect choice for a romantic dinner or a small celebration.

In addition to its rich history and delicious cuisine, La Rose de France also boasts a prime location in the heart of Île de la Cité. This makes it the perfect starting point for travelers looking to explore some of the city's most famous landmarks and attractions. After enjoying a meal at the restaurant, visitors can take a leisurely stroll through the charming streets of Île de la Cité and take in the sights and sounds of one of the world's most beautiful cities.

L'ORANGERIE

This elegant restaurant boasts a stunning location in the midst of the Seine River and provides a unique dining experience that combines exceptional food, impeccable service, and breathtaking views.

L'Orangerie's menu features a range of mouth-watering French dishes that are carefully prepared using the finest ingredients. From classic French cuisine such as escargots and foie gras to more modern twists like poached lobster with black truffle, the chefs at L'Orangerie are passionate about creating culinary masterpieces that will leave a lasting impression on their guests.

But L'Orangerie is more than just a great restaurant – it's also steeped in history and charm. Originally built in the 17th century as part of the Palais des Tuileries, the building that now houses L'Orangerie was once used to house orange trees during the winter months. Today, the restaurant pays homage to its past with a beautiful orange tree display that serves as a centerpiece for the dining room.

The interior of L'Orangerie is equally impressive, with its grand arched windows, opulent chandeliers, and ornate décor that create an ambiance of timeless elegance. The restaurant also boasts an outdoor terrace that provides unparalleled views of the Seine and Notre-Dame Cathedral – making it the perfect spot for a romantic dinner or special occasion.

One of the most intriguing aspects of L'Orangerie is the extensive wine list. The restaurant's sommelier has curated an impressive selection of French and international wines, with a particular focus on rare and exclusive bottles. Guests can enjoy a wine tasting experience to learn about the different varietals and pairings available, or opt for a perfectly matched wine pairing with their meal.

For those looking to experience L'Orangerie in a more intimate setting, the restaurant also offers private dining rooms that can accommodate groups of various sizes. Each room is beautifully decorated and provides an exclusive atmosphere for a special event or celebration.

As with any renowned restaurant, reservations at L'Orangerie are highly recommended. The restaurant can be found at 28 Rue Saint-Louis en l'Île, just a short stroll from Notre-Dame Cathedral. Whether you're a foodie looking to indulge in a gastronomic feast, a wine enthusiast searching for rare and exceptional bottles, or simply looking for a unique dining experience in the heart of Paris, L'Orangerie is a must-visit destination.

To start your meal at L'Orangerie, be sure to try their signature dish - the langoustine carpaccio. This delicate dish features thinly sliced langoustines served with a citrus vinaigrette and fresh herbs, creating a perfect balance of flavors. The restaurant's foie gras is also a standout, served with a fig compote and brioche toast for a delicious combination of sweet and savory.

For your main course, the poached lobster with black truffle is a must-try. The tender lobster is complemented by the earthy truffle flavor, creating a dish that is both decadent and refined. The duck breast with caramelized pear is another standout, with perfectly cooked duck served with sweet, tender pears and a rich jus.

To finish your meal, L'Orangerie's dessert menu offers a variety of sweet treats to satisfy your cravings. The crème brûlée with vanilla and Tonka bean is a classic French dessert done to perfection, while the chocolate fondant with hazelnut ice cream is a decadent indulgence.

Aside from its exceptional cuisine and stunning location, L'Orangerie also offers exceptional service. The restaurant's knowledgeable and attentive staff ensure that guests feel welcomed and well-cared for throughout their dining experience.

If you're interested in learning more about French cuisine, L'Orangerie also offers cooking classes and culinary workshops. Led by the restaurant's talented chefs, these experiences allow guests to learn about French cooking techniques and create their own delicious dishes.

SORZA

The restaurant is tucked away on a quaint street lined with chic boutiques and art galleries, just a stone's throw from the iconic Saint-Germain Church.

Upon entering Sorza, travelers are greeted with an intimate and cozy atmosphere that exudes old-world charm. The restaurant's interior is adorned with exposed brick walls, wooden beams, and soft lighting, creating an inviting ambiance perfect for a romantic dinner or a night out with friends.

The menu at Sorza is a fusion of Italian and French cuisine, featuring a tantalizing selection of dishes that showcase the finest local and seasonal ingredients. The chefs at Sorza are passionate about using only the freshest produce, meats, and seafood to create their dishes, and their commitment to quality is evident in every bite.

Some of the standout dishes at Sorza include the mouthwatering beef carpaccio, the delectable homemade pasta with truffle cream sauce, and the perfectly cooked sea bass with roasted vegetables. And for dessert, the restaurant's signature tiramisu is a must-try.

One of the most interesting facts about Sorza is that the restaurant is named after a small town in northern Italy where the owner's family originated. The owner, a passionate foodie and wine connoisseur, spent years traveling throughout Italy and France in search of the perfect ingredients and inspiration for his restaurant. And his efforts have paid off - Sorza has quickly become a favorite among locals and travelers alike.

In addition to its delicious cuisine, Sorza is also known for its extensive wine list, featuring a carefully curated selection of French and Italian wines. The restaurant's sommelier is always on hand to help diners choose the perfect bottle to complement their meal, and the cozy bar area is the perfect spot to enjoy a glass of wine before or after dinner.

Travelers visiting Sorza will also appreciate the restaurant's convenient location in the heart of Saint-Germain-des-Prés. After a delicious meal at Sorza, visitors can take a leisurely stroll through the charming streets of this historic neighborhood, taking in the stunning architecture, quaint cafes, and world-class art galleries.

Overall, Sorza is a must-visit destination for travelers looking for an unforgettable dining experience in the heart of Paris. From the charming ambiance to the exquisite cuisine and exceptional wine selection, Sorza has everything a foodie could want and more. So if you're planning a trip to Paris, be sure to add Sorza to your itinerary - you won't be disappointed!

Printed in Great Britain
by Amazon